580-4410

D1083493

Contest for Liberty

CONTEST
FOR
LIBERTY

Military Leadership
in the
Continental Army,
1775–1783

Seanegan P. Sculley

WESTHOLME
Yardley

Westholme Publishing, LLC
904 Edgewood Road
Yardley, Pennsylvania 19067
Visit our Web site at www.westholmepublishing.com

ISBN: 978-1-59416-321-0
Also available as an eBook.

Printed in the United States of America.

CONTENTS

INTRODUCTION

LEADERSHIP IN THE CONTINENTAL ARMY
AS A NEGOTIATION OF AUTHORITY

O N JULY 3, 1775, WASHINGTON WROTE HIS FIRST GENERAL ORDER
as commander of the Continental Army. To accurately determine how many men were fit for duty, he told the regiments surrounding Boston to conduct a muster and report their numbers to
his headquarters.[1] The next day he notified the troops that they were
now placed under the command of the Continental Congress rather
than their specific colonial governments. Distinctions (of what was
not specified) by individual colony were to be ignored.[2] A few days
later a court-martial found Captain John Callender guilty of cowardice for his actions at Breed's Hill and sentenced him to be
cashiered from the service. Washington began mentoring his officers,
exhorting them to show courage at all times.[3] In less than a week,
the first and only commander in chief was taking command, in a very
assertive manner, of the Continental Army.

Yet the army Washington took command of that week was not
truly a continental army. It was largely an army from New England
that had just accepted a Virginia planter as its leader. When Washington was finally able to get strength reports into his headquarters
from the regiments, he learned approximately 19,500 soldiers were
present and fit for duty. Five colonies were represented and, while

Pennsylvania had a contingent of 925 soldiers, the rest of the troops were from New England and 60 percent of those soldiers were from one colony, Massachusetts.[4]

The new commander in chief was not pleased with the soldiers and officers he met in Cambridge that summer. The officers lacked courage and the soldiers were "a dirty and nasty people." But he did judge them willing to fight well. Writing his brother on August 20, 1775, Washington claimed these soldiers could have defeated the British regulars at Bunker Hill two months before if they had been led by good, courageous officers ready to provide the leadership needed to win.[5]

Why did these soldiers from New England make such a poor initial impression on their new commander? Perhaps his expectations were too high before he arrived. From the distant colonies of Virginia and Pennsylvania, the battles at Lexington and Concord in Massachusetts on April 19, 1775, must have appeared a validation of republican ideals. As Washington described that day to his friend, George William Fairfax, American citizens under arms successfully defended their liberties and stopped "Ministerial Troops" from destroying private property. The British retreat was a rout, despite reinforcements from Lord Percy's brigade, and Washington hoped this would convince Lord Sandwich that Americans would fight to protect what was rightfully theirs and they would do so successfully.[6]

Of course, this account, based on reports received in Philadelphia just prior to Congress assuming control of these armed men surrounding Boston, did not include an understanding of the difficulties faced by the officers in charge at Cambridge. Artemus Ward, commanding from Cambridge, spent the months from April to July trying to organize a camp of almost twenty thousand soldiers who possessed little experience living in such a large community. Boston was the largest town in the region and its population was no more than sixteen thousand at the time. Ward gave orders regulating latrine duty and other tasks required to prevent the spread of disease among the soldiery while he prohibited prostitution, profanity, and excessive drinking. The men were to attend sermon daily and maintain the protection and sanctity of God.[7]

Convincing the soldiers to follow these rules was not an easy task. Though some of the officers, including Ward, had served during the French and Indian War twelve years prior, most of the enlisted soldiers and many of the younger officers had little military experience. Their conception of military service came from militia drills in their towns and stories told by their elders. David How, a seventeen-year-old boy from Methuen, Massachusetts, was one of these soldiers encamped around Boston. He and his five brothers all served in the Revolution and David was both a minuteman at Lexington and a soldier in Colonel Paul Dudley Sargent's regiment at Breed's Hill.[8] Private How spoke often of the sermons he attended that were given by his regimental chaplain. He described parading in front of the regiment's major to have his musket appraised.[9] While these portions of How's diary suggest elements of discipline were being enforced, other portions of his account illustrate that Private How did not believe his officers were entitled to his unqualified obedience. Instead, there appeared to be little social distance between privates and the officers in charge of them at the company level.

For the next few months after the weapon inspection, Private How sold his original musket to a colonel, purchased a new musket, and then sold it to another soldier, always at a profit to himself.[10] In February 1776, How's lieutenant, David Chandler, died of smallpox. When Lieutenant Chandler died he owed Private How thirteen shillings. A week later Chandler's brother paid How the debt.[11] It is hard to imagine Lieutenant Chandler lowering himself to borrow money from someone he viewed as significantly socially inferior. Instead, these soldiers looked more like young acquaintances traveling together on a military adventure.

While this business of borrowing money and buying and selling muskets testifies to How's personal (and possibly cultural) views on the merits of the entrepreneurial spirit, it also underscores the difficulties faced by more senior officers. Soldiers experienced months of boredom as they waited for the British to make another attempt to attack outside of the confines of Boston. Men paid prostitutes for entertainment, drank liquor excessively, and gambled their money away. Two soldiers combined the sins of drunkenness and gambling, wagering over who could drink the most in the shortest amount of time. Within two hours, one of the two gamblers was dead, apparently from alcohol poisoning.[12] The leadership challenges faced by senior officers were exacerbated by the fact that soon after the first few months of the Army's existence, 3,500 soldiers were reported too sick to accomplish their duties and hundreds more were on furlough. These men not fit for duty comprised about 15 percent of the overall troop strength of the organization.[13]

Other reports from observers not members of the army confirm both the difficulties faced by military leaders attempting to enforce discipline and the cultural bias that could color perceptions of these men mustered to defend Boston. A British Army surgeon, using his position as a doctor to gain admittance to the rebels' camps, described the men he encountered as "drunken, canting, lying, praying, hypocritical rabble" who ". . . without New England rum . . . could neither fight nor say their prayers."[14] Benjamin Thompson (later Sir Benjamin Thompson, Count Rumford), a Loyalist who served with the King's American Dragoons later in the war, claimed shortly after Washington took command that these New England soldiers were "Dirty, Nasty, Insubordinate, and Quarrelsome." According to Thompson, "doctrines of independence and levellism have been so effectually sown . . . and so universally imbedded by all ranks of men" that proper subordination would be impossible to enforce.[15]

While the reality of disciplinary problems probably clashed with his ideal of a virtuous republican army, it also certainly ran contrary to Washington's desire to command a more professional army capable of defeating British forces in a conventional war. Washington's ideas regarding the necessary qualities of a successful army had been developed during the French and Indian War. He spent time serving as a volunteer officer under the tutelage of several British commanders and was the first commander of the Virginia Regiment in 1756 and 1757. During that time, especially while training his regiment, Washington attempted to mold himself into a professional officer and disciplined his men to meet the same professional standards.[16]

Central to his conception of military professionalism was the belief that officers exercised the right to command through social recognition of their personal honor. While honor in some societies can be conferred on an individual through birthrights, for Washington personal honor was gained and retained through personal actions and social status. In his earliest writings as a military leader, Washington did exhibit a belief that a sense of honor could be inculcated in an individual officer if honorable action was found wanting, a task he worked hard to complete with his colonial officers in the Virginia Regiment.[17] If an officer exemplified his personal honor to his soldiers, they would, in return, confer the right to command them on the officer. Personal honor was, then, the prerequisite to leadership because it governed proper behavior for the leader that would be recognized by his followers.

Historian Bertram Wyatt Brown explains this understanding of honor in the southern colonies as a combination of three necessary elements: a sense of self-worth in the individual, a show of that worth to the public, and an acceptance of that worth by the public. A man of honor had first to believe himself worthy of esteem among others in his society and then exemplify that worthiness to his community. Yet that was not enough. The most important component to this formulation was the acceptance of the community that this man's actions adequately proved his worth. If the community agreed, honor was conferred.[18] It was this concept of personal honor that Washington found lacking in the officers and soldiers of the new Continental Army. From his perspective, New England officers did not appear concerned if their actions failed to reflect the necessary sense of self-worth nor did the soldiers convey the proper attitude of acceptance that the officers were worthy of commanding obedience to orders.

Was Washington correct, then? Were the soldiers outside Boston ineffectively led before Washington arrived? Was the New England officer corps devoid of the proper conception of personal honor necessary to legitimize their authority to command? Or were cultural beliefs regarding military service and military leadership simply different? And how would this perception by Washington affect how the Continental Army was led throughout the American Revolution?

To understand these questions and answer them, it will first be helpful to define military leadership. This is no easy task, as several historians explained in their papers submitted for the third Symposium on the American Revolution in 1974. Writing about political leaders during the Revolution, Alfred H. Kelly decided "leadership will be defined somewhat arbitrarily as the combination of characteristics in a public figure which enables him to play an influential role in the life of the state."[19] Kelley gives little in the way of explanation for how he came by this definition, instead assuming several constant characteristics of leadership (courage, the ability to inspire others to action, the ability to formulate myths of social order and give it legitimacy) that he believes belong more in the realm of sociology and psychology than history. He did, however, admit that, despite these constants, there are extensive variations on these characteristics in political leadership between societies, and while American political culture can be seen as extending from western European traditions, there is still something uniquely American about its political leadership.[20]

Marcus Cunliffe, deciding not to define the term in his essay on congressional leadership, instead elected to categorize various forms (character, moral, managerial, intellectual, symbolic, and manipulative).[21] Meanwhile, Gordon S. Wood took the meaning of leadership for granted, focusing on the impact of the Founding Fathers' intellectualization of republican ideals on political life in America. He argued that the end result was a separation of ideas from power.[22] He claims, quite rightly with regard to political leadership, that these men were leaders by virtue of their social status as gentlemen, that their role as intellectual and political leaders was thrust upon them as a responsibility of their rank.[23]

Perhaps one of the most influential military historians of the Revolution, Don Higginbotham, cautioned "He who hazards an absolute, ironclad definition of military leadership is likely to be in for trouble, and doubtless the same warning applies to other fields of leadership as well."[24] European military thinkers, like the Comte Guibert, Marshall Saxe, and William Lloyd, believed generals were born, not bred. Officers at this time were amateurs without formal schooling. Experience was important, but doctrine was somewhat lacking. And breeding that ensured a sense of honor was the most important characteristic of an officer, even in the British Army where the aristocracy led in conjunction with the gentry.[25] He goes on to argue that this idea of who should lead was not radically changed during the American Revolution and Washington, in particular, thought only gentlemen should serve in that capacity as officers.[26]

Higginbotham does admit that this ideal of the gentleman-officer was never reached in the Continental Army, that there was a democratization of office-holding in America that extended to the officer corps.[27] American officers were more civilian than soldier, committed to republican ideals, politicized, with leadership that was not divorced from their society. The American generals faced a unique problem of their time, holding together an army that annually suffered the trauma of losing numbers and reenlistments. This problem forced Washington to convince soldiers of the necessity of their continued participation while the leadership maintained their civilian skills to engage with political and social leaders in order to gain the necessary resources for a prolonged conflict. For these reasons, American military leadership was more civilian in nature.[28]

Despite Higginbotham's warning, it is important to define the term "leadership" if we wish to understand the interactions within the Continental Army between senior officers, junior officers, and soldiers. Since leadership requires communication and agreement between individuals within an organization or society, the term is laden with cultural values and beliefs. The word defines, therefore, a cultural concept and the goal is to strip it of those cultural connotations in order to better define what it meant in the Continental Army, to contextualize it historically without bringing outside cultural understandings into the investigation. To accomplish this task it will be necessary to briefly investigate what an army is in its most basic (and universalist) form. An army is, of course, a type of human organization. To address many large problems, societies create teams of individuals to work together and solve specific problems for the good of the society. Some problems involve food production while others center on spiritual protection and winning the approval of a god or gods. Problems of a more immediate and dangerous nature are related to self-defense and territorial expansion. In each case, the organization formed to tackle challenges requires a system of decision-making that is culturally acceptable to those individuals involved. The system devised to make those decisions can be generally termed leadership.

To make these decisions and then act upon them in an efficient and effective manner often requires the majority of individuals belonging to an organization to accept the decisions made by a minority. Those individuals are, in reality, granting the authority to exercise power to those in a leadership role. People may do this consciously and voluntarily or they may believe they have no choice, depending on their cultural conceptions of power and authority. In the case of armies, this cultural understanding of the appropriate level of submission may differ from most other organizations in their society due to the immediacy of danger to life and limb and the recognition by the group and society that the security of all hinges upon the success of the organization preparing for battle. Furthermore, efficient and effective decision-making can more easily be understood as paramount in a military organization and so the leadership structure is often more hierarchical than perhaps is acceptable in the society from which the military was created.

The relationships between members of an organization often imply some exercise of power and authority. Max Weber famously defined power as "the chance of a man or of a number of men to realize their own will in a communal action even against the resistance of others who are participating in the action."[29] For Weber, power was coercive in nature, a force used to compel some men to follow the direction of others. And as such, power was a universal force, defined once and applicable to all societies. Almost a century later, historian Edmund Morgan defined power as a socially constructed myth with far-reaching consequences for a society when that conception changed.[30] For Morgan, the transformation of English political structure from the English Civil War to the American Revolution served as an example of power becoming reconceptualized. A monarchy based on the ideas of the divine right of kings gave way to the sovereignty of the people. In other words, the basis of power shifted from its origination with God to its foundation within the individual, a belief pivotal to the natural philosophers of the eighteenth century. The result was revolution, both at home and in the colonies.

Both Weber and Morgan explored not only the nature of power but also the relationship between those with power and those without. For Weber, economic means and social status allowed the few to exercise power over the many while Morgan claimed the transformation of Anglo understanding created the unintended consequence of decoupling status from power. Both discussions give important insight into both the nature of power and the authority to use it and are useful to a discussion on leadership. Understanding power as both an exercise of will and a "myth" leads to questions concerning the cultural nature of authority (i.e., the legitimate use of power) and how members of a society work through the differences between an idealized understanding of power and the reality of its use by leaders.

Taking into account the prior discussion regarding organizations, their generalized purpose in societies, and the characterization of power, leadership can be defined generally as the cultural construct within which decisions for an organization are made and actions are taken to effect that decision. More important, leadership is conducted through a negotiation of authority between the leaders and the led to determine how both the decisions and their method of execution are reached. Negotiation is crucial to maintaining the legitimacy of the system in question. This negotiation is cultural in nature because the understanding of power, its origin and the acceptable use of it, are not universal. Both those in charge and those following have agency. They can accept, acquiesce, resist, revolt, and come to an evolving understanding of the acceptable exercise of authority, influenced by cultural norms.

Over time, these organizations can form their own institutional subcultures as the organization seeks to provide continuity between succeeding "generations" of members. The subculture of an organization will usually tend not to diverge too far from that of the greater society from which it was formed because it is constantly assimilating new members that were raised in, and presumably accept, the larger cultural beliefs of their society. But as historian John Lynn pointed out in 2003, military subcultures tend to be more divergent (and accepted as necessarily so by society) due to the extreme nature of their purpose. Still, he noted, that divergence must fall within certain acceptable parameters. If it does not, cultural values will change to meet reality or the society will force reality to come back in line with cultural ideals.[31] This greater degree of divergence can include both a higher elevation of some values (for example, courage, loyalty, honor) and the compromise of other beliefs (for example, freedom of speech or individualism), often in the name of collective security.

The longer an organization remains, the deeper entrenched its subculture can become. As older members of the institution increasingly accept new values and beliefs shaped by their experiences and possible isolation from the larger society, they could encourage and enforce assimilation of those divergent beliefs on new members. Inversely, a new organization will exercise its objectives first with values more closely aligned to those of the larger society and, over time, begin to elevate and compromise certain cultural norms to meet the challenges of their environment. This can be a turbulent time for the members of an organization as they negotiate among themselves and with their society over changes perceived as necessary. The Continental Army would certainly fall within this category of a new organization, with some reservations.

While the Continental Army was a newly formed organization, it will not be asserted here that it was formed in a vacuum, a social experiment to wage war in a purely republican manner. As has already been successfully proven over at least the last thirty years, there was a multitude of military cultures developed in the American colonies prior to 1775 (some more robust than others). Instead, it will be argued that those various military solutions competed with one another for supremacy in the Continental Army as officers and soldiers from across the colonies came together to accomplish the overarching goal of establishing independence from the British Empire. Central to that competition, and negotiation, was how the army would be led.

In terms of military organization, the British model was accepted by all colonies, and then states, concerned. At its heart was the infantry regiment, comprised of ten companies, with between sixty and a hundred men per company. A captain led his company with the help of a lieutenant, an ensign, and several noncommissioned officers, including a first sergeant, sergeants, and corporals. A colonel and his staff of one lieutenant colonel, one major, and an adjutant commanded the regiment.[32] While this basic organization of leadership structure could lead some to assume more similarities between the British and American armies than actually existed, a cultural understanding of leadership as a negotiation of authority will lead to other conclusions. Still, the British Army was highly regarded by all would-be military leaders in the American colonies prior to the Revolution, and a closer look at the British military culture of the eighteenth century is important to understanding the goals of American commanders during the war.

The British Army prior to the Revolution had evolved by way of a growing fiscal-military state that allowed for its expansion in size without threatening the rights of its polity (namely the Parliament). Following the Glorious Revolution, Britain entered a period of almost continuous warfare with France and her allies that resulted in larger standing armies and navies, a permanent national debt with higher taxation, and a large fiscal-military state necessary to administer these wars that made the state the largest borrower, spender, and employer in her economy. While the army grew three to five times its previous size, the populace did not have to face this growth in any direct way because the army remained squarely under civilian control and most of its units were rarely at home.[33] Within the army, gentlemen-officers led private soldiers in a manner that reflected both socially accepted norms of class and Whig ideology concerning rights.

The majority of the officers in the British Army came from the aristocratic and gentry classes. Certainly by the time of the War of Spanish Succession, under the rule of Queen Anne, the qualification for entry into the officer corps was birth, if not wealth.[34] Fully two-thirds of commissions were attained through the purchase system, whereby officers purchased their next higher rank from the current officeholder following the retirement of a superior officer somewhere along their regimental chain of command. All ranks from colonelcies down were subject to purchase, but the Crown retained the right to approve requests for purchase to maintain royal control, evaluate merit, and protect seniority.[35] The cost of purchase was regulated by the government and the cost was not so high as to preclude officers without means to borrow money or rely upon a patron. The other third of promotions came from filling vacancies caused by the death of an officer or his removal and contributed to a "social mélange" that included not only nobility and landed gentry but lesser gentry, gentlemen without means (including foreigners), and those promoted from the ranks (though these officers remained in the subaltern ranks).[36]

The soldiers who filled the rank and file were predominantly lower-class and lower-middle-class workers who found themselves unemployed due to economic developments in both the agricultural and industrial sectors of England, Scotland, and Ireland.[37] These men enlisted voluntarily for life, though during times of war the government allowed for enlistments of three years or the duration of the war. A smaller number of recruits, enlisted under the Press Acts, came from debtor prisons and the indigent poor.[38] The overall result was an army led by the social elite and manned by the lower classes of society.

Officers and soldiers interacted with one another in ways that often mirrored British social interactions outside of military life. Soldiers accepted the hierarchy of rank that required their obedience to officers' commands because they were acculturated to social rank recognition at home. This submission of soldiers to officers was enforced through military regulations that required public recognition of an officer's higher status while barring fraternization between them.[39] Still, officers were bound by their honor as gentlemen to exemplify military virtues of courage, gentlemanly behavior, setting the example, and reputation in order to encourage a sense of military honor among their soldiers (commonly referred to as esprit de corps) while securing their own ambition for advancement.[40] Officers had several means to encourage dependence among their soldiers, building a sense of paternal attachment that combined with unit cohesion to form a distinctly British military culture.[41]

Interactions between American colonials and the British Army during the Seven Years' War both encouraged a belief that the British Army was a superior military organization and that the relationship between officers and soldiers left much to be desired. In fact, many of the colonies had created their own military traditions, allowing them to raise provincial regiments that fought with British regulars on campaigns between 1755 and 1762. These provincial forces developed their own distinct military cultures that organized themselves in roughly the same fashion as their British counterparts but fostered an engagement between officers and soldiers in distinctly different ways. These traditions would have an important impact on how the Continental Army would initially be led. A closer look at several American colonial military cultures supports this line of investigation.

The history of colonial Virginia provides an example of a society that only sporadically invented military solutions to its political problems. While the early history of the colony was marked with violence, first on the Eastern Seaboard and then on the frontier, the need for military solutions to political problems declined in the eighteenth century. Following the end of Bacon's Rebellion in 1676, the colony rarely saw a need to create a military organization to defend its borders or increase its territory. Instead, the political leadership relied on alliances with native powers and its relative isolation from both French and Spanish colonies to avoid the expense of war. While the colony maintained a militia system at the county level, these local defensive measures were focused on prevention of domestic violence (particularly from its enslaved and indentured sections of society) and had devolved into more of a social organization than a military tradition.[42]

The ability to remain aloof from the internecine imperial competition prevalent in the north evaporated in 1754 when George Washington and other investors in the Ohio Company ventured west into the Ohio River Valley. Following a disastrous expedition to the forks of the Ohio River in that year, the governor of Virginia, Robert Dinwiddie, established the Virginia Regiment, a provincial army led by Washington as its colonel.[43] Washington requested to organize the regiment along the British professional model, with two battalions totaling two thousand men. He suggested each battalion would contain ten companies and that three of those companies would be commanded by the field-grade officers of the battalion, again in the fashion of the British professional establishment.[44] Over the next year,

Washington and the House of Burgesses struggled to enlist even a fraction of the required soldiers as social and political realities emplaced obstacles insurmountable to the colonial establishment. Not until 1758, when William Pitt convinced the Parliament in London to approve funding from London, would the regiment be fully manned.[45]

During his tenure as commander, Washington attempted to lead based on the conception of personal honor described by Bertram Brown. He also enforced a code of military justice and punishment similar to that of the British Army. Following accusations of misconduct from civilians living in and around his headquarters at Winchester, Washington issued an order stating any officer witnessing "irregularities" and not correcting the problem would be arrested. Noncommissioned officers who did not enforce discipline would be reduced to the ranks and suffer corporal punishment. Soldiers who fought one another would receive five hundred lashes without the benefit of a court-martial while those found drunk would receive a hundred lashes.[46] The regiment soon adhered to the Parliamentary Act passed in 1754, placing all colonial troops under the British Mutiny Act, and while the officers were initially shocked by the severity of these military laws, the regiment was governed by this system for the remainder of the Seven Years' War.[47]

From 1758 to 1762, the regiment did well in the field, even gaining the respect of the British professional officer corps for gallantry under fire. Historian James Titus argues this success was due to a corps of officers and soldiers who served throughout the war, developing unit cohesion and a degree of professionalism. He also points out, correctly, that with the infusion of funds from London, the regiment was comprised of voluntary, well-paid soldiers who learned to fight on the offensive against their French and Cherokee enemies on the frontier.[48] It is possible he missed one other reason for their acceptance by the British professional establishment. The Virginia Regiment looked very similar to the British Army, led by social elites whose personal honor was accepted by their social subordinates as a legitimate source of authority. While London reimbursed the House of Burgesses for military expenditures after 1758, the soldiers enlisted into the regiment were still taken from the margins of colonial society.[49] The act of voluntarily reenlisting soldiers every year placed limitations of the abilities of officers to enforce military discipline, but the combination of recognized social rank, accepted values of personal honor, and British military punishments allowed for a paternalistic relationship between officers and soldiers that would be recognizable to their British counterparts. Arguably, this was possible because the structure for military leadership did not diverge too far from accepted social and political norms of leadership within the greater colony.

If colonial Virginia's military history could be characterized as sporadic but increasing during the eighteenth century, the history of Massachusetts paints a picture of consistent military tensions from 1636 to 1763. Massachusetts's provincial military system was not created, it evolved over a period of 120 years as the colony took the lead combating incursions from Canada by both the French and their Indian allies. Several times, the colony was even capable of projecting military power deep into French holdings.[50] In 1745 a provincial army from Massachusetts even successfully besieged and captured the French fortress of Louisbourg on Cape Breton with the help of a small squadron from the British Navy.[51]

While the basic concept of the militia in Massachusetts was not unique (with universal male participation between the ages of sixteen and sixty), the colony's ability to raise voluntary regiments to serve for a year or less was exceptional. Following the end of King Philip's War, the General Court effectively stopped the practice of local impressment by militia committees and instead promoted the enlistment of volunteers for provincial service.[52] The local militias served to protect the towns from raids by the French-allied Indians while the General Court possessed the ability to commission officers from the counties to recruit volunteers and create regiments of infantry for campaigns. The rank given to an officer reflected in many cases an assumption by the governor that the officer could raise a certain number of men. In 1748, John Stoddard wrote a letter to Governor William Shirley that illustrates this point. He suggested Ephraim Williams as a good candidate for the rank of captain in the provincial regiment raised in Berkshire County. Stoddard reported that Williams was ". . .thought to be the fittest man . . . I know no man amongst us (except Col. Williams) that men would more cheerfully list under than he. . ."[53] When a person was commissioned a colonel, it was because the governor believed he could raise a regiment of volunteers in his county. Captains were chosen to raise companies, sergeants to recruit a few men for the company. This system worked for over a century with interesting consequences.

As Fred Anderson proved in 1984, men who enlisted in the Massachusetts provincial regiments understood their service as contractual in nature.[54] Young men working to gain some form of economic independence (or competence) willingly enlisted for a short term to earn much-needed cash and, in many cases, because other members of their families were enlisting as well.[55] Units were formed locally and regionally and those in leadership positions were not socially distant from their soldiers. For all these reasons, discipline was not harsh by the standards of the day, with a biblical limitation of thirty-nine lashes emplaced on corporal infractions. Capital crimes were referred to the governor.[56] The result was a rather democratic form of military structure, limited by the religious context of the culture in the New England colonies, and recreated every year of the conflict.

Leading soldiers in this system required much more overt negotiations of authority than in the Virginia system. Soldiers enlisted with a certain officer because they trusted that individual.[57] They would not serve in another regiment or company and if they were moved to another unit, or if their leader died and was replaced by another officer not to their liking, they would resist in various ways. In 1755, following the death of Colonel Ephraim Williams near Lake George, the men of his regiment expressed their displeasure at the temporary appointment of Lieutenant Colonel Thomas Gilbert as regimental commander. The field commander, General William Johnson, selected him for his seniority of rank, but he was not from Hampshire County. Due to their unrest and a petition sent by the citizens of Northampton, Gilbert was soon replaced with the local favorite, Lieutenant Colonel Seth Pomeroy.[58] Pomeroy, as an experienced military leader from Hampshire County, had the reputation among both the soldiers and their town members to effectively take the position.

In other instances, entire companies were known to desert their post, despite the tactical or strategic consequences, if their enlistments were complete. In February 1758, Captain Ebenezer Learned faced a difficult dilemma. The enlistments for his company had just expired. The British commander at their posting outside Stillwater, New York, demanded the company of Massachusetts provincials remain until he received reinforcements. Learned's men told him they were planning to desert if he could not convince the British command to release them. Captain Learned agreed with his soldiers, and when the British officer, Captain Philip Skene, refused to acquiesce to the provincials' demands, Learned left with his company.[59]

In response to the relative power of soldiers to resist those actions by their leadership viewed as unacceptable, and because officers were forced to reenlist soldiers at the beginning of each campaign season, officers were not able to lead through a recognition of personal honor based solely upon social status or with the aid of draconian military laws to enforce discipline. Instead, they led by exemplifying courage, common sense, and religious fortitude to maintain the loyalties of their soldiers and communities. Of course, this system of decision-making appeared inefficient and unprofessional to their British counterparts. While Captain Ebenezer Learned certainly believed his decision to lead his company to desert was justified, the British commander could only see this action as both a betrayal and a cowardly act. While different perspectives give separate meaning to these actions, two points can be reasonably asserted. First, the military system developed in Massachusetts was consistent with cultural expectations from the colony. Second, the style of leadership utilized was one that was both acceptable to the soldiers who served and to the communities from which they came.

These examples drawn from Virginia and Massachusetts serve as useful bookends between which other military systems developed in the various colonies. Though a neighbor of Virginia, the colony of Pennsylvania could not strictly follow Virginia's example during the French and Indian War. Prior to the war, Pennsylvania was one of the most peaceful British colonies in North America. Its Quaker-dominated assembly refused to institute any formal military structure

and the ethnic minorities on the frontier were left to fend for themselves.[60] That is not to say that there existed no military units in Pennsylvania prior to the Seven Years' War. During King George's War,
in 1747, Benjamin Franklin subverted the power of the Quaker Party
to obstruct the formation of a military structure in the colony when
he initiated the Associators. These companies of citizen volunteers
privately funded their own organizations to defend against possible
French invasions, electing their officers and equipping themselves
with swords, muskets, and cannon. As many as ninety-eight separate
companies were formed during the war. While the movement lost
momentum in the years between 1750 and 1755 and none of the
companies actually fought in the war, the Associators maintained
their private organizations up to the American Revolution.[61]

Once French forces moved south into the Ohio Valley after 1754,
colonial politicians were forced to change their position regarding a
publicly funded military force and attempted to create a Pennsylvania
Regiment.[62] Initially, men were enlisted for a year, soldiers often
elected their officers, and discipline was very lax.[63] Following a crisis
at Fort Augusta in 1757, when the regiment refused to remain longer
than enlistments allowed, the governor convinced the assembly to
authorize a more professional model, with three-year enlistments, officers commissioned by the governor, and discipline determined by
the British Mutiny Act.[64] Most of the men enlisted were indentured
servants, poor laborers, and recent immigrants. They were recruited
from all over the colony and placed under the command of officers
previously unknown to them. And the officers were commissioned
by the government for their social status; none of them had any previous military experience. The result was often disorder early on, as
the soldiers lacked any respect for their officers and the officer corps
had to mature through experience and attrition.[65]

These "Old Levies" were augmented one year later with twenty-
three companies of "New Levies," forces generated with the help of
William Pitt's policies in London. The "New Levies" followed a third
structure, similar to those instituted in Massachusetts, with soldiers
enlisted for one year but officer ranks determined by the number of
men enlisted by that officer. This structure was made possible with

the promise of British money to pay for American provincial troops. The result was companies drawn from specific regions that were ethnically homogenous. According to R.S. Stephenson, 50 percent of the companies were Scots-Irish, 25 percent were English, and the remainder were drawn from the Welsh and German communities in the colony.[66]

If experimentation and turbulence characterized Pennsylvania's evolution, studies suggest quite a different story unfolded in the closest neighbor to Massachusetts, the colony of Connecticut. During King Philip's War, the colony drafted large numbers of its men in a war for survival. Following the conclusion of the conflict, however, Connecticut became more secure and found less need for a defensive force. In the early years of the eighteenth century, the military reputation of the colony waned as the colonial government struggled to raise provincial regiments to aid in the projection of British imperial power against their French neighbors.[67] Over a period of seventy years, the colony came to an accommodation. Arguably for fear of losing their political autonomy if they failed to properly support British imperial ambitions, Connecticut created a semiprofessional provincial force structure that induced young men to voluntarily enlist with higher bounties under officers they knew from their communities.[68] The colony still resorted to impressment during the Seven Years' War (until 1760 when it rejected the practice outright) but utilized the practice in a manner that recognized the need to maintain the consent of its populace. Draftees were given twenty-four hours to voluntarily enlist (with the accompanying bounty) and officers consulted with their local militia leaders in an attempt to select draftees from militia companies that had not already enlisted enough men.[69]

In Connecticut, similar to its neighbor Massachusetts, the soldiers who enlisted came from the lower economic strata of society but they were not the permanent poor; they were young men, with an average age of twenty-three years.[70] The officers were all selected for their assumed ability to recruit and came from the same communities as their soldiers and from the same social and economic backgrounds. Their chief difference was in their age, as captains averaged thirty-nine years and lieutenants thirty years old.[71] Many of the officers eventually came from the ranks, promoted for their increasing reputation within their communities as military leaders.[72] Many of the officers who rose in rank during the Seven Years' War balanced the need to persuade men to reenlist with the requirement to enforce discipline, led not through social status (because most of them lacked that characteristic) but through example and charisma, and would serve again in 1775.[73]

British and colonial military organizations interacted with one another throughout the Seven Years' War and their diversity illustrates the variation of military structures and cultures developing in the colonies prior to the American Revolution. It can be argued, then, that both the soldiers who served and their various colonial societies created different expectations concerning leadership in the military. It was within this environment of competing visions and perspectives that George Washington took command of the Continental Army in 1775.

When Washington expressed his displeasure with the officers of New England, he was both expressing a cultural bias and noting concrete examples of poor leadership. In no culture easily identifiable is it considered a virtue for military officers to show cowardice in the face of the enemy, as was the case in the conviction of Captain John Callender. Yet Washington began "mentoring" his officers on the virtues of courage four days after arriving in Cambridge and following one completed court-martial of a captain for cowardice. It can be argued four days was a short time to determine there was a problem of cowardice among an officer corps numbering over 1,300.[74] Furthermore, Washington quickly complained to John Hancock, then president of the Congress, that his delinquency in reporting troop numbers was due to a lack of discipline among the officers.[75] It would appear he agreed with Benjamin Thompson's observation that the lack of social distance between the officers and the men made the enforcement of discipline impossible.

Still, these officers, without the benefit of Washington's guidance, managed to ride a rapidly rising tide of popular force that drove the British regulars from Lexington and Concord back to Boston and then exacted a costly victory on the enemy at Breed's Hill, leaving the British where they started, bottled up in Boston. Certainly, the Provincial Congress of Massachusetts gave command of the forces to Artemus Ward largely because of his experiences in the previous war but also for his political connections to the country party. Yet each regiment fought separately at the Battle of Bunker Hill and for commanders the soldiers chose to serve under. While the officers and soldiers constructing the redoubt on Breed's Hill accepted the leadership of Colonel William Prescott, no general officer or field officer exercised overall command on the battlefield. With Colonel Prescott in the redoubt on Breed's Hill was Major General Joseph Warren who refused to take charge because he had not yet received his formal commission from the Congress and lacked the military experience of Prescott. He fought as a volunteer private. And there was confusion at Bunker Hill, but this was due to an inconsistency of experience and training among the various regiments and an unwillingness to obey Israel Putnam as he attempted to move units from Bunker Hill to Breed's Hill. In other words, failures during the battle were due in large part to a lack of political coordination between the four New England governments and their forces in the field.

Still, the forces occupying the redoubt on Breed's Hill and defending the flanks of that position fought with discipline and courage. Colonel Prescott mounted a defense on Breed's Hill that repelled the British regulars twice and resulted in a victory so costly to the British (1,054 soldiers killed or wounded from a total force of 2,300)[76] that they were eventually forced to abandon Boston, following the arrival of artillery from Fort Ticonderoga. Captain Thomas Knowlton of Connecticut and Colonel John Stark of New Hampshire, defending the left flank behind both a fence and stone wall, effectively defeated every British attempt to overrun their position. But these officers essentially fought their own battles, using their experience from the previous war to inform their decisions on how to defend their positions and when to retreat. On their third attempt, the British regulars gained the redoubt on the hill, despite never flanking the position, in part because the American forces ran out of ammunition.[77] The Americans in the earthen fort fought a rear guard action hand-to-hand against the British with the support of a company that remained in the flaming Charlestown, while Stark's forces still defending the fence and wall on the American left flank withdrew on their own across Charlestown Neck to Cambridge.[78] While American casualties were high at 450 soldiers killed or wounded, the British managed to capture only 31 soldiers, most of whom were mortally wounded.[79]

For over a century, Massachusetts and the other New England colonies fielded forces capable on the battlefield. While these provincial forces often lacked training in conventional warfare, they frequently performed quite well when used as light infantry for skirmishing and ranging. Their most glaring military weakness was in the arena of logistics and transportation, an issue Lord Loudon focused on when he took command of British forces in North America in 1756.[80] Yet Washington initially did not focus on logistics or training (though he was aware of a lack of muskets, ball, and powder), deciding the men would fight well if properly led. But in his opinion these New England forces lacked the proper leadership. Arguably this was a culturally biased perspective that would not recognize that not only was New England leadership devised at the time to lead a soldiery acculturated to the democracy of New England's town meeting governance, but it was actually effective, if only for the short terms necessitated by one-year enlistments.

In fact, Washington faced a serious leadership challenge of his own from the moment he took command of the Continental Army. Due to a conflict of cultural expectations, a *new* negotiation of authority was required between the leadership of the army and those who were led. While the Virginia gentleman was initially taking charge of New England regiments, he would shortly be confronted with the requirement to assimilate forces from almost all of the former colonies into a single army. To do so, he and the rest of the officer corps would need to create a new form of military leadership that could be identified as distinctly American.

Don Higginbotham suggested a similar understanding of this process. Examining several of the generals in the Continental Army, Higginbotham argued that the amateurish nature of their service led to a leadership style more civilian than military in character. While Washington was attempting to create a professional officer corps based on the British model, there was little continuity between the Seven Years' War and the Revolution so the generals were commissioned based on their civilian merits. Amateur generals combined with a civil-military relationship dictated by republican ideals to shape this new and uniquely American leadership style.[81] Yet Higginbotham missed the continuity between these two wars provided by senior officers to include not only Washington but also New England officers like Seth Pomeroy, Israel and Rufus Putnam, John Stark, and several others.

This current examination will go further, considering not only the top leaders of the army, but investigating the perspectives and remembrances of soldiers and mid-grade officers as well. These narratives will show that culturally there was more continuity between the Seven Years' War and the Revolution in the realm of military activities than Higginbotham concluded. Additionally, the formulation of leadership as a negotiation of authority requires an analysis of the evidence from both the top down and the bottom up, continuing a tradition of historical study decades old that enriches our understanding of the agency exercised by people not completely in control of their own destiny.

Other influential historians have investigated the evolution of the Continental Army and concluded that, over time, it grew to look more like the British Army in structure and leadership. James Kirby Martin and Mark Edward Lender make the most compelling case in this regard. Writing what is perhaps the seminal work on the Continental Army (now in its third edition), they contend that the colonial military tradition was becoming Anglicized or Europeanized over the course of the eighteenth century through the practice of enlisting poor and marginalized men for active service in provincial armies during wartime.[82] This pattern of service continued following the short period of the *rage militaire* in 1775 and 1776, as Washington's request for longer enlistments was approved by Congress. "From the point of view of social characteristics, the new Continental soldiery increasingly took on the appearance of a traditional European army while looking less like a republican force."[83] While this position allows for a tension between ideology and reality, it suggests reality won out, making the Continental Army an un-republican institution fighting for republican goals.

The evidence presented here will argue against the conception that a European military culture infused the Continental Army or that reality overcame ideology in its institutional practices. Instead, there was a tension in the army between a republican ideal of the citizen-soldier and the real need for a professional army, a tension that was not as overtly visible in other European armies of the eighteenth century. Among the various groups that organized within the Continental Army there were competing understandings of what proper military service looked like, tensions between professional and popular military cultures that already existed in the colonies before 1775. A cultural discourse concerning the nature of authority and the legitimate use of power was necessary to resolve those stresses or the army would cease to exist. For these reasons, the Continental Army was led in a manner foreign to their European enemies and possibly set the foundation for how the US Army would be led in the future.

For the majority of the War for Independence, the Continental Army conducted its major operations within three distinct departments: North, South, and Middle. The command of the Northern Department fell initially to Philip Schuyler, headquartered in Albany, and his soldiers came from regiments recruited in New England, New York, Pennsylvania, and New Jersey. From Albany, campaigns were launched into Canada and against the forts built along the Lake Champlain-Lake George corridor leading into Canada. Later, Major General Horatio Gates fought the battles at Saratoga as commander of this department and operations finally ended with Sullivan's campaign against the Iroquois in western New York in 1779. The Southern Department was commanded by at least four generals from the Continental Army. Charles Lee first successfully defended Charleston in 1776. The region then suffered a period of civil strife between Loyalist and Patriot partisans until the British attacked Savannah and Charleston in 1779 and 1780. Benjamin Lincoln was in command until Sir Henry Clinton captured Charleston, when Horatio Gates moved south to reassert American control of the region. Following Gates's defeat at Camden in August 1780, Washington chose Major General Nathanael Greene to take command in the South, where he remained until Cornwallis's defeat at Yorktown in October 1781. During this entire period, Continental forces in the Southern Department came from the southern states, and were significantly augmented by state militia forces after the almost complete destruction of the Maryland, Delaware, Virginia, and North Carolina state lines at Charleston and Camden.

The core of the Continental Army occupied the Middle Department, a region spanning between Newburgh, New York, in the north and Yorktown, Virginia, in the south. Called the Grand Army, this main force was continuously commanded by George Washington from 1775 to 1783 and included regiments from Massachusetts, Connecticut, New Hampshire, Rhode Island, New York, New Jersey, Pennsylvania, Delaware, Maryland, and Virginia. This portion of the Continental Army contained the largest number of troops representing the widest cross-section of the states. In fact, one recent study suggests as much as 50 percent of the Continental Army was comprised by men from New England, with another 40 percent originating from Virginia and the mid-Atlantic states, making the Grand Army representational of the whole of the Continental Army.[84] Furthermore, during the periods of winter encampment, many of the other elements of the Continental Army from other departments converged on the Grand Army until the following campaign season. While some attention will be given to the other departments of the army, this study will focus largely on the Grand Army, the general orders given to those soldiers, and their responses to these orders as representative of the whole army.

In an attempt to understand the negotiations of authority at play in the Grand Army, five important areas of army life will be examined to highlight how officers sought to transform the force into an organization capable of defeating the British and how their soldiers responded to these efforts. It seems apparent the first area of focus should be on the developing concept of officership. The term officership will be defined as the qualities and traits of leadership necessary for one man to command another within the confines of the Continental Army during a time of war. Both top leaders of the army and those being led maintained rights to determine those qualities and traits, as general and regimental officers mentored company officers who then faced commitment, compliance, or resistance from their men in the rank and file. Cultural understandings, ideology, and the exercise of authority in camp and in the field all played with and against one another to forge a common understanding of the "good officer."

Recruiting was a topic of much debate during the period. While the war began with states willing to enlist men for only one year, Washington always maintained the view that enlistments for the duration of the war were critical to the success of the Continental Army. The reasons for this will become clear, but they do not all hinge on the creation of a core of professionals. States resisted this change for a period of time for several reasons, but Congress eventually acceded to Washington's request, creating enlistments for three years or the duration of the war. Still, those enlisting maintained, in most cases, the voluntary nature of enlistment and the army always contained men enlisted under various terms, including bounties, pay, and time of service.

Tied to recruiting was the issue of discipline and punishment. This was another topic affecting the governance of the army that Washington again had little authority to change himself. At the onset of war, soldiers were governed by the Massachusetts Militia Act of 1775, a set of military laws viewed as much too lenient by Washington and many of his fellow generals. While this form of discipline superficially followed British forms, with regimental and general courts-martial and both corporal and capital punishments, lashings were still limited to thirty-nine per offense and the sentence of death was an extremely rare punishment. Within a few years, however, new military justice laws were passed, allowing up to a hundred lashes and allowing capital punishment for several infractions, including treason and desertion to the enemy. Still, these laws were much more lenient than those of the British Army and soldiers continued to exert their perceived rights to resist in the face of what they regarded as draconian or illegal uses of discipline by their officers.

In order to fight effectively on the battlefield, soldiers and officers needed training. Operating the smoothbore musket of the late eighteenth century required discipline and courage in the face of a determined enemy. To win on the field of battle, soldiers were required to maintain unit cohesion while maneuvering across the ground in a rapid and precise manner to flank the enemy and force their withdrawal. Initially, training was left to the regimental commanders, while brigade commanders issued orders during the battle to their regiments, assuming the regiments could execute those orders in a timely and effective manner. Due to the lack of regulated and centralized training, the soldiers of the early Continental Army rarely experienced tactical success offensively. Despite notable exceptions at Trenton, Princeton, Bennington, and Saratoga, the leadership and soldiers of the Continental Army were much more confident and successful on the defensive. A change would come in the spring of 1778 when Major General Frederick Wilhelm August Heinrich Ferdinand von Steuben introduced the "Blue Book." The effects of this new emphasis on regular training will be explored to determine the repercussions on officer-soldier interactions and negotiations.

Harder to assess but even more important was troop morale, a subjective measure of the spirit of an army. This difficult subject is the final area of study for this investigation. Morale is defined here as the measure of soldier acceptance to their mission, to their environment, and to the leadership of their officers. Included in their environment was their treatment by civilian society and the legislation passed by Congress. Over the course of the war, it can be safely asserted that the support of neither their political leadership nor their civilian brethren met soldiers' expectations, even superficially. Yet the Grand Army remained in the field and fought until the end. The reasons for this rather amazing fact was the ability of the army leadership to convince their soldiers that the cause was worthy and the officers would take care of the men when the time came for their support. Some historians would argue the core of the army, those who enlisted for the duration of the war and served for longer than six years, became professionalized and institutionalized in the values of the organization. The historians taking this position might also argue those values that compelled these soldiers to remain were handed down to the army by the British establishment (even the pan-European military culture of the West) and were enforced by the economic limitations of those who served. Yet events throughout the war, particularly in 1781 and 1783, contradict this view. Those events will be examined toward the end of the chapter.

The Continental Army was formed initially as an amalgam of regiments from a multitude of military traditions that were either created or evolved during the final colonial war. Above the regimental level there existed few areas of agreement over issues of recruiting, discipline, or training. In order for the Continental Army to become an American army, these disagreements would have to be settled. The treatment of soldiers, and their willingness to serve under that treatment, would have to become standardized throughout the army. Failure to successfully negotiate the terms of authority necessary to determine both how decisions were made and how those decisions were executed would have spelled the end of the army in the face of the enemy. How the Continental Army managed to arrive at a consensus led to a new agreement on leadership that, while imperfect, was distinctly American.

One

Officership in the Continental Army

THE PROPER EXERCISE OF AUTHORITY

IT IS WELL KNOWN THAT GENERAL WASHINGTON WAS LESS THAN pleased with the caliber of officers he encountered when he arrived at Cambridge in 1775. In various letters to his friends in Congress and Virginia, he said that these leaders from New England were cowardly, vain, and only willing to serve for money and promotion. In short, these men were completely devoid of the republican virtues Washington had come to expect given New England was the heart of the Revolution. Furthermore, Washington's despair did not solely derive from disappointed ideological attachments. He also described important cultural differences between himself and these northern men, to the effect that he rarely recognized a gentleman among them. Instead, these officers were much too close to their men and unable or unwilling to order their soldiers to do the tasks required for soldiers to win in battle.

Washington was looking for the right kind of men to lead the Continental Army, men with the proper background to command respect and compel obedience. His experiences in the French and Indian War led him to the conclusion that one factor, personal honor, was the key to effective leadership. Personal honor could be recognized by the social status of an officer, his personal actions, and by his treatment of those placed under his command. Honor, in Washington's opinion, could be taught, instilled in younger officers through mentorship. Of course, these young officers had to understand the necessity for honor first. This understanding often required an officer to have a background that recognized social obligation and gentlemanly honor as marks of social leadership.

This conception of who deserved to lead the army and its soldiers was not readily agreed upon by the majority of those officers in service at the time of Washington's appointment as commander in chief or by the soldiers enlisted at that time. Over the course of the war, Washington and his officer corps worked hard to come to a new agreement on the meaning of their offices, the legitimate sources of their authority, and the appropriate exercise of that authority, all the while responding to the abilities of their soldiers to exercise their own agency. In the first two years of the war, Washington sought to gain more control over who should lead, directing officers to follow his orders while many of them resisted complying in various ways. Though Congress decided on the general officers based upon their social status and the political need to keep the states happy with their quota of generals, commissions for the majority of the field and company officers came directly from their states and were based more on their willingness to serve in the army. These men were often not yet affluent, though their families might have had some modicum of wealth, and they invariably spent more time with their soldiers than they did the commander in chief. As the war continued, officers came to understand the need to follow many of Washington's examples while His Excellency was forced to admit certain compromises both to meet the expectations of his officers and soldiers and to standardize conduct throughout the army.

How this negotiation played out over the Revolution is the topic of a minor debate. One of the more persuasive arguments is presented in a dissertation by Scott N. Hendrix, "The Spirit of the Corps: The British Army and the Pre-National Pan-European Military World and the Origins of American Military Culture, 1754-

1783." As its rather lengthy title suggests, Hendrix argues in this work that before the development of a strong nationalist ideology, honor was the justification for military culture in the pan-European world, including the North American colonies of Great Britain. Gentlemen served as officers to "display their courage and honor" and others served in the rank and file to participate in an occupation viewed as "acceptable and honorable."[1] While Hendrix admits the democratic revolutions of the late eighteenth century served to undercut this culture over time, he asserts that the American military inherited this view of military service and that it remained into the twentieth century.[2]

Yet Hendrix focused almost solely on the British Army to make his point. Only brief attention was paid to the Continental Army, and American military history in general, in his final chapter.[3] Caroline Cox, writing a year earlier, did address the Continental Army and its officers and she did so in much the same vein. She depicted the army as one with a distinct social divide between gentlemen officers and lower-sort soldiers that worked well with the hierarchy necessary in a standing army. Concepts of personal honor were important to her formulation, as well, but where Hendrix viewed personal honor as the purview of gentlemen, Cox argued personal honor existed for the enlisted soldiers too.[4] Discipline was less harsh in the American Army than in the British establishment because all men serving maintained a certain amount of personal honor, a commodity the army could take as punishment for a misdeed. While corporal and capital punishment existed in the American military justice system of the era, public shaming was also important for both officers and soldiers to strip them of their honor.[5]

These two works are the most persuasive studies in an area that has not received much focus. As stated earlier, Don Higginbotham did write an essay recognizing Washington's cultural bias toward his New England officers and suggesting that the amateur nature of the officer corps led to a civilian-like leadership model within the Continental Army. Still, in the realm of military leadership, he focused much more of his attention on Washington's contribution to the American military's traditional adherence to the proper civil-military relationship of subordination to civil control.[6] Other historians, like E. Wayne Carp, focused on the administration of the Continental Army to show how officers in support roles (hospitals, quartermaster corps, and Commissary Department) exercised republican virtue to keep the army alive despite a consistent lack of support from both politicians and civilians during the war.[7] What these works and others investigating the Continental Army ignore, assume, or only imply is the relationship between the officers and their soldiers that we call leadership today.

In every army organized within a construct that recognizes a distinct officer corps to lead soldiers there is an understanding of what constitutes a "good" officer. Of course, the term "good" is difficult to define due to the cultural nature of its definition. In general terms, "good" officers derive their authority to lead from a legitimate source and then exercise authority over their followers in a legitimate fashion to achieve success on the battlefield. Legitimate sources of authority and legitimate uses of authority are areas for negotiation between the leaders and the led, whether or not they are recognized as such in an overt way.

To understand how the Continental Army was led by its officers and how or why both officers and soldiers agreed (or disagreed) over the concept of the "good" officer, it must first be acknowledged that there did exist differing perspectives on the topic. Several distinct cultural visions of officers existed in the colonies up through 1775. While there were variations, three basic conceptions of leadership guided most colonial military institutions in their exercise of authority. In many of the southern colonies up through Maryland and, at times, in Pennsylvania and New Jersey, the gentleman-officer was viewed as a legitimate leader in the military. His authority to lead was derived from his social status. His sense of personal honor maintained that authority over those he led by exhibiting courage and a sense of patronage for his soldiers. In the northern colonies, particularly those that comprised New England, local loyalties and a cultural understanding of a communal contract governed who could lead and how they should conduct themselves. The authority to lead came from local recognitions in towns and counties while the conduct of the officers was regulated by a communal sense of the proper use of authority. An improper exercise of authority was seen as a violation of contract (both communal and enlistment), potentially releasing soldiers from their obligation of enlistment and justifying resistance. The third distinct construct of proper leadership developed in the Pennsylvania Associators, a model that was also employed on occasion in Delaware. Here was the most directly democratic expression of the exercise of authority, where the authority to lead was determined by the consensus of the group and that authority was only exercised legitimately through the same group consensus. An important difference between this model and the other two discussed was that the Associators were privately funded units, often with members derived from similar social strata.

These three solutions for who should lead and in what manner interacted with ideology, reality, and human action during the American Revolution as regiments from the various state lines came together to fight the British. Most of the officers and soldiers serving during the war agreed with a republican ideology that championed citizen-soldiers serving in a temporary capacity as a safeguard against the evils of a standing army. And their service further committed them to an ideology bent on overturning traditional forms of authority in favor of a new paradigm. Yet many of them came to agree with the need to professionalize the service to some degree in order to increase their capabilities to defeat the British Army on the battlefield. This tension between ideology and necessity was further complicated by the realities of officer jealousies over rank, states' political competition for officer appointments, and the real economic consequences of service for both officers and soldiers. Finally, the expectations of treatment expressed by those soldiers in the rank and file limited attempts to increase the authority of the officer corps and tempered movements toward a professionalized standing army. The acceptance of revolutionary ideology that championed a challenge to traditional authority lent legitimacy to soldier resistance against increased officer authority in the army.

After four years of war and institutional evolution, Congress published the drill manual for the American army. Known as the "Blue

Book," this manual sought to standardize drill and make it easier for commanders in the field to control units from the various states. In the back of the book, every rank was described and their corresponding duties were prescribed. These duties set down many of the ideals that the commander in chief sought to instill throughout the Revolutionary War. Still, the manual's approach does not fit easily into a framework that recognizes a gentleman as having a class-based right to lead through personal honor. The private soldier is granted a degree of autonomy. Noncommissioned officers are directed to recognize this autonomy in their methods of instruction and discipline while officers at the junior ranks are taught to protect that autonomy from abuses. Furthermore, the need to publish and reassert these expectations suggests a recognition that the officers in the Continental Army were not bringing with them certain skills, knowledge that a gentleman would conceivably gain through practice in his civilian surroundings.

In the end, the interaction of competing understandings of military leadership produced a new American concept of the "good" officer. He was not necessarily a prominent person socially, though he often was more affluent than his soldiers. He did maintain more control over his subordinates than was allowed outside of the military, but he could not compel his soldiers' obedience to the degree that his European counterparts could. Furthermore, he was constantly aware of the need to treat his soldiers in a manner that did not risk rebellion, endangering the very existence of the force. The result was a new standard formulated in the drill manual of 1779 that codified proper behavior for officers and noncommissioned officers within the regimental structure of the army.

AT THE ONSET OF THE AMERICAN REVOLUTION, there were competing ideas about the legitimate source from which the authority to lead should originate. In the North, the legitimacy of an officer was based on local reputation for leadership (to include military leadership) and was confirmed by the willingness of local men to enlist under his command. In certain regions of the middle colonies, a mixed practice of local reputation and popular election determined who would lead on military ventures. The tradition most prevalent in the South, and accepted by George Washington, agreed with the concept of the gentleman-officer and found validity within the British professional establishment.

At the beginning of the war, in Boston, General Thomas Gage experienced disciplinary problems among some of his officers. In March of 1775, the British soldiers sent to occupy Boston were disgruntled over poor living quarters (many of them were encamped on Boston Commons) and inadequate food. On March 20, 1775, two ensigns were tried in a general court-martial for dueling over an accusation of ungentlemanly behavior. Three days later, a lieutenant colonel and an ensign attempted to duel with swords after the lieutenant colonel struck the ensign, but they were stopped. Attempting to finish the matter, the two officers reengaged with pistols on the Commons and were arrested by the officer of the guard.[8] These gentlemen, with little to do, were beginning to pick at each other's honor and dueling to protect the same.

In February 1777, three Royal Artillery officers were stationed in Quebec for the winter. One night these three young men drank too much and traveled to the home of a local inhabitant who had three daughters. During that evening, while these three men took "liberties" with the young women, their father returned home and ran the officers off his property. In the morning, the father complained to the British commander, Major General William Philips. The general addressed all the officers in his formation, claiming he did not know who these men were and that he did not want to know. Instead, he chastised the group, insisting that gentlemen did not conduct themselves in this manner, nor should they need to do so to gain the affections of a woman. For this reason, those officers responsible should go to the aggrieved father and apologize; soldiers should at all times conduct themselves gallantly. Thus shamed, the three officers went to the accusing father and apologized.[9]

British lieutenant Thomas Anburey recounted this event in his diary and then followed with an anecdote about Colonel Carleton who was assaulted one day while riding in his sleigh. Anburey blamed the senior commander, General Guy Carleton, for this incident, arguing the general's generous behavior with the local Canadians led to insolence on the part of the lower class in Quebec. While he agreed with General Philips that gentlemen should always conduct themselves honorably, the plebeians of Canada needed to be taught to respect the authority of their betters if order was to be maintained during the winter's quarters.[10] And the only way to teach the lower sort was through the exercise of authority and compulsion.

These accounts of British officers' behavior and their superiors' responses highlight a culture of leadership that historians often see as being shared by American officers during the period. For the gentleman-officer, personal honor was paramount. Honor lent the officer his authority to command and guided his actions toward his soldiers, his fellow officers, the enemy, and those civilians with whom he interacted. To maintain his authority, that personal honor required guarding against accusation and demanded examples of courage under fire. For those above him, an assumption of his honor allowed for shaming as the highest form of punishment while the gentleman jealously protected his prerogative from unjust accusations. To attain personal honor, these men had to possess a certain position, given to them either by virtue of their birth or through patronage.

This was the model of officership George Washington initially sought to create when he took command of the Continental Army in 1775. His experiences during the Seven Years' War had taught him that the British model described previously was the professional solution to his current Revolutionary problem. Washington served as a volunteer officer aide to British major general Edward Braddock in 1755 and again as a colonial colonel under the command of British brigadier general John Forbes and Colonel Henry Bouquet. In 1756, while serving as commander of the Virginia Regiment, his letters to members of the House of Burgesses illustrated his adherence to this model of the gentleman-officer. Following accusations by a few politicians that he and his officers were conducting themselves in a dishonorable fashion, Washington defended his actions and insisted he always strove to be the model of a gentleman-officer. If he could no longer command the unanimous support of the colonial government, he would gladly resign his commission.[11] In response, he received several letters aimed at soothing his honor, including one from Landon Carter claiming the accusations made against him came from a few men of little esteem in the assembly and that "A whole croud of Females" sent their regards and were holding a service in his honor.[12] Washington's honor was thus soothed by the assurance that those who accused him did not possess the approbation of his society and that assurance was confirmed by the support of the ladies.

During the Revolution, Washington wanted gentlemen of honor to serve, men with merit and republican virtue, and men with the means and social status necessary to understand and maintain personal honor. He notified his officers early on that their commissions would soon be determined not by how many soldiers they could reenlist but by their social standing. Commissions would be reserved "for such Gentlemen as are most likely to deserve them."[13] Commanders should be easy and condescending with their subordinate officers but not too familiar, as this would breed contempt. With their soldiers, they should strictly enforce discipline, but not in an unreasonable fashion, and they should reward or punish their men by the merit of their actions. Above all, the senior officers must discourage vice and remind their soldiers of the justice of their cause.[14] To state it differently, Washington was announcing his determination to decide who was fit to lead and his decision would be based on a man's personal honor and right actions.

Other gentlemen from the southern colonies agreed with Washington's initial vision. For a week in October 1775, a committee from Congress visited the army's encampment at Cambridge. Their mission was to confer with Washington and representatives from the four New England governments over the issue of raising a new army in 1776.[15] One of the members of the committee, Thomas Lynch from South Carolina, wrote to Washington the next month to inform him of Congress's response to the committee's recommendations. While Congress did agree to pay a bonus to those officers who elected to remain in the service, Lynch hoped Washington was in a position to turn down those New England officers who changed their minds and decided to stay only for the money. He now believed, after visiting Cambridge, that the soldiers of New England could be convinced to follow gentlemen from other states, relieving Washington from the necessity of relying on "bad Offices of that Country in order to raise Men there." Washington should also be pleased to know that Congress approved all the amendments to the Articles of War Washington suggested, so officers would now be required to act and dress like gentlemen.[16] Though not an ideal solution, especially as it acknowledged the necessity to induce officers to serve through payment, the congressional decision to begin following Washington's suggestions regarding officer conduct was encouraging.

Yet despite what appeared to be an early success to restructure the officer corps more to the liking of the commanding general, Washington faced daunting resistance from both his fellow officers and his soldiers in the rank and file. The vast majority of his army understood their service in terms of local loyalties and communal contract and they would only agree to serve under a leadership structure that fit with those terms of service. The strongest obstacle to Washington's designs was the demand for regionally aligned regiments. Writing to John Hancock on November 8, 1775, Washington complained that his efforts to create a new corps of officers were stymied by the refusal of soldiers to serve under officers not from their home colonies. He was seriously contemplating dismissing all those unwilling to serve in an integrated regiment.[17] But within only a few weeks, when faced with the urgent need to reenlist his entire army, Washington admitted defeat on this plan and formed his force with regiments determined by region.[18]

In fact, both New England officers and soldiers were unwilling to let go of their cultural understandings concerning who should lead and how they should be selected. Despite Washington's orders that officers would be selected among the gentlemen with the best merit, junior officers continued through the fall of 1775 and winter of 1776 to compete with one another for enlistments. First lieutenants in the regiments competed with their captains for recruits under the belief that they would be promoted if they enlisted more men.[19] Soldiers petitioned Washington for solutions to who should lead and not for reasons Washington would have agreed with. One group of soldiers from Rowley, Massachusetts, asked Washington to replace their company commander with Lieutenant Cresy, followed by Second Lieutenant Pike, and then Sergeant Bailey. This line of succession in the company would settle the issue of officers properly representing the men of the town who were aligned with two different parishes.[20]

And while Washington viewed these competitions and demands as unpatriotic and provincial, the men serving from New England believed this was the only way for officers to maintain the trust of their communities and for soldiers to be led by men they trusted. During the colonial wars, New England towns enforced their own influence over officer behavior during campaigns. While the local reputation of a prospective officer was important to his ability to recruit, his actions on campaign were equally important to his ability to continue to serve. Officers who failed to perform well on campaign could even face imprisonment upon their return home. Additionally, officers like Colonel Seth Pomeroy from Northampton could enjoy local political support for promotion in the field should that promotion become necessary.[21] This requirement for the officers to continue to serve in the trust of their communities did not change over the twelve years between the end of the Seven Years' War in 1763 and the start of the American Revolution in 1775.

Rufus Putnam, Washington's first chief of engineers and then a regimental commander, recounted his experiences during the Seven Years' War that gives a full account of how reputation, town attachments, and the expectations of those serving all worked together to determine who would lead in a New England provincial regiment. Putnam first enlisted as a private in Captain Ebenezer Learned's company recruited out of Brookfield, a few miles north of Sturbridge, Massachusetts, in 1757.[22] At the end of that campaign, his company deserted their post because they were being held past their enlistments.[23] Putnam enlisted the next year in Joseph Whitcomb's company (Captain Learned having lost his commission for leading the desertion) in Colonel Timothy Ruggles's regiment, again out of Brookfield.[24] The following year, Putnam again enlisted, this time as a sergeant, in William Page's company from Hardwick, again in Colonel Ruggles's regiment (Hardwick is a town just north of Brookfield). But Putnam ended this campaign very disillusioned with his service, having been forced to conduct extra service for the British Army as a carpenter but not receiving the extra pay he was promised for this service.[25]

While he vowed not to enlist again, he found himself in an interesting situation the following spring in 1760. Putnam had moved to the neighboring town of New Braintree and enrolled in the town's militia. When mustered to meet with Captain Page who was again recruiting, Putnam was handed recruiting orders direct from Timothy Ruggles who had been promoted to brigadier general in the provincial service. Notwithstanding his promise never to serve as a soldier again, Putnam also faced the displeasure of his new town if he agreed to follow these orders. Apparently, several other men from New Braintree had applied for the job, as these orders promised the rank of lieutenant should Putnam enlist enough men. Ruggles had refused these older members of the town and they were now angry at his selection of Putnam for the position, claiming it was an insult to the town. Page attempted to recruit in New Braintree with no success, but when several former soldiers acquainted with Putnam claimed they would enlist under his leadership, Putnam accepted his orders and enlisted eight or nine soldiers immediately. Ironically, Putnam made the mistake of enlisting these men not for himself but for Captain Page and when Page failed to make his quota for a company, he took Putnam's recruits, forcing him to go looking for more men late in the season with disappointing results.[26]

Several traits of the New England tradition concerning military leadership and the legitimate source of an officer's authority to lead become apparent through this account. Men known locally recruited companies for the provincial service and their success was determined by their reputation, often as military leaders. Yet the commissions came from the General Court, handed down by the senior military leadership, so local support for applications of commissions did not guarantee rank. A reputation among those senior officers continuing to serve over several campaigns could also provide increasing promotions in the service, as long as a man could maintain the support of the towns. William Page was not able to maintain that loyalty between Hardwick and New Braintree, but clearly Rufus Putnam could. Still, Putnam had to thread his way carefully or he risked alienating himself from his newly adopted town. Finally, the men he recruited were men who had served with him before, at similar ranks, and who worked with him in the towns of the region. While he lost these initial recruits, he was given a commission as an ensign in Colonel Abijah Willard's regiment based on Brigadier General Ruggles's recommendation.

A sense of commonality between officers and men was further strengthened through a shared sense of religious community. The journals and diaries from the French and Indian War often cite which Psalm was preached each Sunday while on campaign. Chaplains were usually designated within the regiments of Massachusetts and Connecticut but it was not unique for a soldier or officer recognized as most able to preach. If the Sabbath preacher was a private, all soldiers, officers and privates alike, were expected to listen. Stephen Cross (a New England carpenter contracted to build ships for the British on Lake Ontario) wrote "attended Worship where a Common Soldier by the name of Williamson Preached I believe a Good Man made many Good observations and good admonitions and councils."[27] In an orderly book kept by Sergeant Josiah Perry in Nova Scotia, "Prayers are to be attended daily at 9 o'clock, A.M. by all the men of the garrison off duty. . . Divine service to be attended every Sunday by all the garrison off duty—11 A.M."[28] This congregation of soldiers as equals was so ingrained in the mindset of colonial soldiers from Massachusetts that Rufus Putnam (writing after the American Revolution) remarked, "Captain Learned prayed with his Company Morning and evening, and on the Sabbath read a Sermon (Oh! How the times have changed)."[29]

Washington experienced this religious component of New England military culture when many of his men celebrated Pope's Day (or Guy Fawkes Day) that commemorated the anniversary of the foiled Catholic plot to blow up Parliament in 1605. Officers and soldiers alike paraded through Cambridge on November 5, 1775, burning an effigy of the pope. Washington scolded his officers, calling their actions "monstrous" and demanding the celebrations stop while there was an American attempt to elicit the aid of Canadian colonists.[30] Still, he recognized the necessity of providing for the religious requirements of his troops when, in February 1776, he formally established a Chaplain Corps, ordering one chaplain be designated for every two regiments.[31]

Certainly not all units present around Boston were from the New England colonies. Companies from the Pennsylvania Associators were among the first forces from outside the northern region to join in active revolt. As many as 924 men were present in the summer of 1775 and grew to several thousands by the summer of 1776.[32] Initially, the Pennsylvania Associators enlisted and trained these soldiers. The Associators were governed by their Articles of Association, a document drawn along the lines of John Locke's natural philosophy where membership was voluntary, the soldiers elected their company officers (approved by the governor), and funds were furnished voluntarily.[33] In the early summer of 1775, following the news of Lexington and Concord, Pennsylvania Associations raised numerous battalions, including light infantry and rifle battalions, training for months, electing officers, and marching to Boston and in support of Washington's Flying Camp in 1776.[34] On July 4, 1776, the officers and privates of the Associations convened and elected their two brigade commanders, Daniel Roberdeau and James Ewing.[35]

At the outset of the Revolution, several military cultures and their various views concerning the legitimate source of authority for officers to lead combined in the formation of a new establishment of the Continental Army on January 1, 1776. Known as the First Establishment, the Continental Army consisted of soldiers enlisted for one year, regiments remained organized by state but were designated as numbered Continental regiments, and the Massachusetts Articles of War governed disciplinary actions. For many, republican ideology was all that linked these different understandings of military service in common cause to eject British forces from the colonies. Perhaps intuiting this reality, Washington encouraged his officers from the very beginning of his time as their commander in chief through the use of republican rhetoric in his general orders. Preparing to seize the Dorchester Heights overlooking Boston in March 1776, he demanded that all of his soldiers display the courage expected of "freemen" fighting for their liberty.[36]

And Washington's republican rhetoric was mirrored by the state legislatures. The Massachusetts General Court congratulated the general for his successes at Boston. In their speech on March 28, 1776, the political leaders of Massachusetts painted Washington as the perfect republican gentleman, one who gained the trust of the people by his reputation from the previous war, for his refusal to accept pay while in military service, and because he always placed himself under the authority of civilian leadership.[37] Just five days after its signing, Washington ordered the Declaration of Independence to be read to the army as a fresh reminder that every soldier now acted to preserve and protect his State, a State imbued with the power to reward his endeavors to preserve the liberty of a free country.[38]

While the General Court of Massachusetts believed Washington embodied republican virtue, Washington believed he needed to inculcate that vision of republican virtue among his New England officers. From his perspective, they lacked the necessary public spirit required to lead soldiers in the Revolution. In fact, he complained vociferously to his friends and congressional leadership that the patriotism he was taught was characteristic among the people of New England was completely absent.[39] Instead, these soldiers wanted to go home frequently on furlough, they refused to enlist for longer than one year at a time, and they refused to continue service unless they were paid. The result in the first months of the war was a much lower enlistment than previously expected.[40] These men were proving their service was based more on local loyalties than true patriotism and Washington believed the reasons for this clearly related to the lack of social status among the officers. How could a man truly understand patriotism if he did not own land or give the proper level of dedication to Congress if his commission was not determined by that august political body?

In reality, when Washington took command of the army in Massachusetts the officer corps was filled with men chosen either through election by their soldiers or for their ability to recruit. In other words, the officer's position was in large part determined from below. Washington quickly came to the conclusion that this system had two major flaws: the officers were just like their men and they were unable to effectively make their soldiers complete necessary tasks. Washington knew gentlemen of sufficient social standing and experience who would make proper officers. If commissioned, their position would be determined in the proper way, from above. Yet their ability to be promoted in the service was hampered by their lack of influence within the New England governments and among New England soldiers.[41]

What Washington felt he needed was a Continental Army beholden to Congress, not the state governments, led by officers committed to republican virtue and personal honor. He needed field officers appointed directly by Congress and company officers commissioned by Congress but appointed by Washington based on his determination of legitimacy. The authority to lead would come from the Continental Congress down, not generated up from the soldiers being led. Still, he initially was at a loss on how to break the model of various provincial regiments led by different types of officers. He decided to canvass his general officers for methods of promoting those he considered the best among the junior officers.

In October 1775, with enlistments just three months away from expiration, Washington saw an opportunity to remold the force more to his liking. He had to reenlist every soldier and either appoint or gain the appointment for every officer. The army of January 1776 would be smaller than the force currently surrounding Boston, so some officers would have to be let go. Washington knew, however, that the soldiers would be reluctant to reenlist until they knew which officers would be kept, which would be promoted, and which would be released.[42]

To settle these important questions, Washington canvassed his general officers. Three days later, the other generals met at a council of war. The decision of all these senior leaders was that they could not make a decision on the promotion of officers because it was too delicate a question.[43] No political decision had yet been made to allow Washington or any other general to commission or promote officers within the army. States still held that power and made their determinations separate from Washington's concerns. The officers themselves were not fully committed to staying in the new army structure, waiting to see what might serve them best, a commission in the Continental Army or service with their local militia. The most glaring problem, however, lay with the need to reenlist all the soldiers for the Continental Army. And these men were going to wait to see who was promoted before they decided if they would continue to fight within the new organization.

So Washington decided to encourage adherence to his understanding of service among his fellow officers, recognizing those who acted in a similar fashion. In his general orders for November 16, 1775, Washington recognized one of his regimental commanders. Colonel Asa Whitcomb had been notified his position would no longer exist in the new establishment on January 1, 1776. His response was first to exhort his men to remain in the service and reenlist under a new commander. He told them he would remain as well and would reenlist as a private in the army due to the righteousness of the cause. In response, Colonel Jonathan Brewer, the newly designated commander for the regiment, offered to resign his commission in favor of Whitcomb remaining in command. Washington agreed to this solution as a good example for the army, agreeing to keep Colonel Whitcomb in command and placing Colonel Brewer in the position of barracks master until a new regimental command became available. These men, through their actions, proved to Washington that they possessed the personal honor and republican virtues necessary to lead in the new Continental Army, characteristics he wished to highlight for the rest of his officer corps.[44]

Interestingly, Washington may have only gotten half of this estimation correct. Whitcomb certainly possessed the republican virtue necessary to step down when asked and then to serve as a private soldier. But would this be the action of a gentleman who prized his personal honor? In fact, Whitcomb remained in service as a regimental commander and was stationed at Ticonderoga in 1777. At that time, his two sons served as his waiters, doing menial tasks and making shoes for their fellow soldiers. The decision by the regimental commander to allow his sons both to serve as privates and to wait on him doing laborious tasks caused his fellow officers from Pennsylvania to deride him over time. On Christmas Day 1777, one of these Pennsylvanian officers, after a night of drinking, destroyed the cobbler's bench in Colonel Whitcomb's office, assaulted Colonel Whitcomb, and caused his soldiers to fire on the Massachusetts regiment as they came out of their barracks. Colonel Whitcomb's response was to accept the insolent officer's apology in the form of a dinner and let the issue disappear.[45] Whitcomb's willingness to allow his sons to labor as common servants and his decision to overlook a challenge to his honor suggest strongly that he did not adhere to a strong sense of personal honor. Whitcomb and Washington may have agreed on service as a republican virtue, but their conceptions of proper action based on social status were worlds apart.

Throughout the war, Washington increasingly worked to inculcate a republican ideology in his officers and soldiers, believing his men would follow leaders who lived the ethics of the Revolution. Outside of the New England states, men like Joseph Bloomfield fit Washington's ideal well. Born to a middling family in New Jersey, Bloomfield was trained in the law and practiced in West Jersey until the start of the war. He joined the Third New Jersey Regiment under Colonel Elias Dayton early in 1776 and served until shortly after the Battle of Monmouth in 1778. He was initially commissioned as a captain and commanded a company first in the Mohawk Valley and then at Fort Ticonderoga.[46] Soon after he joined the regiment, Bloomfield was granted a short leave. He returned home; was engaged to his future wife, Mary McIlvaine; and wrote that, despite the income loss of £250 per year, he would serve as long as necessary based upon his patriotic principles.[47]

When Captain Bloomfield was given his commission and command, he quickly enlisted his full quota for a company among his fellow residents in Cumberland County. He listed the roll of his men in his journal and vowed that these soldiers were now his family and that he would endeavor to treat them all with kindness and humanity to gain their love and esteem, all to fulfill the trust given to him by his country.[48] His initial ideas of leadership certainly followed along the paternalistic lines common in Washington's formulation of the concept.

Yet this young captain did not agree with some of the actions of his fellow officers, actions they might ascribe to their personal honor. In July of 1776 two volunteer officers challenged one another to a duel. The regular officers allowed the contest but turned it into a charade for their own amusement. They loaded the pistols with powder and wadding only, no ball. After the first round, when no one was hurt, one officer said honor was satisfied but the other would not yield. The regiment's lieutenant colonel, also in on the prank, told the two officers honor now required a duel to the death. Again their seconds loaded just powder and wadding. Again no one was injured. The first officer again allowed that honor was satisfied but the second officer was livid. He demanded they fire a third time but at only five paces. The spectators were now openly laughing. The regimental commander and Captain Bloomfield finally stopped the entertainment and ordered the two officers to make up and drink as friends. Bloomfield stated this "Frolick" convinced him more than ever of the absurdity of this kind of behavior. He called it "a ridiculous custom (that) serves only to shew the Passionate Temper and absurd Folly of those who expose themselves to satisfy their brutish thirst for what? Why for nothing else but to keep the world from thinking they are Cowards."[49]

Men like Captain Bloomfield fit Washington's vision of an officer with legitimate authority to lead. He was of the right class, for a junior officer, he volunteered for the right reasons, and he wanted to lead his soldiers in a paternal manner, though his views on dueling hint at a very different understanding on personal honor. With an army so young, Washington believed he needed to take men like this and promote them as their merit allowed.

From the very beginning, he told his officers their ability to rise in the ranks would be determined mostly by merit and not solely through recruiting or time in service. When groups of officers wrote him to complain about promotions, Washington often took the opportunity to mentor them on a new vision for the army. The officers of Brigadier General Joseph Spencer's brigade complained in September 1775 over the promotion of Ebenezer Huntington to lieutenant in the Second Connecticut Regiment because he was junior to other officers. Washington wrote a letter back to Spencer, admonishing his officers for preferring time in service over merit. Instead, this was a young army that needed to promote those best suited for the job over those longest in the line. Seniority may play a part but it would not be the determining factor.[50]

Of course, at this early stage, "merit" probably meant different things to different people. And for those from New England, merit continued to be determined by how many men would willingly enlist under a given officer. Tensions over company-level promotions remained throughout 1776 because Washington and his New England officers did not agree on the issue of merit. One particular case highlighted the problem. While in New York, preparing to defend the city against the Howe brothers, Washington convened a general court-martial for Lieutenant Thomas Glover. Glover was from New Hampshire and the first lieutenant in Captain James Wilkinson's company in Colonel James Reed's Second Continental Regiment (New Hampshire). Glover had verbally attacked his new company commander and refused to obey his orders, believing himself to be the company commander. The reason for this confusion was that Glover had enlisted the most men in the company and Brigadier General John Sullivan promised him he would serve under his former company commander, Captain Ogden, and no other.[51]

To break the institutional link between recruiting and promotion endemic among his New England officers, Washington needed John Hancock to convince Congress to take the power to promote all the officers in the army away from the states. And on May 10, 1776, Congress did so.[52] Still, the issue was not fully resolved for the rest of the year. In this specific case, among others, the soldiers supported the view of Lieutenant Glover. Washington was forced to parade the Second Continental Regiment with two other regiments looking on under arms to dissuade a mutinous spirit from infecting even more soldiers. He sent that regiment up to Albany to remove them from the immediate situation. He allowed Lieutenant Glover to join the unit, as a lieutenant and under the command of Captain Wilkinson, once Glover had formally apologized and agreed to follow the orders of his new commander and influence the men to do likewise. While

Washington believed this decision was too lenient when it came to dealing with Glover, he admitted to Hancock that he was not in a position to completely change the culture of these regiments. As he eloquently stated, "Time can only eradicate and overcome customs and prejudices of long standing—they must be got the better of by slow and gradual advances."[53]

Since Congress had assumed the authority to promote officers in the Continental Army, Washington asked Congress to give him the ability to promote officers at the company level, under their authority.[54] This power would allow Washington to promote the right type of officers, exhibiting the right kind of merit—men Washington understood as legitimate and worthy of emulation. In this attempt, however, Washington failed. Congress never did relinquish this power, forcing Washington to go to them for every promotion for the duration of the war and hampering his direct influence on officer selections. The states were unwilling to cede the power to determine who led their soldiers and many of the state representatives in Congress were worried of centralizing too much power in the army and its commander; Washington's desired changes would be more gradual than he wished.

Eighteenth-century republicans feared nothing more than a professional, standing army. A standing army was the instrument of coercion for the power-grabbing members of the governing body. Yet eighteenth-century linear warfare was not an activity for amateurs. It required discipline under fire and extensive training for the soldiers of the rank and file to perform intricate maneuvers and the evolutions of firing the flintlock musket. This very real need for military competency in the Continental Army clashed with a majority adherence to republican ideology and remained a source of Washington's frustrations throughout the war, both in regards to his officers and his soldiers.

Though the Continental Army was successful forcing the British into an untenable position in Boston in March 1776, it was not until August of that year that the American and British armies would meet on the battlefield while Washington was in command. The American general was clear before the Battle of Long Island: those soldiers who

displayed courage under fire would be rewarded, but those found retreating without the express orders of their commanding officers
would be shot for cowardice.[55] Soon after their defeat at Long Island,
one officer on Harlem Heights attempted to enforce this order, with
almost disastrous results. Sergeant Leffingwell, from a Connecticut
regiment, passed through the lines to retrieve more ammunition, at
the order of his regimental commander. Washington's adjutant general, Colonel Joseph Reed from Pennsylvania, saw the man "retreating" and told him to return to the line. When the sergeant explained
his mission, Colonel Reed refused to believe him, ordering the sergeant again back to the front. The sergeant would not budge and
Colonel Reed drew his sword on the man. Sergeant Leffingwell leveled his musket at the colonel and cocked it. He was arrested, tried
under court-martial, and sentenced to execution. On the day of the
execution, the regiments from Connecticut were paraded to watch,
but Sergeant Leffingwell was pardoned. Private Joseph Plumb Martin
claimed this was a good choice by the officers. If Sergeant Leffingwell's blood had been spilt, more blood would have followed.[56]

Leffingwell's refusal to listen to a countermanding order from an
officer not of his regiment (and not from his state) and his willingness
to shoot that officer in the midst of a battle illustrate his belief that
the only officers with the authority to give him commands were those
he had agreed to serve under. Colonel Reed's decision not to believe
the sergeant came from a different understanding, that his position
as adjutant general overrode the regimental commander's authority.
It may also have come from a lack of experience and a view of common soldiers as mostly liars and cowards. Even if the soldier was
telling the truth, Reed's orders came from the superior authority of
General Washington. And Private Martin's assertion that the regiment would have rioted hints at a possible reason for Leffingwell's
stay of execution; Washington may have understood the court-martial's sentence was not seen as legitimate by the soldiers from Connecticut.

Over the course of the war, training and discipline among the officers increased, though challenges remained. As late as 1779, senior
commanders were still admonishing their junior officers for breaches

of discipline. That summer, while conducting operations in upstate New York, Brigadier General Enoch Poor admonished the officers of his regiments after an embarrassing ambush executed by enemy Native Americans in the area. One regiment was marching through country known to contain hostiles, yet no officers were present with their soldiers. When other officers attempted to regain control of men firing in a less-than-disciplined fashion, some of those officers were almost shot themselves. General Poor wondered "how Exceedingly pleasing it must be to four or five Lurking Savages to See one fire from them produce a wanton Discharge of All the musquets in A number of Regiments without any kind of aim meaning or Order and Leveled at no Object."[57] While this incident documented continued challenges for the officer corps, the composition of Poor's brigade shows growing integration in the army. Enoch Poor was from New Hampshire (though he was born in Andover, Massachusetts) and fought as a private for Massachusetts in the Seven Years' War. His brigade not only contained three regiments from New Hampshire but two regiments from New York, as well.

Still, the individual regiments remained organized, manned, and officered by their particular states. At the lower levels, officers usually came from the same state as the soldiers they led, and when soldiers were forced to complete duty in specialized, integrated units, some commented on the strangeness of the officers and soldiers from other states. This was particularly true for the soldiers from the New England states, where regiments remained homogenous. After the Battle of Monmouth in June 1778, Private Martin from Connecticut was placed in an integrated light infantry battalion. The regiment was comprised half of soldiers from Pennsylvania and half from New England. While he did agree that the officers were gentlemen, the experience made him extremely "homesick." During this short period of service, all he wanted was to return to a Yankee regiment, under the leadership of Yankee officers.[58]

And the demand made by soldiers to remain in regiments affiliated by state was not unique to New England. While at Valley Forge in the winter and spring of 1778, Washington and his officers faced a serious problem with new recruits from Virginia. Initially these men were to fill vacancies in Virginia regiments without regard to their preference. Due to their reluctance to comply with this order, a compromise was reached. The soldiers would initially be placed in the brigade of the officer bringing them into camp. After a period of twenty-four hours, time for the soldiers to determine which regiments contained family and friends, the soldiers would determine which regiment they wished to join. If that regiment was full, they would be given their second choice. Interestingly, this accommodation was reached despite the fact that many of these incoming soldiers were draftees, probably with the hope that this decision would lessen the urge to desert.[59]

Despite Washington's frequent attempts to develop an officer corps throughout the army that derived its legitimate authority to lead through class and adherence to ideology, pressures from state representatives in Congress and from the soldiers serving required a more localized view on legitimacy that remained throughout the war. While he ended the practice of officer elections and eventually loosened the connections between recruiting and promotion, Washington lacked the ability to promote directly. The authority of officers no longer came from below (derived instead from Congress), but states still controlled who was selected to lead and soldiers still demanded they be taken into account for those selections. The closest Washington got to creating a sense of affinity to a larger entity was to design uniforms that reflected a regional alignment of states. In 1779 he issued a general order from his headquarters at Moore's House in New York describing what soldiers would wear, when their states had the funds available to provide the uniforms. Massachusetts, Rhode Island, Connecticut, and New Hampshire regiments would wear blue coats faced with white. New York and New Jersey regiments would face their blue coats with buff. The regiments from Pennsylvania, Maryland, Delaware, and Virginia would have red facings while those from the remaining southern states would face their uniforms in blue with a white stripe.[60]

IF WASHINGTON COULD NOT INSIST that officer commissions be reserved for gentlemen of the proper caliber, he could at least train the officers he had to act like gentlemen once they arrived in camp. Yet his ideal would continue to be challenged, both by his junior officers and by the soldiers that they led. At issue were the expectations of these officers, some with prior military experience and some without, and the expectations of the soldiers and what they viewed as acceptable and legitimate uses of authority.

The fall of 1776 was a very difficult time for the Continental Army. The American forces lost their first conventional battle under Washington's command in August of that year at the Battle of Long Island. The generals were still attempting to defend New York, an untenable position given America's inability to oppose amphibious landings. The soldiers were demoralized and suffered from a nonexistent logistic system, lacking food and ammunition. To compound the challenges faced by the leadership, the Continental Army was actually only a portion of the forces on the ground. Much of the American opposition to the British invasion was comprised of local militia and state levies. These men had agreed to serve for only a short time and while Washington hoped those in the state levies might decide to enlist in the Continental Army, without success on the battlefield most would not.

The regimental commander for the Second Connecticut State Levy at that time was Colonel Fisher Gay. His regiment was one contingent of a large Connecticut force of twenty-five state levy regiments and fourteen militia regiments sent to support Washington's efforts to defend New York. The defeat on Long Island seriously compromised the abilities of the officers in these "New Levies" to control their men and, at times, themselves. Private Martin, serving in one of these regiments, described a lieutenant crying before the battle and his field officers removing any signs of their rank.[61] After the battle, he could not find an officer to tell him and his friend where to go. The only officer he admitted to seeing was an artillery officer attempting to stop him returning to his regiment.[62] The reality was that the officers had lost control of their forces in the aftermath of a

British victory and regimental commanders such as Colonel Gay did not know how to retreat in an orderly fashion.

Washington was both disappointed at the defeat and dismayed by the actions of his officers. Prior to the battle he told the battlefield commander, Israel Putnam, to stop the soldiers under his command from firing at the British in a scattered and undisciplined fashion.[63] The soldiers and their officers were getting nervous, wasting precious ammunition in fruitless attempts to harm their enemy while they were out of range. During the battle, soldiers had retreated to the rear when brigade commanders attempted to reposition regiments to avoid becoming flanked. Directly after the defeat, he told the army that the actions during the battle were intentional. The generals ordered the maneuver not due to a lack of faith in the army's ability to stand firm against the British but to shorten the internal lines of communication.[64] The inability of the officers to translate these commands effectively and the soldiers' lack of trust in their leadership led to a disastrous outcome. This initial fight, mostly on open ground, showed Washington some important weaknesses in the army, not the least of which was a serious problem with leadership.

Washington explicitly addressed this weakness with Colonel Gay directly after the battle. The men of the Second Connecticut State Levy were accused of plundering and stealing. Men were deserting and Gay was not conforming to Washington's requests for information and disciplined action. He stated he could not decide if Colonel Gay was not receiving the general's orders or simply ignoring them and he did not want to know. The ill-disciplined actions of both the colonel and his regiment would end. Gay would send the strength returns Washington demanded immediately and would continue to do so every Saturday from now on. At this point, the method used by Washington to enforce compliance from Gay and his other officers was shame. Appealing to what Washington assumed was Gay's personal sense of honor and attachment to country, he demanded Gay act like a gentleman and an officer and obey orders.[65]

Over time Washington relied increasingly on disciplinary actions to enforce gentlemanly behavior and act as a negative example for right action. During the encampment at Valley Forge, court-martials were held for numerous officers and many resulted in a dismissal from service. Ensign Carson of the Fourth Virginia Regiment was dismissed for falsely accusing another officer of cowardice, becoming drunk, and act unbecoming a gentleman.[66] Major General Adam Stephen was found guilty of being drunk during the Battle of Germantown and ordered dismissed.[67] Washington continued to purge his officer corps of those found guilty of acts unbecoming a gentleman, cashiering at least ten more officers for being drunk, taking shoes from their soldiers, sleeping and messing (preparing meals) with the men, and other infractions deemed to lessen the social divide between officers and soldiers.[68] Still, Washington either reinstated or pardoned those officers who violated some of the Articles of War, specifically Section Seven which prohibited dueling, possibly because these actions where not considered ungentlemanly.[69]

The commander in chief also insisted that his officers lead by example and take care of their soldiers. A serious concern during the periods of winter quarters was keeping the men from going home on furlough and then not returning once that furlough ended. Obviously, not all the soldiers could go home at the same time, but the fewer soldiers present placed less pressure on a fragile logistic system. Officers were required to set the example, planning officer furloughs at the regimental level to ensure there was always one field grade officer present and that each company always had one company officer present.[70] Officers failing to return from furlough in a timely manner could be court-martialed, as was the case for Colonel William Cook, commander of the Twelfth Pennsylvania Regiment, who absented himself from Valley Forge for three months.[71]

Encouraging obedience to orders was also a necessary focus. On June 8, 1777, Colonel Henry Beekman Livingston from the Fourth New York Regiment stood accused of speaking against his brigade commander, Brigadier General Alexander McDougall, for ordering a retreat of Continental troops on March 3, 1777. He was also accused of not bringing his regiment to the battle in a timely manner and, when the regiment did arrive, for not equipping his soldiers with enough ammunition. General Putnam reprimanded the colonel for speaking in an abusive manner to McDougall in front of other officers, because such behavior gave a poor example to the soldiers and encouraged ill discipline.[72]

Perhaps the most important example the officers were required to set for their soldiers was courage under fire. As stated earlier, Washington thought this particular trait was seriously lacking among his officers at the beginning of the war. Initially, he was so concerned that a good example would not be set that he ordered any man caught retreating in the face of the enemy shot. As the war progressed, however, this particular order was not repeated. Instead, Washington and other general officers exhorted the officers and soldiers to fight as freemen struggling against tyranny, praised them (often by name) for their individual acts of bravery, and court-martialed those accused of cowardice. Washington personally recognized Captain Harry Lee for his actions in January 1777, when the cavalry officer reportedly held off two hundred British dragoons at a house with only a corporal and four other men.[73] Following Washington's example, Major General Nathanael Greene made similar comments about his officers after the American defeats at Brandywine and Germantown, though he was sure to thank the soldiers, as well, for their bravery in the face of defeat.[74]

There was also an expectation that the officers would share the hardships of the men, from caring for the sick to marching alongside them during movements. To encourage these examples, Washington made sure it was known he would follow his own rules. During the campaign of 1777 in Pennsylvania, Washington disposed of his baggage, except his blanket, and made his staff do the same to encourage his fellow officers to comply with his order that baggage trains were to be limited to necessary supplies. His actions led Brigadier General George Weedon to do the same, telling his officers that despite the fact that the brigade's wagons were available, all officers under his command would follow Washington's example.[75]

Encouraging the company-level officers to visit the sick was another issue entirely. Smallpox was a constant worry for American forces during the war. Inoculations were dangerous and caused entire units to be unavailable for fighting for long periods of time. Washington was often forced to forbid regiments from attaining inoculations due to campaign requirements, though these orders were sometimes ignored, with serious consequences. The fear of becoming sick when taking care of soldiers who fell ill was, therefore, a very real emotion for officers. In February 1778, Colonel Walter Stewart of the Thirteenth Pennsylvania Regiment was forced to reprimand his officers for their failure to take care of their sick men. He decided after visiting the hospital at Valley Forge to order his captains to visit the hospital themselves on a daily basis and, to ensure they complied, to report the findings of their inspections and their actions to support the sick to him after each visit.[76]

While Washington and his senior officers maintained expectations for the rest of the officers, these more junior leaders had expectations of their own. These men volunteered to serve in the army for various reasons. Some did so from patriotic zeal. Many others sought commissions for money, land, or from a desire to become gentlemen after the war. For all these reasons, most officers expected to have some say in their promotions and were not too shy to complain or resist when they felt their higher commanders did not recognize their proper rankings. This led directly to another common expectation, that senior officers would publicly recognize their good behavior. Junior and senior officers alike could be very delicate when it came to their reputation, leading to public complaints, active resistance, and, in some cases, open fighting among officers if someone thought his reputation was in danger. Naturally these men expected they would be adequately compensated for their service, but they also wanted to serve with other officers they deemed legitimate and who viewed them in the same manner.

As discussed earlier, on the outset of the war, junior officers, particularly from New England, believed they had the right to tell Washington if they felt they should be promoted ahead of their peers. Isaac Bangs, from Harwich, Massachusetts, decided to take the matter of his appointment to lieutenant in his own hands in April 1776 when he volunteered to join the Continental Army. Although he was a lieutenant in Colonel Cary's militia regiment, he told Colonel Bailey he would fill a vacancy in his new Continental regiment left by Lieutenant Shaw if Colonel Bailey agreed. He then walked to Washington's headquarters to get his commission. Since the commander in chief was too busy to speak with him, Bangs spoke with Major General Gates who suggested he fill the vacancy, get a recommendation from Colonel Bailey, and wait until the commission arrived.[77] Gates, a former British officer and immigrant to Virginia, was mentoring this young man to follow the tradition of young gentlemen in Britain and the southern colonies, volunteering their service until a commission came open. Bangs followed his guidance.

But his decision was not appreciated by the other company officers of his New England regiment. Over the next few months, relations between Bangs and the other junior officers of his new regiment were tense. When Bangs attended the third meeting of a new association begun by the company officers of the regiment, he learned that many of the officers were upset with him for presuming to fill a vacancy from outside the regiment ahead of other officers from inside the regiment. While his fellow officers placed much of the blame on the field grade officers, Lieutenant Bangs was guilty of not discussing the issue with his new company commander first. Bangs told his side of the story at the meeting and believed he had convinced most of the audience that he had not intended to offend anyone. The next day a lieutenant colonel in the regiment thanked him for successfully diminishing tensions within the unit.[78] Bangs was guilty of ignoring the regimental line of succession and of failing to follow more traditional methods for attaining his rank, i.e., recruiting soldiers. Still, Bangs was able to remain in the regiment, as his fellow officers gradually accepted his promotion from above, provided he recognize their complaints as valid.

Throughout the war, and not solely in regiments from New England, officers publicly complained if they thought an officer was promoted in an irregular way. In February 1778 a captain in the Pennsylvania Line made a complaint against the promotion of Michael Ryan to the majority as irregular. This complaint forced Washington to suspend the appointment until a board of generals investigated the matter. Eight days later, after hearing the evidence presented, the board recommended to Washington that the promotion was in fact irregular and Washington removed the appointment.[79]

This belief among the junior officers that they had a right to be included in the decisions made regarding promotions could get them in trouble. John Barr was an ensign in the New York Line late in the war. When he returned to his regiment after a furlough in 1780, he refused to comply with an order from Lieutenant Colonel John Conway of the First New York Regiment to be officer of the guard. Barr demanded Ensign Bartholomew Vanderburgh of the Second New York be assigned instead, due to his junior appointment. When Lieutenant Colonel Conway suggested they draw lots, Barr again refused and both ensigns were arrested. At his general court-martial four days later, Barr claimed he chose to force the issue of guard detail to settle a larger problem, that of the date of his appointment to ensign. He produced paperwork from the New York State Council of Appointment placing his date of rank as January 1, 1779. When his appointment date was published in the brigade orders, other ensigns complained to their regimental commander, Colonel Peter Gansevoort, who agreed to push the appointment date to May 15, 1779, and making Barr the junior officer in the regiment. Ensign Barr did not believe Colonel Gansevoort had the authority to do this and so ignored his decision. Barr believed he should, therefore, be acquitted from the charge of failing to obey a superior officer, as his actions stemmed from the need to settle this more important matter and not from a lack of respect for Lieutenant Colonel Conway. A few months later, after Barr had left his regiment to serve in the Quartermaster Department, he received a letter notifying him that he was found guilty of disobeying a lawful order and would receive a reprimand.[80]

Decisions made by junior officers to settle disputes among themselves publicly troubled Washington for the duration of the war. It is well known that many of the generals in the army were publicly jealous of their reputations. Major General Philip Schuyler threatened to resign after his retreat from Crown Point in 1776 because he felt his reputation was being damaged by an inquiry into his decision.[81] Colonel John Stark left the Continental service when other junior colonels were promoted to brigadier general ahead of him.[82] Other senior officers, like Colonel Varnum, threatened to resign when they were not promoted, because they did not want to follow the orders of men formerly their subordinates.[83] Most famously, Benedict Arnold's act of treason can be traced in part to his anger over slower promotions than he thought were fair.

And this sensitivity over rank, promotion, and reputation was not limited to senior officers. Ensigns, lieutenants, and captains also felt a tension between patriotic service and their desires to leave the army with the highest rank possible. The issue became bad enough by the spring of 1778 that Washington felt compelled to make a statement in his general orders. Following the acquittal of one lieutenant accused for striking another, Washington scolded his officers for resorting to violence to settle their personal disputes. He saw a pattern of this behavior among his junior officers that was coming to light in public trials. He wished, instead, that his officers could view one another as brothers, able to settle their problems amicably and thus avoid the necessity of public courts producing public documents that would leave an embarrassing public record.[84]

While some historians believe these disputes to be proof of a sense of personal honor among these men, it is also probable that tensions arose due to the convoluted nature of promotion and a desire among many officers at the more junior level that this system follow some logical line of legality. While Congress and the state legislatures wrangled over who would maintain the right to promote within the army, these men served, often for years, without pay or adequate food and shelter. The situation led to stress and tension within and among those serving due to the uncertainty of their future after the war. Some of these officers abandoned burgeoning professions while others entered the service too young to have begun a civilian career. As the war continued, many officers decided they could no longer serve at the cost of supporting their families while others continued to serve and faced beginning life anew once the war was concluded.

Despite the uncertainty, these men did serve, many for the duration of the war, and they wished to do so with others they deemed fit to be their peers. Captain Bloomfield was placed in an exceptional position to affect who served in his company in 1776. While the rest of his regiment went to Fort Stanwix, Bloomfield was placed in command of his company and a company of militia to guard the rear and await the arrival of General Schuyler at German Flatts. As he was in command of two companies, he placed two of his volunteers (those without commissions but serving as very junior officers) in the positions of adjutant and quartermaster. As soon as the regimental commander left the camp, one of the lieutenants from the militia tested Captain Bloomfield's authority and left the camp for several days against orders. With the support of General Schuyler, who visited for a day while on his way to Fort Stanwix, Captain Bloomfield arrested this lieutenant when he returned and forced his resignation, along with that of a second lieutenant who claimed to be too sick to continue in the service. These resignations allowed Bloomfield to move several officers up to fill the vacancies and secure for his two volunteer officers regular commissions as ensigns. Bloomfield was naturally glad to rid his command of a troublemaker, an officer he claimed was lazy and who only really cared about his appearance.[85]

For the entire war the junior and senior officers to varying degrees negotiated who held the legitimate authority to serve as an officer and what would be a legitimate exercise in authority regarding their relationships to one another. The enlisted soldiers made sure they had a place at the negotiating table as well. What these men expected from their officers with regard to performance and treatment would sound reasonable and, perhaps, obvious. Still the ability of the enlisted soldiers to affect change in the army was greater than in other, more mature military institutions. As mentioned before, these soldiers expected to be led by officers from their region, or at the least from their state. They wanted officers to share their hardships with them and officers they deemed unfit to be removed from the service. They wanted the opportunity for promotion, either to the noncommissioned or to the commissioned officer corps. Most importantly, they expected to be treated with the recognition that, as individuals, they had equal rights. The ideals of the Revolution, and the revolutionary rhetoric they heard, encouraged them to challenge traditional authority. If these expectations were not met, these men, many of them volunteers, felt they had the right to resist, with either their feet or their fists.

In 1775 and 1776, soldiers who had not served in a military before would act like civilians until properly trained and accustomed to military hierarchy. While young men in the colonies were used to the hierarchy of family and work, military service could be seen as an avenue toward greater autonomy, and the aim of the army was to overthrow a traditional form of authority. And resistance by enlisted soldiers when subjected to treatment they perceived as unfair, overbearing, or in violation of contract persisted throughout the war. Late in the war, Joseph Plumb Martin, by then a sergeant, stopped a prank that his soldiers were planning against their company commander, a man often spoken of as overbearing and unwilling to share in the hardships of his men. While working on Constitution Island blasting rock in 1782, these men planned to fill a wooden canteen with gunpowder and explode it under the captain's bed. The canteen was filled with three pounds of gunpowder! Though the men claimed they just wanted to frighten the officer and so make him more "complaisant," Martin was sure this bit of mischief would kill him. While the sergeant did not like his commander any more than his soldiers did, he did not believe the captain deserved to die.[86]

Soldier demands to serve in regiments from their own state, with fellow soldiers they knew or at least had something in common with, and to be led by officers they recognized as legitimate also remained throughout the war. Washington recognized this fact in 1776 when he told John Hancock that Congress should implicitly recognize a regimental line of promotion instead of a continental line. He warned the president that only in extreme cases of merit or failure should Congress ignore this advice, as the men in many regiments would mutiny if the regimental line of succession was not followed.[87] When Private Martin broke his ankle in 1777, he was placed on guard of the baggage train. He said it was bad enough being placed under the command of officers he knew, but it was intolerable to be placed under the command of strangers. He left for his company soon after.[88] While Washington was specifically speaking of his New England troops and Martin did come from Connecticut, the attachment of men to their local leaders was found throughout the army. Incoming Virginia soldiers to Valley Forge wanted to determine which regiment of the Virginia Line they would serve in (hoping to be located with kin and friends) and, at the beginning of the war in South Carolina, recruiters found men in the militias would not serve unless their militia commanders were serving, as well.[89]

Of course, these demands had implications for officers' exercise of authority. To be perceived as legitimately exercising authority once in that position the officer was first expected to share hardship with his men. General Washington recognized this when he took only his blanket with him into Valley Forge, Captain Bloomfield recognized it when he took his pack off the wagon and placed it on his back for the march to Fort Stanwix, and the soldiers expected it in most cases. John Henry from Lancaster, Pennsylvania, enlisted in a rifle company in 1775 and traveled with Benedict Arnold and Daniel Morgan to Quebec. Henry described how they divided rations along the march through Maine as the vanguard of the force. The principal officer would divide the food evenly and in front of the men. He would then turn his back to the men, pick a portion, and ask the group, "Which one is this for?" Henry said in this way every man knew his portion was given fairly and without prejudice.[90]

When officers acted in ways the soldiers believed did not recognize a sense of individual equality, soldiers often complained in imaginative ways. Corporal Lemuel Roberts felt it unfair one night that he had to stand guard outside while General Alexander McDougall slept comfortably inside. The corporal spent the cold evening stomping his feet on the loose boards of the outside porch both to keep his feet warm and to keep the general awake. The general told his aide to make the guards be quiet, but the lieutenant knew better. He came outside, gave the men a bottle of whiskey to stay warm, and asked them to be as quiet as possible. This line of reasoning apparently worked and the general got his rest.[91]

Additionally, soldiers expected to be treated in accordance with their conditions of enlistment. The soldiers of Colonel John Stark's regiment in February 1776 assaulted the paymaster for New Hampshire, Colonel Samuel Hobart, because they feared he would not pay them. Their commander was forced to apologize to the assaulted colonel because he did not do enough to stop them.[92] On December 31, 1776, Corporal Roberts's regiment almost refused to fight because it was the last day of their enlistments. They made a stand before the march, claiming they should be dismissed and allowed to go home. They would, however, be true to their enlistments. They would march one more day and not a day after that.[93]

While there was a recognized separation between officers and soldiers in the rank and file, there was also an expectation that merit, wherever it came from, could get a soldier promoted up the ranks. Lieutenant Benjamin Gilbert entered the service in 1775 as a private, was promoted to sergeant in 1778, and ended the war as a junior officer.[94] Of course he managed to survive the entire war, which helped. Still Lieutenant Gilbert was not a unique example (at least in the Massachusetts Line), nor even an exceptional one, as men serving in the Continental Army died or rotated back to civilian life. This ability of those from the ranks to become noncommissioned and commissioned officers existed because the legitimate basis for authority was changing, allowing a more fluid flow between ranks. Furthermore, this fluidity was based less and less on a person's ability to recruit and more and more on recognized abilities to lead.

THE CONTINENTAL ARMY WAS A TEMPORARY CREATION that only lasted for eight years. It took much of its structure from the European model of regiments and companies, captains and sergeants. Still, its institutional culture did not come from Great Britain. It came originally from New England, because the vast majority of its first soldiers and officers came from New England. While the only commander in chief to ever command this army wished for more integration, the army never achieved it. Regiments remained regionally aligned and the officers who led them did so, as well. Only at the most senior levels did this not hold true, specifically among the major generals commanding divisions. The result was an officer corps from the regiment down to the company with differing understandings of legitimate sources for authority but growing agreement in how their power should be exercised. These issues were always in negotiation with their soldiers, and as accommodations were reached, institutional culture grew.

In 1779, in an attempt to promote more uniformity among the various regiments, Washington ordered the "Regulations for the

Order and Discipline of the Troops" be published and distributed among the officers and soldiers of the army. Drill manuals were not uncommon in the eighteenth century, but this manual had something different at the very end. The last fourteen pages were dedicated to a description of the responsibilities and duties for every rank from colonel to private. While the language is paternalistic, speaking of gaining the "love" of soldiers, the overall tone is one that recognized the autonomy of soldiers who would not follow harsh or tyrannical leaders. Regimental commanders had to ensure their officers watched for the health of the soldiers, while promoting noncommissioned officers for merit and their willingness to teach. His first responsibility was the health of his men and he was instructed to always encamp and march with his soldiers, as it was his example, and the example of his officers, that the soldiers would follow.[95] The company commanders were instructed to listen to their men and address their legitimate complaints. Ensigns were told to protect the men from harsh treatment by their noncommissioned officers if that treatment was not warranted. At the same time, the noncommissioned officer was directed to discipline the soldiers while treating them always with respect and kindness.[96] When teaching the privates to drill, noncommissioned officers should do so mildly, understanding no one would get the movements correct the first time.[97]

There is a leniency in tone, a recognition of the humanity and value of the private soldier that does not contradict Washington's earlier effort to instill personal honor in the officers of the Virginia Regiment. Still, these descriptions acted as a contract between the officers, their commanders, and their soldiers for the legitimate exercise of authority. These drill manuals were issued to all soldiers, not just leaders, so even privates were taught the responsibilities of those appointed to lead them.

The authority to lead these soldiers came not from social rank or status but from Congress and the individual states. Of course, each state had its various reasons for commissioning officers and certainly some of those decisions were made with social status in mind. Still, without a large source of "gentlemen" to draw from, and with many of the wealthier citizens choosing to serve in political positions or to pursue private endeavors rather than risk life or limb in the army, many of the officers could not claim "Esquire" as a moniker. The best they could do was earn some cash, hope for a land grant, and perhaps learn some of the characteristics of a gentleman along the way.

The amalgamation of various cultural understandings of who should serve as an officer and how he should conduct himself while in uniform led to two significant changes in the concept of officership. The authority from which the officer derived his ability to lead soldiers, the basis for his legitimacy as a leader, trended away from civilian social status toward a political foundation based largely, at the ranks below regimental commander, on merit and consensus. An officer's (or noncommissioned officer's) ability to lead soldiers could often determine his promotion into the company grade officer ranks. With regard to the legitimate use of authority while leading, officers navigated between the demands of their commander in chief, peer pressure from other officers, and the willingness to follow (or lack thereof) from soldiers who viewed themselves as volunteers fighting for liberty. The result was a code of conduct, written in the *Regulations for the Order and Discipline of the Troops* that recognized command authority had many limitations in the Continental Army. Soldiers would not be coerced to serve, except in extreme cases, and the success of the Revolution lay with their willingness to follow.

Two

Recruiting for the Continental Army

INITIAL NEGOTIATIONS OF AUTHORITY

O N JUNE 24, 1775, CAPTAIN BERNARD ELLIOTT LEFT CHARLESTON, South Carolina, for nearby Savannah, Georgia. His mission was to recruit soldiers for the Second Regiment of South Carolina Troops in support of the revolt against British control of the colony. As he rode toward the Savannah River, Elliott experienced limited success, enlisting twenty larger men of grenadier size initially, followed by another group of young men before reaching the river. He traveled with a retinue of thirteen people, including musicians. And as he stopped at each settlement, Elliott treated the inhabitants with wine and grog, hosted barbeques, and held "Virginia" dances. When this method was unsuccessful, he gathered the local militia leaders and produced documents describing the abuses of Parliament against the colonies, believing this political avenue of persuasion might convince the local leadership to encourage participation in the revolt. Over the next few weeks, Captain Elliott met another captain on a recruiting mission (agreeing to target only men large enough to serve as grenadiers so as not to compete with his comrade from the First

Regiment) and convinced a colonel of a county militia to resign his commission and serve on the Patriot side.[1]

Elliott viewed the objective of his mission as more political than military. South Carolina experienced serious divisions between Loyalists and Patriots throughout the Revolution, and at the very beginning, the Patriot side recognized the need to convince the populace to choose the policies of the Revolutionaries over their loyalties to the Crown, committing themselves to armed resistance. The manner with which Elliott decided to accomplish this goal was familiar to all in the region. He canvassed the "voters" by treating them. This method of convincing freeholders to choose a candidate for the colonial assembly was common throughout the South, from Virginia to Georgia. It recognized a patronizing form of social leadership where the aristocracy used their wealth and magnanimity to strengthen their relationships with those below them in society. When local elites found it necessary to lead through consent, they treated their neighbors to convince them to follow.[2]

While Elliott experienced some success at enlisting support for military participation in this region along the border between South Carolina and Georgia, much of his time was spent in an attempt to sway local gentlemen to switch their allegiance from a Loyalist to a Patriot position; without this support the other local farmers would not enlist. And even when he managed to do so, as in the case of Colonel Thomas from Halifax, few men were willing to sign up for the state regiment. Most decided to serve with the local militia.[3] In Virginia, similar resistance to enlisting occurred where a militia system was virtually nonexistent, and popular support for the Patriot cause was slow to develop.[4] In the spring and summer of 1775, the House of Burgesses attempted to encourage enlistment into independent companies, but few men elected to participate and the vast majority of those who did were the well-to-do gentlemen of the counties interested in officer commissions.[5]

The ability to recruit men for military service in support of resistance to British rule early on was much easier in the northern colonies. In Massachusetts, where the militia system was robust and participation widespread, mass mobilization in the face of British occupation was rapidly accomplished, especially after Tory-minded leaders like Timothy Ruggles had been ousted from their positions as militia commanders.[6] Likewise, in New Hampshire, Connecticut, and Rhode Island, communities maintained strong militias in their towns that served to provide a wide cross section of their society for temporary military service in 1775 and 1776.

Over the course of the war, from 1776 to 1782, the various states began to approach the issue of recruiting for the Continental Army with different methods, some choosing to maintain the voluntary nature of service to the greatest degree possible while others attempted to coerce service from those living on the fringe of society. In fact, the method used to recruit soldiers always remained in the power of the states to determine. Only the number of battalions required from each state, the amount for enlistment bonuses, and the amount for monthly pay were established by Congress. But states often augmented enlistment bonuses in an effort to induce service. The result was that none of the soldiers serving in the Continental Army did so under the same obligations nor did they receive the same enticements to enlist. Some soldiers enlisted voluntarily for three years, some were drafted for eight months, and some thought they had enlisted for three years but had in fact done so for the duration of the war. Other men signed on early in the war for the $100 bonus offered in 1777 while newcomers arrived in 1779 with a $500 signing bonus in their pockets. These differences did not exist only among the different regiments of the state lines but even among the soldiers within a single regiment.

The methods used to recruit for the Continental Army established much of the foundation for how its soldiers were led. Since leadership was conducted through a negotiation of authority between the leaders and the led to determine how both the decisions and their methods of execution were reached, methods of recruitment initiated that negotiation by setting initial limitations on both the legitimate exercise of authority by leaders and soldier agency to legitimately resist when they believed that authority had been exceeded. Yet the Continental Army was not recruited the same throughout the state regiments and lines. Instead, Congress set state quotas and the states determined the methods used to meet those quotas. These policies were then modified by the willingness of the state's citizens to either support or resist those measures. Some states continued to vote large bounties and allow for short-term enlistments in an attempt to meet their quotas. Other states moved over the course of a few years toward compelling service through classing and drafts.

The biggest change in recruiting came in 1777, when Congress adopted the three-year or for the duration enlistment criteria. In the First Establishment of the Continental Army (lasting only for the year 1776), enlistments remained a year long. Before October 1776, politicians in both the Congress and state assemblies did not believe men would voluntarily enlist for longer periods of time. But following the problems faced by Washington with the fall of New York, the ravaging of New Jersey, and the possible British occupation of Philadelphia, those men elected to Congress determined Washington was correct; longer enlistments were necessary, even if they imposed the danger of a standing army on the newly formed republic. And in some cases, like in Massachusetts and New Hampshire, the same men who served under one-year enlistments did sign up again for three-year terms (though they refused to sign on for the duration of the war) as volunteers. But in other states, like Connecticut and Pennsylvania, the new term of a longer service was a tougher pill to swallow, leading to an inability to meet state quotas for the army and some innovations by the states to induce service. And the further south one went, the harder it became, as gentlemen with means volunteered to become officers, middling farmers avoided service outside the militia, and the lower sorts were targeted for county drafts in states like Virginia.

A combination of cultural views on military service, economic realities at home and across the thirteen states, and the willingness (or lack thereof) of citizens in each of the states to comply with the acts passed by their governments influenced the development of differing methods for recruiting. In New England, recruiting was relegated to the towns and facilitated by large bounties and the acceptance of shorter enlistments when men refused to enlist for three years or the duration of the war. In Connecticut, while recruiting was still a responsibility of the selectmen from the towns, a system of classing was instituted in the militia companies to place social pressure on those eligible to enlist in the state regiments. In Pennsylvania companies were raised by the counties and then combined into regiments as they were completed while Virginia chose to tackle the problem of enlistment by structuring the state into sixteen districts and initiating a draft of landless men. These examples highlight differing cultural views of military service, the variety of social structures in Revolutionary America, and economic realities that influenced solutions found to supply the Continental Army with soldiers.

Yet from 1777 to 1780, these solutions, while rooted in cultural mores and tradition, rarely succeeded in filling the states' quotas. This was due, in part, to the inability of Congress and the state assemblies to meet the monetary terms of enlistment. The rapid inflation of the Continental dollar undercut soldiers' pay while the states found it extremely difficult to supply their regiments with the necessary clothing, equipment, or food. The privations and suffering experienced by Continental soldiers already in service made it harder for the states to enlist veterans and new enlistees as the war dragged on. The result in most states was a repetition of similar acts demanding men enlist in the army with little response from their citizens.

Additionally, as the states shifted policies to meet changing environments at home, soldiers entered the army having received different inducements and under different terms, while older soldiers, especially those with families, suffered from a lack of money, clothing, and food. By 1780, many of these soldiers had had enough of soldiering and believed their three-year enlistments were about to come to an end. Washington would again face a situation similar to the one he faced outside of Trenton in 1776, needing to reenlist the majority of his army while still facing a strong enemy to his front. But this time he would be losing much more, as the soldiers wishing to leave took with them the training and experience gained by three long years or more of service. Meanwhile, many of those soldiers, while eager to go home, were not going to do so quietly if their terms of service were not first met by Congress, to include back pay. The combination of Washington's reluctance to release good soldiers while the war did not appear to be ending and the demands of those soldiers to be released once Congress made good on its initial promises led to a tumultuous year in 1781, a year that thankfully ended with a major British defeat and the ability to downsize the Continental Army.

Through it all, the Continental Army never reached close to a third of the size Congress wished. As was the case in every other labor market of this period in American history, manpower was a constant problem and each state dealt with the situation in ways similar to those chosen to work through their labor issues. In Virginia, the political elites attempted to alleviate their need through coercion of the disenfranchised and, as had happened in the past, resistance followed. In Massachusetts, the towns controlled much of the recruiting, just as they controlled the labor pool. While a few outsiders were brought in, the majority of men recruited came largely from the young laborers waiting for the ability to purchase land and become freeholders themselves. And in places like New Hampshire and Pennsylvania, men enlisted in groups largely connected by kinship and origins of immigration. Yet, overall, the fact that demand greatly outmatched supply allowed the negotiation of the terms of service to continue throughout the war, forcing the officers of the Continental Army to work hard to balance their abilities to legitimately exercise authority against the perceptions of their soldiers regarding their right to resist.

IN THE FALL OF 1775, George Washington knew a serious problem was fast approaching with the coming of the new year. His current army had enlisted under terms that would expire on December 31, 1775 (or thereabouts) and he would be disbanding that force in the face of the enemy while he was enlisting a new army. The regulations governing how this new army, the First Establishment, would operate were intended to be significantly different from those of the previous force, and among the various changes Washington was hoping for, the terms of enlistment was possibly the most important. Could he convince the Congress and state assemblies that enlistments for the

duration of the war were necessary? And would men enlist under such terms? The general was under no illusions about how difficult a task it would be to gain the authority to offer such terms. Nor did he believe, as others might, that this would be the only time he would face this challenge should he fail to achieve that authority. Instead, if Congress elected to maintain the New England tradition of one-year enlistments, Washington would have to convince his soldiers to remain each and every year while their enemy remained to their front. For the commander in chief, this situation was untenable.

The issue began in October while Washington struggled to understand how to motivate his New England soldiers to follow orders, remain in the camp, and continue to support the Revolution through the harvest. At the beginning of the month, he met with a Congressional commission and called a council of his generals to determine how long the new enlistment terms should last and under which officers those enlistments should be served.[7] A few days later, the council (comprised of general officers almost entirely from New England) decided the new enlistment term should last for no longer than one year. In fact, Brigadier General John Sullivan argued for an even shorter term, claiming enlistments should end on April 1, 1776, to facilitate the planting of new crops that spring.[8] While he waited for a decision to be made on the matter from Congress, Washington realized the issue of longer enlistments would probably have to be decided at a later date.

This same council elected not to address the connected issue of which officers to retain in the new establishment. They believed the New England tradition of selecting officers based on how many soldiers were willing to enlist under them made this question too delicate a matter to broach at that time and feared doing so could impede enlisting the necessary soldiers.[9] Colonel William Henshaw sent a proposal of his own to Washington on the same day. Hensaw had been the adjutant general for Artemus Ward. When Horatio Gates was named adjutant general by the Continental Congress, Henshaw offered to resign and go back to Leicester but was asked to act as Gates's second. Colonel Henshaw recommended that Washington gather his major generals and brigadier generals to decide who were the best field officers and retain those needed. Those field officers should then be allowed to pick their company officers for the regiments. Once these decisions were made, the list of officers would be posted for all to see. If this was done, Henshaw argued, the men would then feel comfortable enlisting in the army. If the names of the officers to remain were not determined before December, the men would not enlist and Washington would lose his army.[10]

Washington was unable to follow Colonel Henshaw's suggestion of what would appear to have been an orderly and intelligent solution to the problem, because the council of his generals had already determined they could not make those decisions without risking the popular support for the war at that point. Additionally, Congress decided late in October that "such Officers as have served in the present Army to Approbation & are willing to stay be preferred" and "that they signify in Writing as soon as possible which of them will continue to serve." As long as these officers met with the approval of Washington, they were to immediately "inlist their Men into the Continental Service upon the same Pay & Allowance of Provisions as is now given—The Service to continue to the last Day of December 1776."[11] As the question of promotions was not specifically addressed, interpretation on that matter was left open.

What ensued was a rather chaotic few months with junior officers competing with one another for enlistments under the belief that their rank would be determined in the new establishment by how many soldiers they enlisted. Despite Washington's every attempt to convince his younger leaders that this was not the case, recruiting competitions continued into 1776 and led to soldiers enlisting in more than one regiment, officers refusing to obey their company commanders because they believed they were the commander, and generals being forced to adjudicate between officers when one claimed another had "stolen" his soldier. Still, the confusion did not appear to impact recruiting to an extensive degree, as Massachusetts managed to keep the total number of soldiers in the field above eight thousand going into January and February of 1776.[12]

Washington's personal involvement in one enlistment issue shortly after moving the army down to New York was representative of the larger issue he had with all his New England regiments, especially those from Massachusetts. In May 1776, Colonel James Varnum, commander of the Ninth Continental Regiment (Rhode Island), complained to Washington that fifteen men enlisted for his regiment by Captain John Lane (one of his company commanders) had instead been enlisted into Colonel Edmund Phinney's Eighteenth Continental Regiment (Massachusetts). Varnum was in New York at this time while Phinney was still headquartered in Boston. Captain Lane claimed one of Colonel Phinney's officers, Lieutenant Daniel Merrill, had stolen his soldiers, but when he petitioned Artemus Ward for redress he was unable to produce the required enlistment papers. Ward refused to release the soldiers for service in the Rhode Island regiment and Varnum wanted Washington to force the issue.[13] Despite Washington's request that these men, who had been enlisted from towns located in present-day Maine, be returned to Colonel Varnum, Ward insisted there was no proof of Captain Lane's story and so he refused to do so.[14]

While the competition for enlistments among his officers from Massachusetts and Rhode Island complicated an already challenging problem, another New England state presented a different challenge. When the war began, Connecticut enlisted six thousand soldiers organized into six regiments. Each soldier was enlisted for seven months, paid £2 a month, and given £2.12 shillings as an enlistment bonus. These six thousand soldiers represented fully a quarter of all the men in the state eligible for military service.[15] Yet, by December 1775, most of these men were disgruntled and heading for home. In the Northern Department, under the command of Philip Schuyler, Connecticut soldiers began leaving weeks before their enlistment term had expired as a form of protest against the perceived mistreatment of their commander, Major General David Wooster. Wooster, whose rank was derived from his state's militia, resented being placed under the command of Schuyler (who was both a brigadier general in the Continental service and a New Yorker). Schuyler did nothing to soothe the anger of either Wooster or his men and the result was that fully two-thirds of the Connecticut contingent assigned to attack Canada in the autumn of 1775 left before their enlistments were finished.[16]

In the vicinity of Boston, Washington also had little initial success retaining his soldiers from Connecticut, though for different reasons. Writing to the governor of the state Jonathan Trumbull, Sr. on December 2, 1775, Washington reported many of the soldiers had deserted for home and, while most were brought back, about eighty soldiers from Israel Putnam's regiment managed to escape, taking their weapons and ammunition with them.[17] Despite assurances from the officers, it appeared the soldiers were unwilling to reenlist under the new terms for the First Establishment (a full twelve-month enlistment with only a twelve shilling bonus to purchase a new blanket) and they were exercising their agency to demand a return to higher pay.[18] And, perhaps, these men from Connecticut were disillusioned by the new leadership that had arrived a few months earlier. Simeon Lyman refused to reenlist that December after no less than Charles Lee addressed his unit to demand that the soldiers remain past their enlistment term. When less than a hundred men said they would reenlist, Lee called them "the worst of all creatures" and threatened to have the riflemen from Pennsylvania shoot them! When Simeon and his friends refused to budge their food rations were curtailed and a mutiny almost ensued. Finally, the officers were forced to allow them to leave.[19]

In his reply to Washington a few days later, Trumbull claimed that both the state assembly and the towns were ashamed of their soldiers' conduct (though "a New England man beats high for Liberty") and gave assurances that the deserters would be dealt with under the state's laws.[20] In response to these difficulties with enlisting for the First Establishment, the Connecticut Assembly passed new acts on December 14, 1775, to both support the upcoming campaigns and encourage voluntary enlistments (despite Washington's call for more coercive measures).[21] Anticipating that the decision by Congress not to offer enlistment bonuses for those choosing to join the Continental Army would slow recruiting, the assembly decided to raise one-quarter of its militia into minuteman regiments, electing their own officers and held in constant readiness to fight both in and out of Connecticut for twelve months. Additionally, any soldier enlisting in the Continental Army would be exempt from poll taxes and immune from imprisonment for debt, while those deserting their regiments could expect immediate imprisonment.[22] The result was a return to 90 percent strength of the Connecticut regiments located around Boston and the recruitment of five regiments for the new establishment at three-fourths strength.[23] So while Connecticut managed to maintain its military support for the war, the ability of its soldiers to influence the terms under which they served in support of the war remained strong. And many men, like Joseph Plumb Martin, felt that while "Soldiers were at this time enlisting for a year's service. . . I did not like that; it was too long a time for me at first trial" and so they chose to join either the state forces or wait until the enlistment terms better suited their desires.[24]

In Pennsylvania, the state first relied heavily on the associations to supply soldiers in 1775 and 1776. From June to November 1775, the state assembly first moved to gain control of these private organizations, paying for their services and equipment with public money and encouraging all white males between the ages of sixteen and fifty to join.[25] On November 25, 1775, the assembly approved the Rules and Regulations for the Better Government of the Military Association, determining the rank structure of the association officers and adopting the Articles of Association that enumerated military laws and punishment. Furthermore, a fine of two pounds ten shillings was legislated against those men unwilling to join the associations.[26]

Using the associations that immediately formed throughout most of the counties in the state as training bands, Pennsylvania first raised one battalion of riflemen, known as Thompson's Battalion of Riflemen, which it sent to Boston in the summer of 1775. Recruiting efforts were so successful the battalion was increased from six companies to nine and the men enlisted for a twelve-month term from June 1775 to June 1776.[27] But these men were recruited from the central and western counties of the state, while the more urban populations from the southeast chose to remain in their associations.[28] When Congress requisitioned the state for more Continental regiments to serve in the First Establishment, Pennsylvania responded by raising six new regiments, utilizing their county structure and a growing fear of British invasion to mobilize support.[29] These regiments were authorized in October and December 1775 and January 1776 and recruited over the winter, with enlistments lasting for one year. Again, support came mostly from the Scot-Irish and German populations outside of the southeast, while debates over the issue of independence split the state politically and hampered a more robust military organization.[30]

Farther south, Virginia also was able to raise regiments voluntarily when the war first began. In July 1775, the Virginia Convention raised two regiments totaling a thousand men to fight against Governor Dunmore and the redcoats stationed in the colony. Initially, the new state was divided into sixteen districts with a very rational system for recruiting that allowed the deputy of the district to appoint the company officers and then direct those officers to enlist a total of sixty-eight men for each of their companies. No officer was allowed to recruit outside his district until the company from another district was complete. These sixteen companies formed two regiments. Seniority among the officers would be determined by who brought their company to the appointed rendezvous first.[31]

Following Dunmore's Proclamation, in December 1775 the Convention attempted to raise another six regiments. Wishing to voluntarily enlist these three thousand soldiers, the state abandoned the concept of districting, allowing officers to recruit wherever they could find the men willing to join for two years. Along with a twenty-shilling bonus, soldiers would be exempt from taxes and their families would be cared for at the public's expense if they were maimed or killed.[32] But according to the muster rolls for the army, by September 1776, less than one-third of that number were present and fit for duty.[33] In fact, the politics of recruiting the right kind of army in Virginia worked against providing regiments for Washington's use. As in other states, Virginia was concerned with self-defense and had devised a minuteman system to encourage middling farmers to enlist for local defense while looking for poorer whites to join the Continental service. But the new battalions would not elect their officers and the pay for private soldiers was very low compared to officers, illustrating the disregard governing elites had for the lower enlisted that discouraged freeholders from participating.[34] With the failure of this experiment, the state convention demanded that Congress pay for an increased number of Continental regiments but that they remain in Virginia to defend against Lord Dunmore and his British regulars. Congress refused and enlistments for 1776 stalled.[35]

On the heels of his difficulties reenlisting veterans and enlisting new men, Washington expressed his frustrations to John Hancock in February 1776. Across the army, soldiers were refusing to submit to the level of authority Washington believed was necessary in his officer corps if he was to succeed. He needed longer enlistment for three important reasons. The most obvious was that yearly enlistments forced him to disband his army in the face of the enemy while enlisting a new army at the same time. Washington thought it a miracle that over the winter of 1775 to 1776 General Howe had not marched out of Boston and attacked the American army when it was in this state of confusion. Another important problem with short enlistments related to discipline. Distinctions between officers and soldiers could not be properly maintained because the officers were always aware of the necessity to retain the loyalty of their soldiers in order to reenlist the same men the following year. If soldiers already serving did not reenlist, the officers were forced once again to train and instill proper discipline in raw recruits. And short enlistments had a final shortcoming. When a man's enlistment was about to end, he began to think of home and perhaps how lucky he was to survive the last year. He became careless of his equipment, careless of the camp, and more difficult to lead.[36]

CONGRESS LISTENED TO WASHINGTON'S ARGUMENT for longer enlistments, though an attempt to enlist some regiments from various states for two years without the inducement of a large bounty had largely been a failure earlier in the year. In the fall of 1776, it authorized terms for three years or the duration of the war, and this time recruits were offered an enlistment bonus of $100 for three years or a land grant if they enlisted for the duration of the war. Still, Washington continued to struggle through 1776, again enlisting a new army (known as the Second Establishment) in the face of the enemy in the winter of 1776 to 1777. The year had begun well when morale reached a high point in March 1776 following the British withdrawal from Boston. Washington was glad to receive a report from Lord Stirling that soldiers were enlisting from both the east and the west on the heels of the American victory.[37] But by the winter of that year the British had successfully seized New York and the Continental Army was forced to retreat across the Delaware River, leaving New Jersey's harvest vulnerable to the foraging of the British and their Hessian allies. Washington's decision to attack that Christmas at Trenton and then at Princeton came with great risk but had been absolutely necessary to raise morale and give impetus to his recruiting campaign.[38] And after his success, Washington lost no time using the event to encourage those soldiers whose enlistments would expire in a few days to reenlist immediately.[39]

Given the circumstances, Washington could not continue to fight the war building a new army every year, allowing the terms of enlistment to drive his strategic and tactical decisions. He needed stability and he needed trained soldiers. Another consequence of the policy of shorter terms was that it forced Washington to rely on militia. On November 6, 1776, Washington told Hancock he was forced to call in the militia of the eastern states to shore up his forces because he did not believe he could reenlist his army following their defeats in New York.[40] Throughout the war this was a problem for Washington and several historians have convincingly argued that the issue with the militia was its unreliability against British regulars. While this was certainly the case in many instances, there were some important battles in which the militias and state levies from New England and the middle states fought quite well (Lexington and Concord, Bunker Hill, Bennington, and Cowpens, to name a few). Perhaps a more serious problem for Washington with these state forces was who controlled them.

Two examples serve to prove this point. In New York, during the failed campaign in 1776, Washington's forces were greatly bolstered by a large contingent of state levies from Connecticut. A good portion of those forces were organized as light dragoons, on horses that Washington could not afford to feed. But he did need the soldiers and these soldiers were meant to ride to battle but fight on foot. Washington ordered them to send their horses back and remain as an infantry regiment. The officers of the regiment refused, claiming the laws of their state exempted them from duties required of common infantry soldiers. If Washington did not need their services as cavalrymen, they requested leave to return to Connecticut.[41] Exasperated, Washington replied that if they thought themselves too good to do their duty as needed, he did not care how soon they were dismissed.[42] And all of this occurred while the British were about to land on Staten Island!

Two years later, during the summer of 1778, the Continental Lines of South Carolina and Georgia attempted to partner with the militia of Georgia to attack British forces in Florida. Their goal was to forestall further British attacks on Charleston and other ports in the South. The expedition was a spectacular failure. Brigadier General Robert Howe led the Continental forces while the governor of Georgia, John Houstoun, led the militia. Over the course of the campaign, Houstoun refused to comply with congressional mandates to place all militia forces under the command of the Continental leadership while operating with the Continental Army. Instead, his militia took the best of all local supplies, attempted to charge the army for their own wagons, and stole horses and food from the army. The result was an aborted campaign.[43] The American forces never reached the British fort and the next year British forces were free to march north and support the seizure of Savannah. Problems with enlistments led to the need to rely on militia forces not under the control of Continental officers. The results were usually disappointing.

Washington's arguments did not fall on deaf ears at the Continental Congress. Late in 1776 the delegates did pass resolutions to demand more men for the army and to allow enlistments of three years or the duration of the war but this time in exchange for large bounties, to include a hundred acres of land for every man who stayed in the army until the conclusion of the war. Still, Congress did not have the authority to enlist soldiers directly. As John Hancock wrote to the Massachusetts General Court on October 9, 1776, all Congress could do was help the states induce enlistment with increases of pay, issuances of clothing, and grants of land. It was still the responsibility of the states to garner recruits through their own resolutions.[44]

The result was the continuance of a haphazard system of enlistment, determined by state, which often placed soldiers at odds with one another over the different terms of service. Once Congress set the initial numbers of regiments required from each state and the base bounties for enlistment, the states then set out their individual terms of service. Massachusetts initially voted to supplement the salaries of their soldiers with an extra twenty shillings per month and a new blanket annually. It also mandated that officers failing to meet their enlistment quotas would be forced to forfeit their commissions and send their soldiers to other companies.[45] Connecticut followed this example, also voting to supplement their soldiers' pay with twenty shillings.

This attempt to encourage enlistment was not repeated in the other states farther south. In October 1776, the initial act was passed establishing Virginia's requirement to provide fifteen regiments to the Continental Army. Since the state already had nine battalions in the field, those soldiers in service would be reenlisted under the new establishment and another six battalions were needed. Officers would be selected by the county militia officers and commissioned by Congress, provided they enlisted their quota of soldiers. The state offered no additional inducements for enlistment, but the act did enumerate the bounty and benefits offered by Congress.[46]

The rest of the states outside of New England followed similar strategies and the result was disgruntlement among their soldiers, particularly those serving with New England regiments in the Northern Department. Congress passed a resolve in November 1776 (at the urging of Washington)[47] requesting Massachusetts revoke its previous promise to raise soldier pay through state funding.[48] Both Massachusetts and Connecticut complied, revoking the supplemental pay, though Massachusetts did add an additional £20 enlistment bounty, absolving its soldiers who enlisted the previous month of their commitment and encouraging them to reenlist under the new terms.[49] But while the governments of New England were convinced to lessen their enlistment inducements to help the southern states, Congress was forced to raise soldier pay to bring the rest of the army in line with New England standards. While soldiers from New York, Pennsylvania, and the rest of the southern states were initially recruited at a monthly salary of $5, the soldiers of New England received $6.67 per month. Due to the refusal of soldiers from New York and Pennsylvania to march north to Canada unless properly compensated, Washington was forced to request that Congress standardize soldier pay and raise it to meet New England's rate.[50] Shortly thereafter, Congress did so.

Despite the change in enlistment terms, Massachusetts succeeded in enlisting more men for the Continental Army in 1777 than it had in 1776. While the length of enlistment was altered to allow for both three-year and one-year enlistments, the vast majority of soldiers from the state enlisted for three years and almost half of those were veterans from 1775 and/or 1776.[51] By the fall of 1777, Massachusetts began encouraging enlistments from another angle. As inflation continued to accelerate, soldiers' families suffered from an inability to support themselves on soldier pay. In September 1777, the General Court passed a resolve ordering the towns to give families half their soldiers' pay to buy goods at a reasonable rate. If a soldier was enlisted to fill the quota from another town, the hometown could petition the court for recompense from the enlisting town.[52] While the state did work to increase soldier and officer pay through state lotteries,[53] throughout the remainder of the war Massachusetts recognized a need to support the families of soldiers currently serving if they were to have any chance to continue enlisting new soldiers.

One of the few states to support the war with its own soldiers as effectively was Connecticut. Initially, Connecticut recruited in a fashion similar to its neighbor, Massachusetts. Connecticut also started by granting a twenty-shilling supplement to soldier salaries and then rescinded the offer at the request of Congress. For the first eighteen months of the war, Connecticut struggled to meet its required manning voluntarily, through higher bounties and caring for families. In December 1776 the assembly voted to add £10 to the congressional enlistment bounty.[54] In the same month, the assembly sent a committee to its soldiers, asking those unwilling to reenlist to stay for a period past their enlistment, with additional allowances.[55] On March 18, 1777, at a meeting of the governor and the Council of Safety, it was recommended that the towns establish committees to care for soldiers' families as an inducement for more voluntary enlistments.[56] Despite these attempts, the state quotas could not be filled, necessitating a new approach to the problem.

On April 22, 1777, the governor again met with the Council of Safety. They decided to solve their problems with enlistment in a new manner. The commissioned officers from every militia company in every town would meet to determine how many soldiers they were short to meet their town quotas. The field officers would then evenly divide the militiamen into classes, one for each man needed to fill the quota. These officers were instructed to divide the men as fairly as possible and then gather all the militiamen together, separate them into their classes, and instruct them to produce a man for enlistment within three days. If a recruit was not forthcoming, one man from that class would be drafted into service for the remainder of the year.[57]

This system of "classing" was enforced in May, but not without a few caveats. First, men from the towns were encouraged to find recruits on their own. Any two men who produced a recruit by May 26, 1777, would themselves be exempt from service for the term of their recruit's enlistment. The recruit would count against the quota of his town, unless that quota was complete, in which case he would count against the town of those two men presenting him. After May 26, the militia companies of those towns still requiring men would meet, class their militiamen, and produce the required enlistee. If a man refused to enlist despite being drafted, another man would be forced to enlist and the first man would be penalized under the same laws governing those enlisting and refusing to march. All those men enlisting for three years or the duration would receive all bounties allowed and those agreeing to enlist for the rest of the year would receive £3.[58]

By the end of 1777, the towns were still being given quotas to fill, but the overall responsibility for recruiting was given to the six militia brigades in the state. Officers from the Continental Line were not required to leave the service to recruit. Instead, the field officers from the six brigades canvassed the towns, enforcing the quotas, classing, and drafts. In October 1777, still attempting to meet its obligation, the assembly agreed to draft three hundred men from the First Militia Brigade and three hundred men from the Second Militia Brigade for two months, with service in Peekskill, New York, under the command of General Israel Putnam.[59] Additionally, in an effort to induce soldiers to voluntarily enlist, rather than continue to force a draft, the state made it legal for towns to impress food and clothing from those who could afford to give it (but were unwilling to sell at reasonable prices) and give those goods to families of soldiers serving in the Continental Army.[60]

The results from this year of experimentation with a more coercive form of enlistment (though well short of compulsory service in a draft) gave the nine Connecticut regiments a total of about four thousand soldiers.[61] The results were so disappointing that, by 1778, Connecticut was again allowing one-year enlistments to encourage voluntary service and modified classing by directing the officers involved to draft men, taking into account those who had already served in some capacity. According to the spirit of the law, if a man had already served for a period of time, another man should be selected based on his lack of service. If a draftee felt his selection was not in concurrence with these guidelines, he could argue his case with the officer in charge of the draft and the officer had the authority to pick another man from the militia. Draftees would receive a bonus of over £5 and had ten days to either voluntarily enlist or produce a substitute.[62]

During this same period, the state that provided many of the most ardent Patriots in the public arena began a struggle to raise even a third of the soldiers those Patriots promised in the Congress. While the surviving muster rolls are incomplete, it is clear by May 1777 Virginia managed to place less than 3,600 soldiers in the Continental service, and 938 were listed as too sick to conduct their duties.[63] Over the next year, Virginia state legislators leaned on their county structure and moved quickly toward solutions to solve their manpower problem that mirrored the colony's previous solutions to labor shortages. In response to the shortfall of volunteers, the convention began a draft of militiamen by county. Any two militiamen who convinced a man to enlist in the original nine battalions would be exempt from further drafts for the militia. The county magistrates would draft the remainder of the soldiers from among the men most readily available and fit for service.[64] Importantly, the magistrates picked these men; they were not selected by lottery or through classing.

The result was resistance by those targeted for coerced service. While some men attempted to disrupt the drafts that occurred around the county magistrates, most ran away to neighboring states or to the Ohio Territory. Newspapers were rife with advertisements of draftees that were at large, and this first draft failed to produce more than a thousand new soldiers.[65] As a result, in October of that year, the rules for the draft were refined, defining eligible men as those without children, allowing for a lottery among those men, and providing higher bonuses for those who volunteered while allowing enlistments as short as six months. Those volunteering instead of being drafted would also be allowed to select which regiments they would serve in, providing the inducement of possibly serving with relatives and friends.[66]

But the number of soldiers enlisted still remained abysmal. In the fifteen regiments Virginia was responsible to raise, there existed only a total of 4,908 men by December 1777. Of those soldiers, 672 were reported as sick and present while fully 1,521 were on the rolls as sick and absent.[67] With the number of soldiers enlisted remaining static into May 1778, the convention decided to rescind the draft completely and begin to court potential enlistees with state-funded bonuses. Any man willing to enlist for the duration of the war would receive a $150 bonus and would be exempt from taxes and levies for life. Any man willing to enlist for three years would receive an extra $100. And any soldier disabled in the service would be placed on full-pay pension for life and widows would be cared for by the state.[68] When this measure also failed to produce the desired results, the state returned to a draft but with divisions this time (similar to Connecticut's system of classing) and including shorter enlistment terms and even higher bonuses.[69]

By 1777, Pennsylvania had moved away from the association model of militia service to an encouragement of regular service in the Continental Army. In the new structure of regiments recruited for three years, a total of twelve regiments were recruited, but each was formed with companies raised separately in the various counties. One study shows that 155 companies were raised in total for the state over the course of the war but that each regiment averaged only 250 soldiers apiece.[70] Officers found that while men on the frontier were willing to serve, inhabitants from the southeast of the state were not, particularly within the urban areas of Philadelphia.[71] The result was that many of the soldiers serving in the Pennsylvania Line were immigrants of German or Scots-Irish origin while their officers were more affluent gentlemen from the east who had originally begun their service in the Pennsylvania Associations. Of the records that still exist showing origins of birth, the number of soldiers claiming Ireland as their place of origin outnumbered those claiming Pennsylvania as their birthplace.[72]

While recruiting remained a constant effort for the next few years, Washington had gained a small corps of soldiers and noncommissioned officers across the various state lines who had enlisted for longer terms. Still, his regiments in the Massachusetts Line maintained the greatest stability due to their success recruiting in 1777. Connecticut had a strong mixture of men rotating in on twelve-month enlistments, Virginia was chronically short of men and mixed draftees with short-term men, while Pennsylvania appears to have the majority of its soldiers enlisted for the longer term but were also at one-third strength. And the records show very little evidence that many soldiers volunteered to enlist for the duration of the war. This meant that by the fall of 1779, along with the continuous need to enlist new men in an attempt to fill the required quota, all the states would again face the need to begin reenlisting those men whose three-year terms were about to expire.

By September 1779, enlistment negotiations between those serving for Massachusetts and the General Court began anew as most of the soldiers had enlisted for three years and their enlistments were about to end. Major General William Heath from Roxbury, Massachusetts, wrote to the court at the beginning of the month, warning the politicians that there would be serious challenges reenlisting those soldiers already serving. A committee of three was appointed to visit their soldiers at West Point, New York, and offering both an additional $300 enlistment bonus (additional to those bounties offered by Congress) and a promise to address those entitlements in arrears by January 1, 1780.[73] The committee met with the officers and soldiers and then submitted their report to the court on November 12, 1779.

In their report, the committee disclosed the grievances of those serving in the Massachusetts Line. Both officers and soldiers were no longer willing to remain in the service. Their families were destitute and support from the towns was insufficient. Officers were broke, paying for their own clothes and feeding their soldiers without recompense from the government. Soldiers claimed their weapons were paid for from their enlistment bounties. Furthermore, soldiers who deserted were not actively pursued. Instead, they were readily hired as laborers by the towns at lower wages and protected by the towns from prosecution. Despite the promise of $300 for both those enlisted for the duration and those willing to reenlist, the committee did not believe enlistments would be adequate unless the court could provide their soldiers with good clothing and good food quickly.[74]

While the court did agree to forward $500,000 to General Heath and to fund a visit to Boston by a committee from the army to continue the discussion of grievances, the state of Massachusetts was saved from being forced to address all the complaints from their soldiers by the ending of the war. Still, their inability to honor their promises continued to remain an issue, stirring discontent that fed into Shay's Rebellion in 1786.

Meanwhile, Connecticut continued to struggle to recruit more soldiers to meet even a decreased quota from Congress. Even short-term enlistments of three and six months could not induce men to serve. The assembly attempted to detach militia on active service to the Continental Army, but officers in the militia refused to follow the order. While the number of men enlisted for six months did grow to over 1,700 men, this was still considerably less than the 2,500 soldiers needed and it appears that even this number was only reached by the towns raising their own local bounties from among their residents.[75] But the effect of this strategy was to bankrupt many of the towns, and while the assembly gave those same entities the ability to raise the required men through classing, they were reluctant to do so and enlistment in the Connecticut Line dropped to below eight hundred by 1781.[76]

Throughout the remainder of the war Virginia passed a series of laws that attempted to combine social pressure and political coercion but never succeeded in creating the regiments Washington needed. By October 1780, the enlistment bonus went as high as including one free slave between the ages of ten and thirty years of age, sixty pounds of gold or silver, and three hundred acres of land for those successfully completing their service of three years or the duration (the land grant was only offered to officers).[77] Despite this attempt to give an enlistment bonus less vulnerable to inflation (in the same act soldiers were offered $12,000 for simply enlisting), the draft continued until May 1781 when Lord Cornwallis's invasion of the state apparently forced the issue and made the draft no longer necessary.[78]

In the Pennsylvania Line, the issue of reenlisting soldiers coming up on the end of their three-year term famously came to a head with the Pennsylvania Line Mutiny of 1781. Following the march of the entire line toward Philadelphia on January 1, 1781, and the subsequent agreements made between the soldiers and the Pennsylvania state government, the majority of soldiers left the service and while six regiments remained on paper, only three provisional regiments truly remained in the army. Those soldiers who remained did so somewhat fitfully, as another aborted mutiny outside of Yorktown that fall can attest.

THROUGHOUT THE REVOLUTION, Massachusetts approached the challenge of enlistment from a perspective similar to its approach in the past and in line with its perspective on labor as a whole. Towns were responsible for labor management and they remained responsible for soldier quotas and for the maintenance of their soldiers' families. While participation in the militia was compulsory, enlistment in the Continental Army remained largely voluntary, forcing the court to negotiate terms throughout the war. These negotiations were expensive, overextending both the state and the towns well past their abilities to honor their own terms. Still, Massachusetts consistently maintained the largest number of soldiers in the field throughout the war.

The result of these methods of recruiting was a representation of the full spectrum of Massachusetts society. According to one investigation of both the enlistment and tax records of 4,071 soldiers from four regions of Massachusetts conducted by historian Walter Sargent, 30 percent of all men who enlisted for any form of service (Continental, state, and militia) enlisted in the Continental Army.[79] And the highest number of those soldiers enlisted in 1777 under the new longer terms of service. Refusing to enlist for the duration of the war, most of these men enlisted for three years, though others agreed to enlist once eight- and nine-month enlistments were allowed.[80] The median age of enlistees was twenty-three years of age and overall their ages were representative of the state's population.[81] While it is difficult to determine the economic status of men that young in New England, Sargent traced the family backgrounds of those soldiers who enlisted in 1777 and determined that these soldiers fell within the median economic status of both the soldiers who had served in 1775 and 1776 and within the median of the rest of the state's population.[82] Finally, very few enlistees were black, Native American, or foreign-born, accounting for only 37 of 1,536 soldiers whose records specifically annotated origin (2 percent of the population).[83] In other words, the strategy of recruitment followed by Massachusetts led to a voluntary force of men who were largely representative of their towns and state.

The decision to move quickly from an all-volunteer force to a compromise between volunteerism and compulsory service in Connecticut is interesting, given its military tradition. As a colony, it mobilized forces in much the same way as Massachusetts, abandoning universal service for financial inducements to encourage enlistments, though it did not stop impressments completely until 1760.[84] But during the Revolutionary War, the state increasingly struggled to meet its obligation where the Continental Army was concerned and its response was to innovate through classing.

While Connecticut did institute a more coercive form of recruiting during the War for Independence than Massachusetts, it exercised that plan in a similar fashion to her neighbor. Though legislation was utilized to give authority to military officers to force enlistments, the assembly attempted to avoid resistance to their use of political power by encouraging the use of social pressure instead. Private Joseph Plumb Martin enlisted for the duration of the war in 1777 under this model. In the spring of 1777, Martin's town instituted classing by separating their militia company into squads, classed by ratable property. Each squad had to enlist a man for three years or the duration. If no one volunteered, the squad could collectively hire a man to fill its requirement. If the squad failed to hire a man, one of their members would be drafted. In Martin's case, he was included in his grandfather's squad but was hired by men from a wealthier class to volunteer, thus increasing his enlistment bounty.[85] Social pressure (centered on town culture) allowed Connecticut to raise more men than any other states except Massachusetts and Virginia, though by the end of the war its towns were largely bankrupt and the vast majority of men remaining refused to serve for more than six months at a time.

The political elites of Virginia, in similar fashion to their northern counterparts, approached the problem of enlistment in ways that embodied their cultural norms for organizing labor. Poor whites were necessarily targeted, as it was viewed as too dangerous to arm enslaved blacks. The result was that one-sixth of all recruits were substitutes, paid to serve in the stead of the gentry and richer yeomanry not interested in attaining a commission as an officer. One-third of those who enlisted were adolescents and fully 80 percent of the soldiers were younger than twenty-five years of age. Additionally, 20 percent of all recruits were foreign-born, most of these men coming from the Scots-Irish immigration of the early 1770s. In other words, the men recruited or drafted to serve were the young and poor of Virginia society.[86] In particular, draftees were akin to indentured servants, landless young men who were given money at the beginning of their indenture and promised a bounty to begin their life anew when their time of service came to an end. Of course, this form of military indenture competed with other forms of labor servitude that placed wealthy landowners at odds with the needs of the Revolution. Military service outside of the county militia, when compelled by a draft, was viewed as forced servitude by those freemen drafted, explaining the extreme difficulty experienced by the state to either execute the draft or meet its congressional requirements. While Virginia did manage to field the second-largest state line in the Continental Army (through a combination of financial inducements, social pressure, and drafting), its attempts to negotiate the initial terms of authority for service to the Continental Army left the leaders of the army with significant leadership challenges and created a large social gap between the enlisted soldiers and their officers.

In the case of Pennsylvania, initial support from the central and western counties allowed the state to raise up to twelve regiments, though never at anything close to full strength (not counting Thompson's Battalion of Riflemen in 1775). The result was a state line filled with at least as many foreign-born soldiers as native sons, all serving often under regimental commanders from the east who gained their commissions through voluntary service in Associations. Still, many of these men in the rank and file for Pennsylvania initially enlisted under the assumption that they would fight to protect their homes in the west. Though these men enlisted under a three-year term of service, they soon began to believe their use in other theaters was a violation of the terms under which they had agreed to serve.[87] This belief, combined with the lack of pay and support over the course of the war, led to their extreme decision to mutiny in 1781.

RECRUITING FOR THE ARMY set the initial terms of service within the force. Men entering the service either agreed that their enlistment came from a legitimate exercise of authority from their state government and recruiting officers (and were more willing to follow their regimental officers) or they did not (and resisted that exercise of authority over them). During the earliest stages of the war, the vast majority of soldiers from every state were enlisted voluntarily but for short terms and high bounties. The result was a motivated force that was undisciplined, untrained, and often unwilling to remain in the field once the terms of enlistment had ended. Over time, some states maintained the voluntary nature of enlistments (though at a continued cost that grew increasingly unsupportable) while others attempted to coerce enlistments that were met with resistance both before and during service. The result was an overarching inability of the states to meet their obligations, either to Congress or to their soldiers.

Toward the end of the war, Lieutenant Benjamin Gilbert observed firsthand the problems that both Virginia and Massachusetts had recruiting for the army. As an officer in the Massachusetts Line, by October 1780 he was quite disillusioned with the insistence by his state to maintain voluntary enlistments and the state's inability to honor enlistment obligations. In a letter to his father, Gilbert explained that morale was low among the officers because they had not been paid in months and they were forced to constantly train new recruits. Many officers were resigning their commissions, his company commander Daniel Shays among them. Gilbert claimed his days were filled drilling raw recruits that were coming in daily, men unaccustomed to army life and most likely to break under fire. These new soldiers slept while on guard duty and were not trustworthy. Gilbert felt relegated to the position of a drill sergeant, training men whose enlistments were so short, they would likely leave the service just as Gilbert finished training them. In his estimation, Massachusetts would be better served drafting enlistees, like Virginia, if the war was ever to be concluded successfully.[88]

Less than a year later, Lieutenant Gilbert experienced a campaign that changed his perspective considerably. By May 1781, Gilbert's unit, the Fifth Massachusetts Regiment, was fighting in Virginia. He witnessed the difficulty that Virginia had mobilizing a regular force through drafting. Washington's Grand Army, of which the Massachusetts Line was the largest component, was forced to stand by as the British plundered the countryside because, according to Gilbert, Virginia was incapable of fielding regular regiments capable of fighting. Virginia could not enlist men for three years or the duration. Their soldiers were not well trained, as a result. Furthermore, this inability to recruit was mirrored in the other three southern states. Gilbert blamed the lack of voluntary enlistments in the South for the fall of Georgia and the Carolinas. The key to Revolutionary success was New England and its volunteer soldiers.[89]

The sentiments expressed by Gilbert over that last year of fighting highlighted the importance of enlistment methods for leadership in the Continental Army. For eight years the officers in the army negotiated terms of authority with their soldiers, developing norms in the exercise of power through discipline, training, and experience that ended with a distinctly American way of leading soldiers. Negotiations began with the terms of enlistment and continued to be shaped by those terms over the course of a soldier's service. Washington understood the impact of enlistment terms on discipline and training, though he did not show in his correspondence that he recognized the importance of local requirements on the methods of recruiting. Expectations were established based on promises made when a soldier first entered the army, though those contractual agreements were rarely met. Still, most of the soldiers who enlisted for three years or the duration remained in the army despite their disappointments. This was because while leadership as a negotiation of authority began with enlistment terms, it continued through the actual experience of service, as soldiers and officers built cohesion in discipline, training, and hardship.

Three

The Use of Discipline
in the Continental Army

THE TERMS OF SERVICE VIOLATED

O N THE MORNING OF JUNE 28, 1776, THOMAS HICKEY WAS marched to the gallows erected in a field near Bowery Lane in New York and hanged for the crimes of sedition and mutiny. Formerly a member of Washington's personal guard, Hickey was implicated in a plot to sabotage American fortifications, to possibly kidnap or kill the general, and to desert to the British Army once imperial forces landed in the state after he was arrested for trying to counterfeit money. His execution was completed in front of a crowd of twenty thousand spectators, including much of the Continental Army then occupying the city. He was the only soldier implicated in the plot and he was the first soldier executed in the Continental Army.[1]

The execution of Thomas Hickey is historically interesting for many reasons. Thomas Hickey was not originally from the American colonies; he was an Irish immigrant who had previously served in the British Army. His "Old Country" origins led Washington to decide to only allow "Natives," especially native-born Virginians with some property, to serve in his personal guard for the remainder of the war.[2] While he was the only person executed, several civilians were also implicated (including the mayor of New York) but never prosecuted.[3] And the crimes Hickey was convicted of were not capital crimes.[4] In fact, the two crimes of which the defendant was expressly convicted (Articles V and XXX) did not become capital crimes until new Articles of War were approved by the Continental Congress three months later.[5] Regardless, Hickey's accomplice in the counterfeit charge, Michael Lynch, was never brought to trial; the mayor of New York, David Mathews, was imprisoned in Connecticut but he escaped; and no other persons were punished.

Washington and his council of generals used the occasion to parade their troops to the field to observe the administration of justice.[6] The next day Washington admonished his soldiers to avoid "Lewd women," Thomas Hickey's excuse for traveling down a bad path.[7] Newspapers such as the *Constitutional Gazette* applauded the execution of an enemy to liberty and hoped "the remainder of those miscreants, (now in our possession,) will meet with a punishment adequate to their crimes."[8] Finally, almost as many people reportedly attended the event as lived in New York at the time. This very public event was an occasion to enforce the most extreme form of discipline in the new army against a person who probably did not have many relatives in the country, for a crime most Patriots could agree was unforgivable, and during a time of extreme duress when the enemy was quickly approaching.

Initially, Washington and other senior leaders believed stricter and more punishing military laws were necessary to shape civilian recruits into Continental soldiers, but over the course of the War for Independence, most officers evolved their views on military discipline and how to achieve success within their formations. At first, some senior leaders perceived a requirement for more authority (codified in stricter military regulations combined with longer terms of enlistment) as the way to enforce discipline among soldiers who lacked training or experience. These officers viewed the combined coercive power found in reducing the need to reenlist veterans every year and the legal abilities to exact more physical and mental punishment as necessary to drive soldiers' efforts in the absence of individual training and unit cohesion. But there were other leaders who believed there was a more complex relationship between regulations, training, experience, and morale and that coercion was more useful as a method to reform those soldiers who failed to adhere to military standards agreed upon and inculcated over time. And indeed, the initial focus on more stringent regulations proved insufficient to the development of an army that looked and acted like a professional force. Despite Washington's early evaluations, the soldiers in his army did not respond well to the use of coercion as a method to drive their efforts. Instead, they often resisted the use of punishment by their officers, illustrating the need for their officers to provide leadership, develop unit cohesion, and inspire motivation—requirements which soon became apparent and altered the focus of many Continental Army leaders.

The term discipline as it was used in relation to military leadership in the Continental Army had several meanings. When used as an adjective (a *disciplined* unit), it was the measure of commitment by both the leaders and led to the negotiated agreement of standards and the proper exercise of authority. Well-disciplined troops were identified as those who maintained their appearance, obeyed the orders of their officers quickly and efficiently, withstood attacks by their enemies, and performed their duties according to established standards. Poorly disciplined soldiers failed to maintain their cleanliness, were unwilling to follow orders or stand against the enemy in combat, and could not be counted on to maintain their duties in camp. At the same time, *to discipline* was an action, the ability to use coercion through a strong set of military regulations that allowed officers to enforce standards, either as a method to reform soldiers who violated those regulations or as a deterrence to those soldiers who needed to be driven to do their duty.

The definitions of disciplined and undisciplined troops illustrate the connections between punishment, training, and morale to discipline and highlight the levels of commitment or compliance to the standards negotiated between those serving in the army. Soldiers who were trained to perform well on campaign and during encampments were confident in the abilities of themselves, their fellows, and their leaders. These were the men who would stand against the British in an open field and follow directions under fire. Still, their morale (often determined by how well they were provisioned and paid) could detract from their willingness to obey the orders of their officers. This led in some cases to regiments exhibiting the worst breakdowns in discipline despite their relatively high levels of training. Soldiers who were well trained with high morale were committed to the standards expected by their leadership and acted with little need for officers to resort to harsh treatment. Soldiers experiencing low morale or who had not received training were much less likely to show any traits of good discipline and would only comply with army standards when faced with the stringent enforcement of disciplinary actions, but this often led to further resistance by the soldiers to the orders of their officers.

From the beginning of the war, Washington understood this relation between training, morale, and punishment, but he believed he could overcome his army's initial inability to face the British on the offensive (due to their lack of training and experience) by resorting to a stronger authority to drive them into compliance through punishment. He knew the first Articles of War, passed by Congress in June 1775, lacked the power to compel his soldiers, unused to military life, to obey regulations and orders with which they did not agree. He wanted the authority to enforce his standards to a degree that perpetrators would be reformed and their fellows would be deterred without the time needed to gain their commitment to those military requirements. His perspective on this issue was formed from his experiences as a plantation owner in Virginia and as a colonial officer in the Seven Years' War. Yet Washington's view on the need for stricter military regulations was not shared by some of his other officers and soldiers, many of whom shared a more consensus perspective on military service. And while Congress would eventually strengthen American military regulations by the end of 1776, the increase in the severity of punishments would be tempered in important ways and their use would not always result in an increase in unit discipline.

In 1775, the Massachusetts provisional government created their own Articles of War to govern their militia forces that were relatively weak (in comparison to the British Articles of War passed in 1774) and harkened back to the colony's military laws from the Seven Years' War. Since the vast majority of the soldiers being reenlisted for the campaign of 1776 were from New England, the Continental Congress chose to adopt the Massachusetts Articles of War for their army. Over the course of seventeen months, Washington petitioned Congress to strengthen those laws, arguing he needed regulations more in line with British practices if he was to form an army capable of defeating his enemy. By the fall of 1776, Congress complied, rewriting their Articles of War to be almost identical with the British model. Still, despite an increase both in the number of regulations categorized as capital and in the severity of corporal punishments, limitations remained that would restrict the administration of punishment in ways nonexistent in the British system while the other half of this coercive coin (longer enlistment terms) never fully materialized as Washington had envisioned. Certainly, as the war progressed, the Continental Army became more disciplined and more capable, and while some of the credit for this improvement could be given to stronger military regulations (and longer enlistments), a reliance on the use of coercion remained insufficient to effect the changes required for the Continental Army to succeed during the war.

THOMAS SIMES, A CAPTAIN IN THE BRITISH ARMY, published a book on military leadership in 1776 titled *The Military Guide for Young Officers, in Two Volumes*. While his work included excerpts from other famous British officers and illustrated in detail the duties of senior officers, junior officers, noncommissioned officers, and soldiers, he began his piece discussing discipline. According to Simes, discipline was the soul of an army. He argued it was a false assertion that complete subordination of a soldier to his superiors was a debasement of courage. To the contrary, the armies with the strictest discipline had made the greatest achievements. General officers did more than give orders; they needed to instill the severest discipline by upholding justice with impartiality. If he could do this, a commander would engender both the love and fear in his subordinates necessary to succeed in war.[9] This perspective on the use of coercion to shape the relationships between officers and soldiers worked well in a British social environment of paternalism and hierarchy. The use of harsh punishment by socially distant officers reinforced both their position as father figures (instilling love and fear in their soldiers) and their class separation from those men they led. From the beginning of his tenure as commander of the Continental Army, Washington adhered to these very same beliefs, stating in his first general order to the newly established army that "Subordination & Discipline (the Life and Soul of an Army) [will] make us formidable to our enemies, honorable to ourselves, and respected in the world."[10]

Some historians have emphasized Washington's outlook on discipline and they have given some credit to the increasing severity of disciplinary actions in the Continental Army for its success as the war dragged on (or at least for its ability to remain in the field year round). Combined with longer enlistments and an increasing number of the lower sorts serving in the ranks, this growing authority over soldiers could be viewed as indicative of the army's growing professionalism based on a European (or at least British) model. It could also help us understand why those serving in the army submitted to the harsh realities of a war in which little support was given to soldiers in food, clothing, or pay. According to this line of argument, the Continental Army remained largely intact because the soldiers serving had nowhere to go, they were legally bound to remain, and the consequences of resistance were quite high.

But while military regulations and punishment were certainly important, discipline in the Continental Army was instilled through a combination of leadership, training, esprit de corps, and disciplinary actions. Still, a comparison of the differing ideas of how the Continental Army should regulate itself when discipline broke down is useful to understanding how leaders sought to enforce discipline and to what degree the rank and file would tolerate disciplinary enforcement. When the Revolutionary War began, officers and soldiers from the various states entered the service with widely different views on this subject. Regiments from the state lines approached the issue of coercion separately, but over time consensus was reached that standardized the administration of justice and acculturated the members of the army to its deployment, but still left room for negotiation up to the end of the war.

Washington took charge of the Continental Army with his experiences from the Seven Years' War clearly at the forefront of his mind. During the last colonial war, Virginia instituted military laws very similar to their British counterparts. Starting in the summer of 1755, the Virginia assembly passed new military laws for their provincial force that authorized corporal punishment against those soldiers found guilty of mutiny, desertion, or sedition. The death penalty was mandated for those convicted of treason. While this new act of the colonial legislature imposed much stricter regulations on men conscripted for the Virginia Regiment compared to their colonial militia, these laws were not enough for the regimental commander, George Washington. By October 1755, he threatened to resign if the assembly did not impose harsher penalties more in line with British military regulations, claiming the current regulations failed to impose proper subordination of the soldiers to their officers and of the officers to Washington. Governor Dinwiddie agreed, directing the House of Burgesses to pass a new Mutiny Act that increased the number of capital crimes and allowed for harsher corporal punishments. The result was a new set of regulations passed in October 1755 that mirrored British punishments, making treason, mutiny, insubordination, and striking an officer all capital crimes. Additionally, the use of the lash was increased, allowing punishments as large as a thousand lashes and giving officers the latitude to summarily administer corporal punishment in certain cases.[11]

Continental forces being raised in the Southern Department followed this tradition in 1775 and 1776. South Carolina began the Revolutionary War with similarly harsh forms of punishment allowed within its regiments. When the colony raised regiments in 1775, the South Carolina Assembly passed regulations based on the British military laws of 1774. For the next year, courts-martial held in South Carolinian regiments passed down sentences as high as eight hundred lashes. While these harsher sentences were often pardoned or lowered, actual punishments still exceeded the current Continental restrictions of thirty-nine lashes, resulting in punishments of fifty to a hundred lashes. Furthermore, soldiers were not allowed to leave their camps without written passes and white civilians were asked to stop soldiers and demand their passes. If a soldier was caught without a pass, the civilian was entitled to a reward when he returned the soldier to his commander. Severe punishments remained the norm in South Carolina until November 1776, when General Robert Howe arrived with the new Continental Articles of War. He insisted the new laws be read aloud to all soldiers in the South Carolina Line, lowering the levels of punishment and bringing South Carolina in line with the rest of the Continental Army.[12]

Yet Washington was not taking command in the South and the vast majority of his army came not from South Carolina or Virginia but from the New England states of Massachusetts, Connecticut, Rhode Island, and New Hampshire. Officers and soldiers entering the Continental Army from the New England states were used to a relatively lax form of military justice that evolved as a result of short-term enlistments under locally known and supported officers from their communities. In Massachusetts during the Seven Years' War, the governing military law was initially the 1754 Mutiny Act. Riding the wooden horse, running the gauntlet, or other like forms of punishment could punish all infractions not designated as capital offenses. This was understood to mean that the use of the whip was not to exceed a biblical limitation of thirty-nine lashes.[13] This set of laws did declare the crimes of mutiny, desertion, and sedition as capital crimes. While a court-martial of eleven officers could adjudicate these crimes, the sentence had to be approved by the governor of the colony before it could be carried out. Though the British Articles of War officially regulated all provincial regiments serving with British regular forces after 1755, New England officers attempted to protect their men from British justice (particularly in cases of capital offenses). In one instance when a British officer did issue such a sentence on a New England soldier, the provincial officers begged him to stay the sentence until the governor could be informed. The refusal of the British commander to wait led to a significant increase in desertions at Fort Oswego (on the shores of Lake Ontario) and, when the British officer was killed a few weeks later, the fort surrendered to the French immediately thereafter. His epitaph from a New England carpenter working at the fort read "thus the man who this week had the lives of valuable men in his hands, and would not extend Mercy to them, now had not time, not even to sue for his own life."[14] For New England colonial soldiers, the death penalty seemed cruel for all but the most heinous crimes, and no officer wished to return home and explain to his neighbors he had executed their son. The result of this lighter form of coercion was that the discipline of New England provincial troops during this period relied on the solidarity of the soldiers with their officers, training in proper military conduct, entreaties of officers to their soldiers to maintain their duty, and the enforcement of community expectations when they returned home.[15]

The only state to provide troops to Washington at Boston from outside the New England tradition was Pennsylvania, and Pennsylvania initially did not allow severe corporal punishment within their Associator regiments. In November 1775, the Pennsylvania Assembly adopted new Articles of Association, incorporating thirty-two articles that worked as their articles of war. Article 15 stipulated two privates or noncommissioned officers would participate as voting members during courts-martial, a practice in use in the Prussian Army at the time but certainly not the British Army, nor would it be adopted for the Continental Army.[16] Furthermore, punishments would be limited to fines, dismissals, and reductions in rank.[17] It is important to note, however, that the Associators were initially comprised of men with relatively equal social and economic statuses given the requirement for enlistees to provide their own equipment.[18]

In the Seven Years' War, Pennsylvania had initiated more severe forms of punishment within the regiments of their provincial army. Following the failure of Pennsylvania soldiers to remain in service at Fort Augusta in 1757, Governor William Denny used the crisis to attempt the creation of a provincial force more in keeping with the professional British model. He formed companies known as the "Old Levies" with men enlisted for three years who were regulated under the British Articles of War and officers commissioned by the governor. This foray into a nascent standing army ended fairly quickly, however, once William Pitt began flowing British resources into the colony. At his suggestion, the "New Levies" were instituted in Pennsylvania, with one-year enlistments and officers selected based on their ability to recruit. Still, these forces within the Pennsylvania provincial structure remained under the regulations of the British Articles of War.[19]

Similar to the issues of recruiting and enlistments, the various traditions of colonial military regulations initially worked against the establishment of an immediate standard in the Continental Army. The vast majority of the officers and soldiers that comprised the early force were from New England, men who understood punishment as a method to reform those who failed to adhere to recognized military standards and were unwilling to subject themselves to a system they viewed as contrary to liberty. General Washington, as their new commander in chief, believed soldiers necessarily subordinated themselves to a more stringent standard of punishment compared to those allowed in civil law or militia regulations. Officers needed more authority to administer harsher punishments as a method to instill discipline in soldiers and drive them to action when they came under the fire of British muskets and artillery. And they needed the ability to exercise their authority in a manner that highlighted the hierarchy of the army, creating more social distance between the officers and the soldiers they led. The resultant tension between these differing views would eventually lead to a negotiated middle ground where military discipline rested not only on the fear of punishment but also on other means to convince soldiers to adhere to military standards.

As WASHINGTON WORKED TO PULL TOGETHER the various groups within his army, he focused on two primary issues he believed were at the heart of a disciplined force. As discussed in the previous chapter, recruitment and enlistment terms had led to his desire for enlistments for the duration of the war. His second concern, spoken of almost in the same breath, was his desire for a more stringent set of military laws. This perceived need for harsher regulations that reflected those of the British Army came from Washington's experiences, his cultural acceptance of a more violent civil law regime, and his understanding that he was taking command of an army that was not consistently well trained or always reliable under fire. Yet the representatives in the Continental Congress decided initially to adopt the military laws developed by the Massachusetts provincial assembly. The Continental Articles of War approved in June 1775 authorized only three offenses as capital crimes, limited lashes to thirty-nine for any one person convicted of a lesser crime (and a court-martial could not circumvent this restriction by giving thirty-nine lashes per offense if multiple infractions were annotated), and retained mutiny, desertion, and sedition as capital crimes. Finally, in recognition of the limited powers of the Congress, Article I stated that while all soldiers were to be regulated by this new system, regiments unwilling to submit themselves to this standard could, with the concurrence of the commander, remain under their particular state regulations.[20]

These initial Articles of War were far less draconian than the British regulations issued each year under the Mutiny Act of 1765. These British military laws enumerated many more offenses under capital punishment and allowed for an unlimited number of lashes to be administered for corporal offenses, sometimes leading to sentences of a thousand to two thousand lashes. Furthermore, the approved Continental Articles of War provided much less authority for Washington to force compliance from his officer corps than he wanted. After being informed that Congress had decided to adopt the Massachusetts Articles of War for the entire Continental Army, Washington immediately began complaining of the lack of discipline among his New England soldiers and officers.[21] While he worked to convince a visiting Committee of Conference to strengthen the laws, in October 1775 that committee from Congress upheld the decision to restrict punishment to thirty-nine lashes.[22] At this point, Washington took a different tack. He issued demands in his general orders for soldiers to behave in a disciplined and orderly manner, appealing to their sense of duty and their adherence to the tenets of the Revolution.[23] He implored his officers to follow his general orders and to train with their men.[24] When his orders were not followed, he threatened the arrest of his officers and cancelled his soldiers' furloughs.[25] Furthermore, he issued an order on the eve of his seizure of Dorchester Heights that notified his army that soldiers retreating on the battlefield would be summarily shot for cowardice.[26] Finally, the general worked through general courts-martial to make an example of those refusing to comply with regulations (both officers and soldiers), cashiering, fining, and whipping (within the legal limits) those found guilty of desertion, cowardice, and failure to stay awake on guard.

With Congress, Washington focused on arguments to increase the terms of service for his incoming soldiers, realizing that training and experience would be needed to inculcate discipline in the face of relatively lax military laws. Writing to Joseph Reed on February 1, 1776, Washington claimed the reason he could not attack the British in Boston was due to his inability to enforce the harsh discipline necessary do so. Without the threat of severe punishment, only longer enlistments would give him the leverage to train his soldiers properly.[27] Washington informed John Hancock that training his soldiers about the proper subordination necessary to win battles could not be achieved while constantly worrying about recruiting and introducing new recruits each year.[28] If Washington could not convince Congress to give him greater authority over punishments, he could still argue for greater authority to control who were the members of the organization and under what terms they would serve.

Still, he had to face the campaign season of 1776 with a Continental Army under the First Establishment, with soldiers fighting under generous terms of temporary enlistments and military punishments that appeared to lack much strength. And his difficulties in discipline only increased when he moved his army to New York. By that time, the number of regiments from states outside of New England increased dramatically, as did the need to convene general courts-martial on a more frequent basis. Over the course of six months, from April to September 1776, Washington reported in his general orders the results of no less than 108 general courts-martial that tried 20 officers, 13 noncommissioned officers, and 130 soldiers for desertion, mutiny, cowardice, theft, striking an officer, and attempted murder. These men put on trial came from Connecticut, Massachusetts, New York, Pennsylvania, and Virginia. In many of the cases, the officers were acquitted, but when they were not, all were cashiered. For the soldiers, punishments ranged from a week's imprisonment on bread and water to fines to repay bounties to lashes from between ten and thirty-nine. The increase in punishments culminated just prior to the British landings on Long Island with the execution of Thomas Hickey for activities that were in reality treasonous.

Despite Washington's use of coercion to instill military discipline, significant portions of his army continued to act in ways contrary to military order. Soldiers and officers regularly visited a part of New York known as the "Holy Ground," a district near Trinity Church where prostitutes plied their trade. On April 26, 1776, the soldiers rioted in this neighborhood after two of their number were found murdered and another castrated. The number of soldiers involved during the riot limited Washington to issuing a general order admonishing his army to rely on legitimate redress for wrongs committed by civilians.[29] Following the reading of the Declaration of Independence to the various regiments, soldiers again rioted, tearing down a statue of King George III. Again, Washington beseeched his men to maintain discipline and order.[30] Yet many of his officers failed to listen. Lieutenant Isaac Bangs in the Second Massachusetts Regiment either did not hear Washington's admonishment or did not agree. From his perspective, the result of the riot that tore down the hated statue was four thousand pounds of lead that could be used to make musket balls. And this would be a fitting use, making ammunition to poison British and Tory soldiers whose minds and souls had been poisoned by the lies of the king.[31]

The result of these breakdowns in military discipline during the army's occupation of New York was a continued distrust between Washington (and his closest advisors) and his soldiers. Facing the impending British invasion, Washington increasingly relied on threats of summary punishment for acts of cowardice or failure to comply with orders. He attempted to appeal to republican ideology to convince hungry soldiers not to loot from nearby farms and houses, and he promised rewards to those who acted as good soldiers. Meanwhile, soldiers like Sergeant Leffingwell and Private Martin resisted orders from officers not in their regiments even in the face of potential summary execution. Still, while Washington continued to struggle with how to instill discipline in this new organization, Congress was about to grant both his requests for longer enlistments and more stringent military laws.

Though Washington appeared at a loss to enforce discipline in the majority of his army during the First Establishment, some officers did manage to produce well-disciplined units at the lower levels. Captain Joseph Bloomfield was one officer who apparently discovered how to instill order despite lacking the authority to enact harsh punishments. Leading a company in the Third New Jersey Regiment, Bloomfield marched his men from New York to Albany on May 3, 1776. Benefitting from the leadership of his regimental commander, Colonel Elias Dayton, who served in the Jersey Blues during the Seven Years' War, Bloomfield was proud to report his regiment was recognized as the best disciplined unit in Albany by General Philip Schuyler.[32] In July 1776, Bloomfield was given a separate mission from the rest of his regiment, to command his company and one militia company guarding the rear of the regiment near German Flatts.[33] A few days later, two more provincial companies joined him, making Bloomfield a *de facto* battalion commander.[34]

For the next two months, Bloomfield worked hard to maintain order within the four companies. He issued daily orders, conducted roll calls and exercises, appointed volunteer officers as adjutant and quartermaster, and held courts-martial when necessary. He even paraded his companies on Monday, July 15, to read the Declaration of Independence.[35] During this period, several disciplinary problems confronted Bloomfield, requiring him to make hard decisions given his relatively junior rank and experience. Many of those problems resulted from drunkenness, with officers and soldiers sleeping outside of camp and absenting themselves from exercises and roll calls. In every case involving an officer, Bloomfield managed to force their resignation. In the case of his soldiers, Bloomfield sentenced them to lashes, imprisonment, and reduction in rank. Yet not a single form of physical punishment was actually carried out. The two corporals reduced in rank were restored shortly thereafter. And imprisonments were limited to the time spent waiting for trial. The only exception to this last point involved Private Michael Reynolds. After his corporal punishment was rescinded, Reynolds claimed he was being punished out of spite and Bloomfield immediately imprisoned him again. Still, after only three days, Reynolds publicly apologized for his comments, stating his remarks were aimed at his fellow soldiers, not his commander.[36]

Captain Bloomfield resorted to group cohesion and identity rather than coercion to maintain discipline over those two months. He repeatedly brought men to the whipping post, admonished them in front of the companies, and then forgave them. He kept the men busy building a fort at their encampment and celebrated the completion of the work with a parade and a toast. Furthermore, he continuously required his officers to share in the exercises and duties of the day. His biggest crisis occurred the day after four months of pay arrived at camp. The following day, five soldiers crossed the river from camp and began drinking. Bloomfield immediately sent a guard detail to return the wayward soldiers. When Bloomfield rode to meet them, one soldier did attempt to flee but Bloomfield subdued him with the flat of his sword. Threatening a general court-martial, Bloomfield again convinced his soldiers to apologize and fall back in line with the rest of their fellows.[37]

Officers like Captain Bloomfield were able to more directly connect with their soldiers, negotiating the use of coercion (or threat of its use) with the known levels of training and morale within their units. And his actions illustrate a desire to utilize punishment as a method to reform poor behavior rather than compel them to accomplish their duties. Bloomfield and many of his soldiers came from the same region in West Jersey, so their relationships were easier to establish and his willingness to drive his soldiers to their work was nonexistent. His mentor was an experienced colonial officer who apparently taught Bloomfield the necessity of daily orders and exercises. While Bloomfield's "regiment" did not encounter an enemy during the period discussed, there was ample opportunity for this small command to degenerate into a disorderly crowd. Yet, despite Bloomfield's obvious distaste for inflicting physical punishment, only two soldiers deserted and Bloomfield was recognized for his success when he was promoted to deputy judge advocate for the Northern Department by General Horatio Gates in November 1776.[38]

BY 1777, THE CONTINENTAL ARMY began operating as the Second Establishment. Two resolves from the Continental Congress worked together to provide Washington and his generals more authority over their soldiers. The first, discussed previously, was the enlistment of soldiers for three years or the duration. Of course, many soldiers continued to enlist for much shorter terms, but a core of enlistees was created that would remain in service for the most difficult period (both while on campaign and in winter quarters) of the war. The second piece of congressional legislation transformed the American military legal system to mirror their British counterparts.

The Continental Congress approved a revised Articles of War on September 20, 1776. While the original Articles of War drew directly from the laws set by Massachusetts, the new regulations reflected a dramatic shift to a more stringent and coercive set of military laws. More specifically, the new Articles of War were based directly from the British Articles of War passed by Parliament in 1774.[39] Many more crimes were specifically noted (from thirty-nine to fifty-nine enumerated offenses), both regimental and general courts-martial were strengthened in their abilities to punish (lash limits were increased from thirty-nine to a hundred), and the list of capital crimes was increased (from only three to seventeen enumerated offenses). The effect was to give more authority to officers over their soldiers and more autonomy to those officers from the Continental and state governments to determine proper behavior within the army.

Martial law in the Continental Army, as in other European armies, was exercised in regimental and general courts-martial. Due to the nature of colonial provincial armies, disciplinary actions usually resulted from regimental courts-martial, with few general courts-martial being held outside of British authority. Provincial generals were few and their colonial assemblies largely held their authority in check, requiring governor approval for capital sentences. In other words, previous courts-martial were rather limited in their abilities to both adjudicate infractions of regulations and in their abilities to punish those found guilty. After over a year of war waged by a Continental Army, Congress recognized the necessity for the generals in the army to administer justice in a more efficient manner and acquiesced to Washington's call for stricter punishments and increased autonomy. Still, the delegates from the new states required that all records and sentences from general courts-martial be sent to Philadelphia as a method of retaining supervision over sentencing.

The most striking change in the military regulations enacted in September of 1776 was an enormous increase in crimes that could result in the execution of a soldier. Eleven crimes previously categorized as corporal were moved into the capital crime list and one of those offenses (doing violence to those supplying the army) moved from a crime initially adjudicated in regimental courts-martial to a capital offense requiring a general court-martial. While this serious increase in army authority is important, the new laws also increased the abilities of army leadership to punish offenders in every other way. If generals, operating through their courts, could condemn men to execution for many more crimes, regimental commanders also gained more power to punish their soldiers. Originally, regimental courts-martial were the venue to punish those who left their platoons without leave, failed to appear at the parade ground on time, and were found drunk on duty. By 1777, regimental leadership could also punish soldiers for speaking traitorously against the Congress, hiring others to do their duty, and destroying private property.[40]

The authority of senior officers over junior officers was also strengthened by 1777. Initially, officers could be cashiered for a total of eight enumerated offenses, while they could be fined for an additional four violations and imprisoned for one crime (behaving badly in a place of worship [second offense]). The new regulations reduced the use of fines or imprisonment for officers to one offense and removed any violations that could reduce an officer in rank. Instead, officers now faced one of two punishments in the Continental Army; they could be cashiered for fifteen separate offenses (and face publication of their crimes in their home state) or be executed.[41] Washington may not have ever achieved the authority to choose his officers but he certainly had gained the power to remove those commissioned officers he found inadequate to the job.

While the regulations that helped usher in the Second Establishment of 1777 did initiate a new era of authority for commanders, they also continued to place restrictions that recognized a compromise between the various military traditions found in the former colonies. Gone was the stricture of thirty-nine lashes for corporal punishments. Instead, a maximum of a hundred lashes were permitted. This increased authority for the use of the whip was important, but when compared to British practices of a thousand and two thousand lashes for corporal crimes, the Continental limitation becomes more apparent. Furthermore, while a two-thirds majority in the court-martial could sentence a soldier to execution, no sentences passed by a general court-martial could be enacted before the presiding general informed Congress.[42]

Washington received the news that Congress had approved his requests for longer enlistments and stricter military regulations in a letter written by John Hancock on September 24, 1776. Hancock wrote, "that without a well disciplined Army we cannot rationally expect Success against veteran Troops" and that "Congress . . . (is) . . . fully convinced . . . our Militia is inadequate to the Duty."[43] Washington received the letter on September 28, 1776, and ordered the "new Rules and Regulations" disseminated to the regimental commanders and read to all the officers and soldiers that very day.[44] A week later, due to either the lack of efficiency in the army's orders process or some reluctance on the part of his officers to relay the new articles to their soldiers, Washington was forced to again order the reading of the new regulations.[45] The new Articles of War went into effect on Monday, October 7, 1776.

Yet to what degree did officers actually exercise their increased powers of coercion (or reformation and deterrence as it was thought of at the time) to force compliance of the contractual obligations soldiers entered into when they enlisted? Many officers certainly wielded more legal authority than they had ever practiced in their civilian lives. For officers from the Southern and Chesapeake states, corporal punishment was largely a private affair, practiced by masters over indentured servants and slaves. As the labor system in these regions moved increasingly from a majority of white indentured servants to black slaves, whipping moved further into the realm of the owners, with laws allowing masters to act as judge, jury, and executioner on their plantations. Still, most Continental Army company officers from these states were not slave owners. Furthermore, their soldiers were often lower-class freemen, laborers used to a racial legal system that consciously separated them from the slave class by limiting their vulnerability to suffer private corporal punishment.[46]

In the New England states, particularly Massachusetts, corporal punishment was reserved for the state, practiced in public, and administered by the county courts of quarter sessions. Guided by John Winthrop in the seventeenth century, the free labor force was subjected to a rational, legalized form of public punishment aimed at reforming behavior to produce better workers. Families delegated their coercive authority over their children to the town, arguably creating a culture that, by the late eighteenth century, relied less on whippings and more on an acculturated, self-disciplined workforce.[47] In other words, many of the officers and soldiers serving in the Continental Army from New England were not accustomed to administer, suffer, or witness frequent events of corporal punishment. They were, however, accepting of the concept that such punishments were necessary (if only in a limited fashion) when they were the result of a deliberative justice system and executed in public for the edification of everyone.

Still, there were two groups within the army more accustomed to a frequent use of the lash to both reform and deter bad behavior. The senior leaders, regimental commanders and general officers, often had experience with either military justice as it was practiced in the Seven Years' War or with administering justice in a civilian capacity. George Washington was both a plantation owner and a former regimental commander. Colonel Rufus Putnam and most of his fellow regimental commanders from Massachusetts previously served under the British in provincial battalions. Some of these men came up from the ranks while others gained their positions due to their political and social status; these senior officers were no strangers to witnessing and/or administering military and civilian justice.

Additionally, many of the men drafted into the Continental regiments from Middle Atlantic and southern states, particularly in Pennsylvania and Virginia, were immigrants from Europe and some were former soldiers in European armies. These men, particularly those who were veterans, may have been used to a more draconian form of military justice. Jeremiah Greenman, from Danbury, Massachusetts, observed that men from the "Old Country" often had to be flogged a hundred lashes apiece else "Sum will git drunk stab the genl horses wen on Sentry at the door."[48] While his observation is rife with the xenophobia common among New England soldiers, observations of the tougher attitude toward corporal punishment exhibited by veterans from other armies was common.

As recorded in many of the general and brigade orders that survive today, justice was rarely carried out at even close to the letter of the law, particularly in the case of capital punishment. In fact, offenses like desertion or enlisting in two regiments simultaneously rarely resulted in executions unless attended by the additional crime of doing so in order to change sides and join the British effort. Capital punishment could only be adjudicated in a general court-martial and the decision of the court had to be published in the general orders, making it easier to determine how many soldiers were actually killed for a crime. The general impression left from reading hundreds of general orders from 1777 to 1783 is that, while many crimes were committed that were classified as capital, very few resulted in a sentencing of death. In fact, after an initial analysis of 776 courts-martial held from 1775 to 1783, only 54 death sentences were adjudicated and 11 of those were pardoned. Meanwhile, 243 cases were held for the offense of desertion alone (a capital offense) and resulted in 39 of the 54 death sentences (five of which were pardoned and all of which included the attending crime of either treason or mutiny).[49] As British lieutenant Stephen Adye warned in his famous *A Treatise on Courts Martial* in 1769, making too many crimes capital offenses would only encourage humane officers to hide infractions and protect their soldiers.[50]

During the difficult winter at Valley Forge, not a single instance of the execution of a soldier is recorded in Washington's general orders. During the winter and spring, over thirty general courts-martial were held, trying at least sixty-three officers, soldiers, and civilians. Four of those indicted were sentenced to die for their crimes. The first was a civilian, Joseph Worrell, accused and convicted of acting as a spy for the British. His conviction was confirmed by over the two-thirds majority required and he was sentenced to be hanged.[51] On March 2, 1778, Washington stated in his general orders that the execution was postponed but, as historian Theodore J. Crackel annotated in his digital edition of Washington's papers, Captain Samuel Kearsley reported to Lieutenant Colonel Aaron Burr the next day "Joseph Worrell is no more but hangs as a spectacle for Buckscounty torys."[52] Given Washington's order, Worrell was possibly a victim of vigilante justice camouflaged with the veneer of military sanction.

The other three capital sentences were passed late in the spring over three soldiers convicted of desertion. On May 5, 1778, John Morrell and Thomas Hartnet were sentenced to die, while William McMath was presumably sentenced during a general court-martial in the artillery. The next day, following the announcement of France's decision to openly support the American states, Washington publicly pardoned Morrell and McMath.[53] While no record exists to definitively show what happened to Hartnet, the lack of a general order establishing the execution site or requiring the soldiers to attend the execution indicates the possibility that the killing was not carried out. When executions were conducted, general orders invariably told all soldiers and regiments not conducting some form of special duty to attend. Such a momentous event was important as a lesson to be seen and experienced in order to reform (if the convict was pardoned) and/or deter (for the rest of the audience).

Soldiers, both enlisted and commissioned, were executed most frequently for spying or encouraging others to desert to the enemy. Still, executions were rare. Furthermore, threats to shoot soldiers retreating in the face of the enemy were not carried out. It was common for Washington to publish such threats in general orders prior to battle, as observed before the battles of Long Island, Brandywine, and Germantown, yet the case between Colonel Joseph Reed and Sergeant Ebenezer Leffingwell during the Battle of Harlem Heights stands out due both to its singularity and the fact that the soldier was not, in fact, shot. Furthermore, following the renewed training regimen established at Valley Forge and practiced throughout the army from 1778 until the end of the war, such threats ceased to be published in general orders, at least from Washington and from Nathanael Greene.

Some soldiers accused of other capital crimes were forced to sit on the gallows for periods of time or were pardoned at the last moment. The most common form of punishment for capital offenses was, however, corporal punishment. Desertion was the most frequent offense and, as the war dragged on, it drew an almost automatic punishment of a hundred lashes. Officers were very reluctant to actually execute their soldiers. As an example, in the summer of 1777, General Putnam's command along the Hudson River had many opportunities to exercise its ultimate coercive power, but only four individuals were sentenced to death. Of those four soldiers, one man was executed and he, Edmund Palmer, was actually a British officer caught as a spy.[54] The other three men, American soldiers, certainly broke the law in rather spectacular ways. Amos Rose attempted to shoot his lieutenant, Elisha Brewster.[55] Lemuel Ackerly admitted he was a robber and a spy.[56] Finally, James Duggan fired on a fatigue party as it returned to camp and then reloaded his musket and fired again.[57]

While the charges against the soldiers involved either attempting to kill a fellow soldier or turning to the enemy, none of these men were executed. Duggan admitted he was trying to kill a fellow private. His excuse was that Private Barns had threatened to kill Duggan's wife; Duggan was acting in a form of self-defense. The result was that the court had pity on Duggan, ordering him to sit on the gallows for thirty minutes with a halter around his neck and then receive fifty lashes.[58] The other two soldiers suffered a more protracted fate. Over the course of seven weeks, these two men had their execution date postponed three times and when their day actually arrived, on September 9, 1777, they were placed in front of their graves, pardoned, and sent to a prison ship.[59]

The fact is, officers did relate to their soldiers, suffered with their soldiers, and were not raised to see their soldiers as completely separate members of their society, particularly if they were from the northern states. Brigadier General John Stark, after taking command of the Northern Department, spent months attempting to alleviate the suffering of his soldiers and officers. Writing to Major General William Heath, Stark notified his commander that he had just stopped a mutiny and captured the ringleader. While he knew he would have to punish this one man for the deeds of many, he was loath to do so, because it was unfair. Besides, Stark agreed with the men; they were being treated in a disgraceful manner and felt abandoned by their government and fellow Americans.[60] It was true that the social distances between southern officers and their soldiers were greater than the distance between New England officers and their men, yet recruiting practices maintained a certain agency for many soldiers to mitigate abuses and excesses, petitioning their officers and governments for redress of enlistment contract violations, participating in mutinies for legitimate grievances, or simply insisting to go home at the end of their term of service and refusing to reenlist.

Additionally, the elites of American society (Washington and a select few others accepted) did not serve in the army as officers or soldiers. The majority of officers, especially ensigns, lieutenants, captains, and majors, were drawn from the middle class or came from the ranks. This was particularly true in the regiments from New England, where over 50 percent of those who agreed to serve for Massachusetts after 1777 were veterans of the first two years of the war and whose median wealth (measured in real estate, livestock, and acreage) fell within the median wealth for their fellow civilians in the state.[61] And Washington's attempts to facilitate further separation by paying officers more and soldiers less failed. While there was a significant difference between the salaries of an officer and a private, it really did not matter. No one in the Continental Army received pay on anything close to a regular basis, leaving almost everyone (officers and soldiers) in debt, ill-clothed, and ill-fed.

Still, time would separate officers from soldiers socially to some degree due to the privileges afforded them. Possibly the most visible sign of this was housing during winter encampments. Throughout the war, regiments arrived at their encampment sites late in the season and the soldiers always built cabins for the officers first. Additionally, a more powerful cause for separation occurred as recruiting practices moved more toward the states enlisting soldiers in quotas and away from individual commanders recruiting for rank. Lieutenant Benjamin Gilbert, serving in the Fifth Massachusetts Regiment at West Point in 1780, was very unhappy with the new recruits arriving in his company. They were inexperienced and enlisted for terms so short they would head home before he had them properly trained. More to the point, he could not trust them, for they slept while on duty and he was sure they would run at the first sight of the enemy. Gilbert wanted soldiers he could trust, soldiers with whom he could courageously rush into battle.[62] He wanted men with experience. Some of the New England traditions were breaking down at the regimental level by this late date in the war. Under the pressure to continue recruiting in a war that had lasted almost six years and during which time the government had failed to meet its obligations, men were unwilling to either remain in the service or enter on longer terms. And officers from the regiment were no longer enlisting men directly for their regiments; recruiting officers were responsible to meet the needs of the state and while they were most often from the region within which they recruited, they were not necessarily serving in the regiments within which their recruits would serve. The result was a growing separation, not necessarily between officers and men but between the regiments of the army and their communities back home.

There was always the possibility that the power to punish would be abused. At Valley Forge, several sentences were overturned or revised because they went beyond the hundred-lash limit.[63] During a failed expedition to Florida in 1778, six men were shot and one man hanged for attempting to desert. Their sentences were determined by a hasty court-martial and Major John Grimké defended the harshness of the sentencing as necessary to avoid a mass desertion.[64] Perhaps most egregious, news quickly spread throughout the New York Highlands in August 1780 when a man from the Tenth Pennsylvania Regiment was hanged without the benefit of a trial.[65] While some of these abuses could be explained by a lack of experience on the part of the presiding officers or due to a sense of desperation when operations began to unravel out on campaign, probably a more comprehensive explanation was that over the eight years American soldiers and officers served, rationalized and legalized public violence exercised by leaders over the led became normalized for the core of the army. Excesses were more likely to occur as punishments became more acceptable. Yet, for the vast majority of cases, those excesses were curbed or stopped by senior leaders.

Nor would soldiers and junior officers willingly submit to arbitrary or extreme forms of coercion. While Washington and others saw the military regulations as a tool to reform offenders and deter their fellows, most American soldiers viewed their service as contractual and certain offenses as legitimate forms of protest against a failure by their government and army leadership to meet contractual obligations. The two most common forms of protest were desertion and mutiny. While desertion was usually an individual form of resistance, mutiny (or truly a labor strike) was the group manifestation of discontent. Attempts by senior army leadership to reform and deter such actions through coercion were fraught with peril, for the organization and the individuals involved.

Throughout his eight years of service, Joseph Plumb Martin annotated many instances of both soldier resistance and reactions to what they viewed as the unwarranted exercise of coercion from above. He claimed his regiment would have revolted had Ebenezer Leffingwell been executed for leveling his musket at Joseph Reed.[66] In the late fall of 1779, he described the hanging of a cavalry trooper for desertion during which the soldiers in attendance pelted the executioner and presiding officer for their attempt to take the trooper's boots before they had even lowered the body.[67] Perhaps more distressing for army leadership, during the Connecticut Line Mutiny of 1780, Martin claimed attempts to stop the protest with the Pennsylvania Line failed when officers realized it was more likely the soldiers from the two states would join together against their officers.[68]

There did exist a core of soldiers who had enlisted for three years or the duration despite the fact that the Continental Army always relied on soldiers with shorter terms to fill out their ranks. These soldiers, noncommissioned officers, and junior officers became increasingly acculturated to army standards and willing to enforce compliance within their ranks. Lieutenant Gilbert served as a private and then sergeant from 1775 to 1780. He reentered the service as an ensign after a six-month furlough. He wrote letters to his hometown friends shortly after arriving back in camp that it was hard adjusting again to military life and discipline, though it was much easier now that he had several years' experience.[69] A few months later, in the winter of 1781, he wrote to his father supporting his soldiers' arguments against the government for lack of food, clothing, and pay, stating that while all were suffering, at least they had moved out of their tents to the barracks.[70] Joseph Plumb Martin, promoted to sergeant in the Sapper and Miners Corps by the winter of 1781, was sent home by his colonel to recover two soldiers who had not returned from furlough. Martin's leave was left open-ended but, not wishing to take advantage of his commander's generosity, Martin refused to stay away too long. He returned to his encampment to find the regiment gone, marching south with the Marquis de Lafayette in support of Washington's siege at Yorktown. Martin was pulled between his nostalgia for home and his desire to be with his unit. He chose the unit, walking south to meet them at Annapolis.[71]

While advertisements were placed in local papers to encourage civilians to return deserters, many regions failed to do so. Noncommissioned officers and junior commissioned officers were sent on furloughs to collect deserters. Sergeant Martin was sent to Connecticut to collect a few of his fellow soldiers because he knew the area.[72] Ensign John Barr of the Fourth New York Regiment searched Duchess County looking for several deserters after his furlough ended in the summer of 1780, finding two in Fishkill and returning them to camp.[73] Additionally, the use of one part of the army to force other regiments to continue to serve was sometimes necessary. The Massachusetts Line was used to surround the New Jersey Line during its Line Mutiny of 1781, forcing the surrender of the New Jersey soldiers and resulting in the execution of two of its ringleaders.[74] At times portions of the army could be counted on to enforce order in another part of the army when the time or the reason was viewed as compelling, though these forces were never from the same state lines.

These examples of both resistance and commitment to army service highlight a change in the understanding of punishment and its use during the period of the Second Establishment (1777–1781). Officers from Washington down to his lowest lieutenants realized that the use of coercion to drive soldiers to their duty was most often met by resistance rather than compliance. Courts-martial were reluctant to punish soldiers to the extent of the law and instead tempered their sentencings in attempts to reform soldiers and maintain support for the army's cause. In fact, over time many soldiers came to agree with the need to enforce standards and became committed to the army. This led to a decrease in the need for officers to resort to harsher punishments, relying on their fellow soldiers to police the ranks and maintain order.

THROUGHOUT THE REVOLUTION, even following the rules and regulations that created the Second Establishment of 1777, soldiers' ability to resist through desertion, mutiny, and refusals to enlist for longer terms meant they could effectively limit the actual practice of coercion within the Continental Army. Officers found, even at the level of the commander in chief, that the soldiers in the Continental Army had to be convinced they were being led and not driven to success. Compliance through force would not work; soldiers' commitment to the army, its cause, and their fellow soldiers was key. While the number of courts-martial increased dramatically from the middle of 1776 on, sentencing remained lighter than the laws allowed in the vast majority of cases. The leadership of the army was always cognizant of the fact that they never had enough soldiers in the line, enlistments were an ongoing challenge, and soldiers could resist if and when they believed their leaders were violating contractual obligations or exercising their coercive powers too harshly.

The exercise of coercion and its relation to discipline within the army was important. Yet while its authorization was increased within the Second Establishment, its use was uneven, usually practiced less than was authorized, fraught with resentment and resistance from the soldiers, and not truly connected to an increase in discipline within the army. Instead, commitment would have to be gained through leadership rather than compliance through coercion (with notable caveats when officers failed to join with their men in the face of obvious failures to hold to contractual obligations by the state).

Training and unit cohesion gained over time would become more instrumental to achieving this goal. A new form of leadership evolved and soldiers' agency reinforced its requirement. Senior leaders in the army, to include Washington, began to see that the army would become more disciplined through training rather than through harsh disciplinary actions. Despite what others may have concluded when investigating Washington's desires, he never received a gentleman-class officer corps. Instead, he was relegated a lower middle-class and middle-class officer corps, particularly at the ranks of major and below, that never fully separated itself from the rank and file. Additionally, the focus some historians have placed on concepts of honor assumes that a southern colonial culture was infused into the Continental Army because Washington was the commander, erroneously connecting the culture of the army to a larger European tradition. But the majority of the men serving in the army (both officers and soldiers) came not from Virginia and the Carolinas but from New England and the middle states. These soldiers were not willing to follow officers in recognition of their social station or perceptions of honor, nor did the majority of officers agree with this conception. For these reasons, a strict exercise of coercive authority never became acceptable to either the officers or the soldiers of the Continental Army.

Still, officers and soldiers did grow more distant from one another, due to enlistments coming from the state and due to officers remaining in service while many of the men rotated out with shorter enlistments. By 1780, many of the company officers were men who had risen to their rank as a result of their longer service. Additionally, those men who agreed to enlist for longer periods of time were from the lower economic and social strata, either agreeing to serve for wages or forced to do so through state drafts. Yet this widening of the social gap was more apparent outside the New England state lines. In the Massachusetts and Connecticut Lines, the men and the officers remained rather close. As will be illustrated later, this may explain why the Connecticut Line did not successfully mutiny in 1780 and the Massachusetts Line remained loyal to the army during the New Jersey Line Mutiny of 1781.

Furthermore, the Continental Army, for the reasons stated previously, was distancing itself from the rest of American society. As E. Wayne Carp (among many other historians) has expertly shown, the Continental Army was never publicly supported during the war. He argues a culture of deferential politics that favored localism, a fear of standing armies, and a belief that property equaled liberty remained at odds with the political requirements to win the war (i.e., political centralization, a standing army, and property confiscation).[75] The result was often public animosity toward the army and a refusal to support that army with food, clothing, or money that soon isolated members of the army from their fellow citizens. Officers and soldiers in the Continental Army soon came to believe that if they were to succeed in the Revolution (and in the face of almost persistent destitution), they would have to agree to a standard of disciplined action that would rely more on commitment than compliance. Leadership, not coercion, would gain this commitment through training and shared experience.

Training in
the Continental Army

THE NEGOTIATIONS OF AUTHORITY SETTLED

E ARLY IN SEPTEMBER 1775, A TENSION GROWING BETWEEN regiments from New England and the sole regiment from Pennsylvania (comprised of riflemen from both Pennsylvania and Virginia) nearly exploded into violence. The Pennsylvania Rifle Battalion (known as "Thompson's Battalion of Riflemen") was encamped away from the rest of the army on Prospect Hill and excused from conducting fatigue detail due to the special nature of their mission as sharpshooters. Since their arrival, several riflemen had been arrested for misbehavior but were either broken out of their confinement by their companions or pardoned by their regimental commander. Finally, the senior officers decided to end the undisciplined actions of their soldiers. After a sergeant was again released from his confinement by a group of his fellows, the regimental commander, Colonel William Thompson, and several of his officers seized the sergeant and ordered a guard detail to march him to the main guard at Cambridge. Less than half an hour later, thiry-two soldiers from one of the rifle companies loaded their rifles and ran off after the prisoner, vowing to release him or lose their lives trying. While the officers stayed with the remainder of the regiment to restore order, the Second Rhode Island Regiment located nearby was ordered under arms in case force was necessary and General Washington re-inforced the main guard with five hundred more soldiers. Washington, Nathanael Greene, and Charles Lee moved to meet the mutineers with a portion of Greene's brigade about half a mile from Cambridge, ordering the riflemen to drop their weapons and submit to the authority of their officers. Surrounded by a company from their own regiment, these thirty-two mutineers did drop their weapons and all were placed under arrest.[1]

Writing of the event, Jesse Lukens, son of the surveyor general of Pennsylvania and a rifleman in Captain Mathew Smith's company of Thompson's Riflemen, declared "You cannot conceive what disgrace we are all in and how much the General is chagrined that only one regiment should come from the South and that set so infamous an example."[2] The genesis of this dangerous occurrence was the lack of trust among the regiments from the separate colonies and the feeling among them that Washington favored those soldiers from his region above the rest of the army. Particularly among the soldiers from Massachusetts, many believed Washington favored the soldiers and officers from Virginia and was taking pleasure in court-martialing the officers from New England.[3] To make the situation worse, the majority of the army soon came to believe the reputation of the riflemen was greatly exaggerated. Instead of being the greatest marksmen in America, the regiments of New England soon believed they could produce better marksmen from their own ranks.[4] While the Continental Army succeeded in forcing the British from Boston the following spring, trust and cohesion within the army were clearly lacking during this initial phase of its formation.

A few years later, the army marched out of Valley Forge after enduring the hardest winter encampment of its short history. The British were evacuating Philadelphia and moving their forces back to New York City to prepare for the campaign season of 1778. After consulting with his generals, Washington decided to harass the British rear guard in New Jersey, and what followed is known as the Battle of Monmouth. Joseph Plumb Martin was there, having been attached to a new, integrated corps of light infantry comprised of the fittest soldiers from the various regiments. His captain was from Rhode Island, "a fine brave man . . . [who] feared nobody nor nothing."[5] During the battle, on June 27, 1778, General Charles Lee was placed in command of the detachment assigned to attack the British rear guard, but Lee quickly decided to retreat before engaging the enemy. Martin remembered that before the fight the "men did not need much haranguing to raise their courage" and that Lee's order to retreat was "Grating . . . to our feelings."[6] Two brigades from Connecticut were ordered to defend at a fence while Washington reversed Lee's decision and brought his army into a more general engagement, and when the British attempted to overwhelm this force, officers "had to force them (the Connecticut soldiers) to retreat, so eager were they to be revenged on the invaders."[7] Martin and his light infantry company pursued the British after a long artillery barrage and forced their general retreat after a heated engagement.[8]

While Martin did feel it necessary to include in this portion of his memoirs that it was soldiers from New England who defended the fence and not soldiers from Virginia (correcting a mistake made by David Ramsay in his *History of the American Revolution*, published in 1789), his story of that battle illustrates that a very different Continental Army existed in 1778 from the one first formed just three years earlier. Martin was himself a very different soldier; his experiences and feelings during the New York campaign in 1776 discussed previously were vastly divergent from those remembered on that hot June day in 1778. He and his fellow soldiers were much more confident and their desire to engage the enemy was much more heightened as they entered their fourth year of the war. And the most important cause for this change was their training completed during the previous winter.

The dangerous requirements of eighteenth-century linear warfare necessitated training. Firearms were unpredictable and needed constant maintenance from fouling and damp. Disease, the biggest killer during campaigns, could run rampant in a camp not properly managed. The realities of communication technology made effective administrative processes necessary for generals to know the state of their armies and for soldiers to know the orders of their generals. Finally, for those infrequent occasions when regiments and brigades actually faced one another on the battlefield, the tactics developed to take advantage of eighteenth-century military technology required men to move in unison and in close order, at the commands of an individual, quickly and efficiently in the midst of fire and death to outflank the enemy and force his withdrawal. For all these reasons soldiers needed to be trained in their jobs, but training did more than simply impart the skills necessary to survive in warfare.

Training in the Continental Army was the most important step in acculturating its soldiers to military leadership. As discussed earlier, the recruiting process initiated the negotiation between the leaders and the led over the proper exercise of authority and the use of punishment could enforce compliance with regulations. But officers used training to establish standards and create an agreement between themselves and their soldiers concerning those standards that engendered trust in their authority and confidence among the soldiers in their capabilities on the battlefield. Training accustomed new soldiers to a power structure that was certainly foreign to most of them. They learned to listen to the orders given and to obey them in the face of imminent danger. In general, soldiers and officers learned to accept more authority over their actions than they were used to in their civilian lives. And training engendered trust among the regiments within the army as they operated together.

After signing his enlistment paper, a Continental soldier began his training, whether he understood it as such or not. This experience was not the same for every soldier, as regiments from different states had disparate methods for initially introducing new soldiers to the army. Importantly, new soldiers were not only trained (or not) in rudimentary drill, they were taught *different* drill commands and procedures. This was because, prior to 1778, the regiments of the Continental Army followed the drill manuals of their colonial predecessors and these manuals were not standardized. As soldiers came into the army's camps, some may have received basic training at a rendezvous for a few weeks prior to their arrival while others marched straight from their place of enlistment into a winter encampment and then on to a campaign with little formal training. While many of the soldiers coming from New England may have received training as members of the militia, often there was not time for the companies and regiments from the Continental Army to train together as a unit. And as the army enlisted more men with less property (especially in the southern regiments), some new soldiers arrived without even the rudimentary knowledge of handling a musket required from their local militia companies.

While the British Army struggled with long lines of communication and could not always train their soldiers properly before they arrived in America, for the first half of the war they did take advantage of relatively safe winter encampments, properly supplied by the British Navy, to train for upcoming campaigns. In the late winter and early spring of 1777, General Burgoyne's army trained daily, despite the cold and snow. Instead of working on the parade ground, regiments drilled on the ice; it was rough enough in texture to allow men to maneuver without slipping.[9] Additionally, while on the marches out of Canada, regiments were instructed to conduct training in wooded terrain, learning to adapt their tactics to the new environment.[10] Additionally, the British Army benefitted from the maturity of its institution. Administrative functions were well established and every regiment trained under the same drill manual, allowing regiments to work well together.

In contrast, the Continental Army spent its first two winters conducting a siege or on the march, without adequate supplies or shelter. While the British Army began adapting its tactics to the realities of war in America, the American army struggled to balance the establishment of its organizational structure with a competing requirement to train its soldiers to fight together in a unified fashion. After a rough start in 1775, the British Army was able to quickly transition its tactical focus from engagement to maneuver, to train for light infantry maneuvers and bayonet charges that took advantage of the close terrain and mitigated American strengths on the defense.[11] The Continental Army needed first to create administrative functions, establish logistical systems, and train its officers and soldiers how to work within these new environments before eventually developing its own standard drill manual that simultaneously accounted for the leadership peculiarities of their soldiers and allowed the regiments to perform better in a cohesive fashion.

Training in the Continental Army evolved over the war despite the challenges of constant recruiting and uncertain logistic support. Initially, Washington and his generals focused on administrative and organizational training, establishing camp discipline, administrative efficiencies, and standards for officer and soldier conduct. Washington was forced to assume that regiments arrived with a modicum of tactical training, particularly with regard to individual soldier skills in marksmanship and maneuver, because he did not have the time or the resources to train these skills while on campaign. His orders necessarily focused on regimental rolls, guard details, dissemination of general orders, officer and noncommissioned officer duties, and equipment maintenance. Certainly, shortages of muskets and gunpowder precluded even rudimentary target practice, but he did not appear concerned over this issue of tactical training until after the Battle of Long Island in the summer of 1776. Once recruiting laws began to produce soldiers who enlisted for longer terms and administrative practices began to settle into a semblance of routine, Washington and others began to focus on standardizing drill and maneuver to avoid defeats like Germantown in 1777, where two brigades converged in a fog and then fired on each other. While other defeats certainly weighed on his mind, other victories had allowed Washington to focus on other reasons for his tactical problems. It was following Germantown, in October 1777, that Washington began to think seriously about the problem of drill and training his soldiers to march and fire their muskets in the heat of battle. With the publication of Baron von Steuben's "Revolutionary War Drill Manual," in 1778, the army began a more intense focus on combat training with notable success.

All of these areas for military training (administrative, disciplinary, and tactical) led to a Continental Army able and willing to face the British and their allies on more equal footing. Of equal importance to the increased capabilities of the Continental Army was the increased confidence of the soldiers in their abilities to survive the war and their trust in those officers who led them. Over the years of the war, soldiers grew to believe that they were capable of defeating the redcoats in a conventional manner. They became angry when they believed their officers did not make the correct tactical decisions to succeed on the battlefield and they willingly endured extraordinary hardships for those leaders they trusted to comply with the agreements reached through their training. The officers, too, committed to those agreements, often taking time to explain to their men why they made the decisions they did and recognizing the laudable actions of their soldiers regularly to reinforce their growing trust in one another. The result was that, by 1781, the Continental Army was able to march into Yorktown, conduct a prolonged siege, and defeat the best field commander in the British Army at that time, and none of that was achieved by threatening to shoot a single soldier moving back out of the line.

HISTORIANS HAVE COME TO DIFFERENT CONCLUSIONS about how and why the colonial forces in 1775 succeeded in both containing the British Army in Boston and then inflicting such devastating losses upon them in the Battle of Bunker Hill. Some authors argue that the British were surprised in 1775 when the New England militias were so capable because the effectiveness of New England forces contradicted Thomas Gage's expectations that were based on his observations during the Seven Years' War. During that conflict British officers interacted with provincial troops, largely from New England, and viewed them as militarily incompetent, useful only for digging ditches and building roads. The key difference between the incompetence of the earlier provincial regiments and the effectiveness of the New England militiamen in 1775 was in the caliber of person recruited. During the Seven Years' War, those provincial troops were the landless poor and indigents unfortunate enough to run afoul of new colonial legislation that allowed the drafting of men without property into what were essentially colonial regular forces. At the battles fought in the spring and summer of 1775, the British fought middle-class militiamen, defending hearth and home and willing to fight to the death.[12]

It is more likely that the differences between British expectations and colonial actions resulted from both a British bias against New England leadership discussed earlier and the fact that many of the senior leaders from New England in those first few months of the war had served regularly throughout the colonial wars on the northern frontier. They gained both training and experience prior to Lexington and Concord, which they brought with them when tensions broke into conflict in 1775. When viewed in more detail, a better explanation for why the British encountered a stronger military resistance than they expected initially is that the New England forces combined a popular uprising with trained and experienced leadership to offer a force capable of withstanding a British attack, at least for a short period of time. Particularly among the militias of eastern Massachusetts, training in marksmanship and loose-order tactics increased following the passage of the Coercive Acts as New England towns prepared for the invasion of British regulars to seize stores of weapons and gunpowder.[13] The fundamental difficulty faced by the American forces after 1775 resulted from both the British abilities to adapt tactically to fighting in America and a lack of institutional cohesion within the Continental Army itself. Long and difficult training would be required to overcome both administrative and tactical challenges, particularly once the initial popular support for military enlistments evaporated with the Second Establishment of 1777.

The issue of cohesion in terms of training was further complicated by the militia traditions of the other colonies. Of particular note, as mentioned previously, was the Associator tradition in Pennsylvania and Delaware. While these were ostensibly private organizations raised to meet particular defensive needs of these colonies, some of these associations probably remained in existence after 1747 and were revived during the first year of the Revolution. These units maintained a continuity of organization and possibly training that allowed Pennsylvania to provide specialized troops, in the form of artillery and rifle battalions, from the onset of hostilities. This may, in part, explain why Pennsylvania was the first state outside New England to send fully formed regiments to Boston in the summer of 1775.

The Philadelphia Artillery Association remained in continuous service following its inception in 1747 due to the need to defend the harbor of Philadelphia from potential attacks of both the French and the Spanish during the colonial wars. Furthermore, artillery use required extensive training to allow crews to operate the cannon with any semblance of expertise. Regular practice of specialized skills and some knowledge of mathematics were needed to operate the guns and hit targets at range. Sheds, equipment, and ammunition were maintained in the city and practice was regularly attended during the interwar years between the Seven Years' War and the Revolution.[14] Throughout the state, following the adjournment of the First Continental Congress, various associations began forming cadre companies to train soldiers. The Philadelphia Greens, the Quaker Blues, and the York Blues associated, founded rendezvous (training sites), and began drilling twice a day under the direction of veterans from the previous war. For the York Blues, a man named Dytch, a veteran of the Royal American Regiment, was chosen as the fugleman (the model soldier used to illustrate drill movements).[15] For the next few months, in the summer of 1775, the number of training companies increased to drill recruits for the Pennsylvania Line, giving soldiers as many as three months of training before heading north.[16]

While this state system enacted to provide trained units to fight the British could be viewed as initially beneficial to the Continental Army, these men trained to a particular standard. In 1775, the Associators of Philadelphia funded the publication of the *Prussian Evolutions*, a two-volume work that included infantry and artillery drills, along with military law and regulations enacted by the Prussian Army in 1756.[17] While the use of this particular drill manual standardized training in much of the Pennsylvania Line, its use exacerbated a problem of various state lines using different training manuals throughout the Continental Army.

There were at least three other drill manuals in use throughout the American forces in 1776 and 1777. Some state regiments, particularly in the South, used *A Plan of Discipline Composed for the Use of the Militia of the County of Norfolk*, otherwise known as the *Norfolk Discipline*. Printed in London in 1760, this drill manual was an attempt by gentlemen in the English county of Norfolk to simplify training for militias formed in England and Wales during the Seven Years' War. During the Jacobite Uprising of 1745, few militias responded to Parliament's call to defend England from a Highlander invasion that supported the young Charles Stuart. To encourage a better popular response for homeland defense should the French invade during the Seven Years' War, William Pitt and his Whig allies in Parliament passed the Militia Act of 1757. English and Welsh counties were instructed to create local militias through a ballot system that compelled individuals to serve in the militia for a period of three years.[18] In the county of Norfolk, William Windham developed and published a simplified drill manual that would allow part-time soldiers to master the Prussian drills with less time to train.[19]

At the end of the Seven Years' War, the British Army revised its own drill manual. Originally published in 1764, *The Manual Exercise, as Ordered by His Majesty* was published throughout the colonies in 1774 and 1775 to facilitate training for militia units that were increasingly preparing for conflict.[20] The manual was considerably shorter than the *Norfolk Discipline*, modernized by British experiences in the Seven Years' War, and contained a shorter series within the manual exercise (a series of movements used to train soldiers to use their muskets in combat) than the militia drill manual.[21] While this would appear to be helpful to those attempting to quickly form military regiments from inexperienced civilians, *The Manual Exercise* took certain matters for granted and so ignored portions of the *Norfolk Discipline* necessary for leaders who were not professional soldiers. Of particular note was the omission of any instructions to officers with regard to their training or their responsibilities to train their soldiers. Still, given its publication in Philadelphia, New York, and Boston between 1774 and 1775, it was easily accessible to state regiments within New England and the middle states of Pennsylvania, New Jersey, and New York.[22]

In 1775, Thomas Pickering of Massachusetts published his own version of drill, entitled *An Easy Plan of Discipline for a Militia* for the New England militia and minutemen. Pickering acknowledged his study of both the *Norfolk Discipline* and *The Manual Exercise* to develop his drill manual, but he claimed these preceding works missed the mark in their attempts to simplify Prussian drill for ease of training. He claimed both manuals continued to favor appearance on the parade ground over utility on the battlefield, leading to overly complicated exercises that wasted time and confused soldiers.

> But to anyone who considers the principles and foundation of exercise, it will be obvious that the Norfolk exercise and that of the army, are neither of them so short and easy as they might be. In the latter it must be acknowledged that divers motions are retained *merely for show* : and in the former some motions are not only *useless*, but *inconvenient*, and directly repugnant to one of the main principles on which exercise is grounded (simplicity and use in battle).[23]

Pickering's manual was in use by many of the New England regiments.

These various manuals contained similar instructions, but none of them were the same. Every manual contained a manual exercise. The manual exercise was a routine of movements designed to acculturate soldiers in close formation to unified motions at the command of their officers. Within all of the various versions, the manual exercise contained the essential commands for loading, priming, and firing a musket. In the *Norfolk Discipline*, the manual exercise consisted of fifty separate commands, each comprising between one and ten motions.[24] As an example, the command "Take up your Firelock!" comprised two motions. First the soldier was instructed to "Step forward, bending the knee, and seizing the firelock above the swell, in the position of the first motion of the former explanation" and then "Raise yourself and firelock, flipping your right hand up to the muzzle, and turning the barrel behind."[25] *The Manual Exercise* contained thirty-five commands with between one and four motions each while Pickering's manual comprised forty-two commands of between one and ten motions each.[26] They all contained similar commands (Fix your Bayonets! Present! Fire!), yet these commands contained a variety of motions dissimilar from one another. In *The*

Manual Exercise, priming and loading the musket was conducted through separate commands totaling twelve motions. In the two manuals focused on militia training, "Prime and Load!" was a single command comprised of nine motions.

The dissimilarities in the manual exercises created at least three problems for the Continental Army. Soldiers from one regiment could not transfer to another regiment with any assurance they would follow the same motions for the same command as the rest or understand a command that was not present in their previous training. Furthermore, regiments from various state lines would be easily confused by orders given by different officers on the field should consolidation be necessary. While battalions like Thompson's Battalion of Riflemen and Dearborn's Light Infantry could operate as separate units, these differences prevented the creation of elite units such as battalions of light infantry that drew men from many different regiments for temporary use during a battle.[27] Rather than increasing cohesion, these separate forms of training manuals only highlighted the regional differences of the state lines and complicated training for an army struggling to coalesce in the face of the enemy.

Other problems arose from further disparities. The British manual omitted any mention of officer exercises with the fusil. While both Windham and Pickering recognized a necessity for officers to practice with their firearms, the British Army discouraged this because they believed officers should focus on commanding their units and not firing as individuals in combat.[28] Before commencing his march on Albany in 1777, General John Burgoyne reinforced this guidance in his general orders. Officers were responsible for leading and directing their men, not firing their fusil. Only in extreme cases of self-defense should an officer fire his weapon.[29] Windham included descriptions of the responsibilities for privates, corporals, and sergeants while on guard duty but failed to discuss officer responsibilities within the regiment. Recommendations were made for officers with regard to training their soldiers in the manual exercise.[30] Any instructions for the responsibilities of various ranks outside their positioning within the formation were omitted from both *The Manual Exercise* and *An Easy Plan of Discipline*.

Linear combat during this period consisted of more than simply standing still and firing volleys. Maneuver was essential to attaining the advantage and forcing an enemy from the field. All the manuals of this time included detailed descriptions of wheeling, turning, and transforming columns to files and files to columns. Again, within the various drill manuals, disparities existed on how these movements should be carried out. These differences would create problems for the Continental Army when various regiments joined together on the field under a brigade structure. As will be discussed shortly, the defeats at Germantown and Brandywine finally convinced Washington a new drill manual was necessary to standardize training throughout the Continental Army and promote that training to increase American chances for victory while on the offensive.[31]

Before the winter of 1777 to 1778, the Continental Army relied on defensive tactics and *petite-guerre* to achieve success. These were the tactics many of the leaders were accustomed to from previous experience. In New England regiments, particularly, these skills fit well with their colonial military tradition. British forces retreating from Lexington and Concord were beset with a running ambuscade executed by militiamen along the road to Boston. At the Battle of Bunker Hill, New England soldiers positioned by their officers behind fences, walls, and within redoubts exacted a terrible toll on British forces before retreating back along the Charlestown Neck. New England officers prepared a good defensive position on Breed's Hill, maintained discipline among their men, and gave orders to aim for British officers, firing at the last possible moment. The result was that General William Howe lost his entire staff in the battle, along with 1,054 soldiers killed or wounded.[32]

What few American regiments understood was how to soldier through a winter, how to act in an encampment composed of thousands of soldiers, how to manage such large forces, or how to operate as a cohesive army on the offensive during a conventional linear battle. For the first two years of the war, Washington and his generals were forced to rely on regional differences in tactical training while they focused on institutional training to achieve both standards in administrative practices and begin instilling organizational cohesion.

Their first goal was to form an American army capable of withstanding defeats, retreats, and harsh winters without experiencing large-scale desertions and mutinies that would sink the Revolution. Once they felt they had achieved a modicum of success in these regards, they then chose to focus on tactical training. The result of their exertions in all these areas (administrative, organizational, and tactical) was a uniquely American solution, one that trained leadership to the officers and noncommissioned officers, recognized the demands from below of the soldiers in the rank and file, and led to the development of a training manual that incorporated more than the manual exercise. Encapsulated within this work was the final agreement between the leaders and the led on how the American army would operate for another forty years following the end of the war.

WHEN THE FIRST ESTABLISHMENT of the Continental Army began on January 1, 1776, Washington began to implement administrative and organizational changes immediately. Impeded by the requirement to complete the reenlist of the army by that day, Washington waited until January 2, 1776, to begin a new plan for training these men to act like soldiers in a unified army. He ordered the officers to provide an accurate account of their men and told them to limit the number of soldiers allowed to go home for furlough. At the same time, he initiated a reorganization of the regimental structure to standardize it across the army. Regiments would contain a colonel, a lieutenant colonel, a major, an adjutant, a surgeon, a surgeon's mate, and a quartermaster. Within each of the eight companies, there would be a captain, a first and second lieutenant, an ensign, four sergeants, four corporals, and seventy-six privates.[33] Furthermore, the regiments lost their distinctive names. No longer would a regiment be known by the name of its commander; now every regiment would be a numbered Continental Regiment. The next day he issued the new Continental Rules and Articles of War, ordering copies be made for each of the regiments and companies and that these new regulations be read aloud to the men once a week. On January 5, 1776, Washington insisted his regimental commanders enforce uniformity and discipline through their noncommissioned officers by dividing their companies in fourths, with one sergeant, one corporal, and nineteen privates.[34] While he concentrated on these issues, he left the details of tactical training to his regimental commanders who were directed to attend to the training and exercise of their men. The soldiers were to be drilled on "the Evolutions and Maneuvers" with the admonishment that "many practices in *Regular Service*" were worthy of emulation.[35] Not specified were which drills to use, how often drills should occur, or what skills should be focused upon.

Yet this effort to standardize training in the army continued to bog down due to a lack of compliance from officers within the regiments and a dearth of resources (time and equipment) available. Comments of drilling or listening to orders are conspicuously absent from diaries of soldiers until much later. Private David How first mentioned being read general orders in October 1776 and he did not note any training until November 18, 1776.[36] Elisha Bostwick, who served as a sergeant and then lieutenant in 1776 for Connecticut, never mentioned drilling or orders, though he did recall Colonel Scott always exhorting the men to aim for the enemy's legs to avoid shooting over their heads. According to the commander, one wounded soldier was worth three soldiers, as it would take two others to remove him from the line.[37]

Certainly a major problem with regard to drill was a severe lack of muskets among those willing to reenlist. Soldiers feared they would have their personal arms seized by the army if they enlisted with them. Washington was forced to offer one dollar to every soldier for the use of their personal muskets, permitting them to take their weapons home when their enlistments expired, and reimbursing them for muskets lost through no fault of the soldier.[38] Still, despite a lack of weapons and sporadic compliance with following orders, training did appear to occur, at least with the manual exercise but to the exclusion of other areas of training. By February, Washington ordered his regimental commanders to focus more on maneuvers and less on the manual exercise in preparation for the seizure of Dorchester Heights.[39]

Washington often noted a consistent lack of compliance from his officers on various occasions and of equal or greater concern was the lack of administrative skills among them. Repeatedly during the siege of Boston, Washington attempted to gain an understanding of his muster rolls and to disseminate his orders throughout the army. He ordered books be kept at the regimental level to track the number of soldiers enlisted and their disposition (on furlough, sick, deserted, etc.).[40] He then instituted a new system for guard details. All guard posts would be assigned to the same soldiers in shifts that began at eight o'clock every morning. Each morning, the new guard detail would parade before the field officers of the regiment, then parade in front of the brigade field officers. These officers would inspect the uniforms and weapons of the detail, before permitting them to parade in front of the brigadier of the day. The brigadier of the day would instruct the field officers of the day on their guard inspection duties and then report to Washington personally.[41]

These initial attempts to train the army in military procedure and protocol necessary to maintain security and discipline in camp highlight several challenges that would continue to plague the Continental Army for the rest of the year. The required focus on building institutional knowledge took much of the attention away from tactical training and centralized decision-making at the highest levels. Washington was consumed with devising and disseminating plans and orders to organize the army and oversee compliance with those orders, compliance being quicker to gain than commitment though less reliable when not supervised. Frustration with his officer corps was the result as they resisted attempts to centralize authority and erase regional distinctions. Furthermore, the army encamped around Boston was only the largest portion of the Continental Army. In March Congress divided the states into three departments, with a major general in charge of the Southern and Northern Departments, leaving Washington in control of both the Middle Department and the army at large.[42] His attempts to standardize activities within the army through general orders meant his plans only immediately affected the regiments directly under his control while often only advising his other two commanders on his techniques for instilling discipline. Finally, while the soldiers in his army admired Washington, his orders were not automatically followed. As highlighted by several historians, the American lack of institutional knowledge or of a civilian culture of subordination meant, unlike in the British Army, senior officers lacked a noncommissioned officer corps acculturated to discipline or able to pass down their experience and training to privates and junior officers.[43]

The Continental Army continued to struggle establishing regularity in training when Washington moved his army down to New York in the spring of 1776. And his challenges increased as new regiments joined him to defend the city from state levies. His orders for regular returns of soldiers fit for duty were often ignored or given late.[44] Despite his demands that orders be read daily to the soldiers in the regiments, many claimed ignorance when confronted for disobeying regulations.[45] Fatigue and guard details were consistently late reporting for duty, with soldiers falling asleep on guard and officers failing to supervise the work. In short, Washington was facing an uphill battle made worse by the nearby presence of the British.

By the early summer of 1776 the Continental Army was composed of sixteen regular regiments, mostly from New England, four state regiments, and some New York militia, totaling over ten thousand soldiers present and fit for duty.[46] Congress directed Washington to send the remainder of his forces, an army of an additional six regular and nine state regiments, to Canada under the command of Major General Horatio Gates.[47] In preparation for his first battlefield encounter with British general William Howe, Washington began training his men in a variety of tactical tasks, including drill, marksmanship, guard duty, and maneuvers. He ordered officers to assign the same defensive positions to the same soldiers, to practice moving to their posts in the dark, and to ensure every soldier maintained his ammunition and pack in readiness for the impending attack.[48] On July 1, 1776, the general allowed each regiment to fire two rounds per soldier from their muskets both for target practice and to ensure their muskets were in good working order, despite the severe lack in both powder and ball.[49]

One of the soldiers in the Continental Army at that time was the ambitious Lieutenant Isaac Bangs. After Lieutenant Bangs smoothed relations with his fellow officers in the Twenty-Third Continental

Regiment (Massachusetts), he spent the early summer supervising fatigue details on the New Jersey side of the Hudson River and getting into trouble in a seedy part of New York City known as the Holy Ground.[50] He did not actually supervise a fatigue detail with his soldiers until May. And he did so only because the men were complaining of abuse at the hands of the assistant engineers.[51] When he next was assigned a fatigue detail, in June, Bangs mentions little to nothing of the work or the soldiers. Instead, he spent his time wandering the Jersey banks of the Hudson and visiting a gentleman named Arent Schuyler who owned a copper mine north of New York City.[52] He also supervised the marksmanship training Washington authorized. His brigade was allowed to fire two shots per man on July 4, 1776. Apparently some of the men were not familiar with firearms, as one man killed himself with his own musket during the practice.[53] A week later, when the British armada attacked the Grand Battery, Bangs saved one man from a bouncing cannonball while witnessing another six artillerymen who accidentally killed themselves when their cannon exploded; they were all drunk.[54]

The challenge faced by Washington and the Continental Army in general was that training standards were being negotiated within the leadership and between leaders and soldiers during this early period. Those negotiations began at the top, between Washington and his generals and between the generals and their regimental commanders. And they continued all the way down to the rank and file. These junior officers and soldiers were proving resistant to following orders or committing to training regimens if they had not been first convinced of their efficacy. And due to the various military traditions within the army, standardization did not exist above the regimental level. Some regiments were viewed as well trained, with a reputation for success while on campaign. Other regiments did not perform well initially and were not trusted by their adjacent units. Additionally, regiments from different regions were distrustful of one another, making it difficult for them to operate together within the same brigade.

Brigadier General Nathanael Greene confronted problems on Long Island that underscore these disparities. When Washington reorganized his regiments into brigades, he placed a New Jersey state regiment under Greene's command. The regiment, under the command of Colonel David Foreman, originally belonged to Brigadier General Nathaniel Heard, also from New Jersey. Heard had been giving permission to soldiers in Foreman's regiment to take furloughs, despite the threat of British attacks on Long Island and without consulting Greene or Foreman. Greene wrote to Washington in August 1776 asking Washington to control Heard. His actions were causing morale to fall within Foreman's regiment. While the men were expecting to go home, Foreman and Greene were forced to deny the furloughs, looking like "tyrants" to their soldiers.[55] The next week, Greene wrote to Washington again, asking the commander to rescind an order to move Colonel Daniel Hitchcock's Eleventh Continental Regiment (Rhode Island) to Fort Washington. Greene claimed Hitchcock's regiment was well trained and disciplined. Furthermore, they knew the terrain and were attached to the rest of the soldiers in Greene's brigade, having been on Long Island for the last month. Greene feared the replacement regiment would not be well trained and, without an attachment to the rest of the brigade, would not fight well when the time came.[56] A combination of training, shared experience, and regionalism combined to form cohesion in Greene's brigade that he was loathe to break.

These issues with training and discipline caused Washington to increasingly centralize decision-making authority to the highest levels. Starting on August 11, 1776, regimental commanders were ordered to submit furlough requests through their brigade commanders to Washington.[57] Additionally, throughout this period, Washington continued to experience other administrative problems. Regiments habitually failed to submit their muster rolls. For this reason, Washington decided to muster every regiment on their parade grounds at one time, on the evening of August 30, 1776, to force regimental commanders to follow his order and gain an accurate account of their men.[58] To put an end to undisciplined firing in camp (and the frequent incidents of fratricide), Washington demanded every regiment discharge loaded weapons at the same time during retreat. Writing specifically to Major General Israel Putnam, the commanding general ordered his division commander to put a stop to undisciplined firing by gathering the colonels together, telling them to control their soldiers and disseminate their orders to the other officers.[59]

During this period of the First Establishment, Washington was trying to gain control of his various forces and to train them to act as a unified army by centralizing authority. While he mentioned noncommissioned officers at various times, his focus was on the responsibilities of commissioned officers to disseminate and enforce orders, to obey the orders of their higher command, and to train and lead their soldiers by their presence and their example. Yet Washington was facing not only a problem of training but a problem of military culture and effecting a change of culture took time, especially in the face of imminent attack by the enemy. By September, Washington continued to face a lack of compliance to his desires, eventually threatening to arrest junior officers and publicly shame regimental commanders should brigades continue to fail to report on time to receive orders, submit musters, and appear for guard and fatigue details.[60]

THE SECOND ESTABLISHMENT of the Continental Army began with the initiation of three-year enlistments, the revised Articles of War, and the reorganization of regiments into state lines (with enumerations that again recognized the states from which the regiments were formed). By the summer of 1777, some of Washington's initiatives appear to have taken root, even in forces outside of his direct control. Israel Putnam was placed in command of the New York Highlands, guarding against a British incursion from New York in support of Burgoyne's invasion from Canada. Putnam's forces operated under specific circumstances, some familiar and some new. Due to the decision made by Congress to enlist soldiers for three years or the duration, some soldiers were veterans of the year before (mostly from Massachusetts) but many were new to the army. Still, this portion of the Continental Army was under less pressure than at any time previous. British forces were maintaining some presence north of New York City, but the majority of their forces were preparing to operate farther south in a bid to occupy Philadelphia. Putnam had time to focus on training.

Drummers and fifes were ordered to practice twice a day, in the morning and afternoon. Following Washington's mandate, only one wagon and four horses were allowed for the baggage for every hundred men, officers included. Furthermore, Putnam was confident long general orders would no longer be necessary; what was necessary was for officers and soldiers to follow standards already set, to "do their Duty."[61] Officers were appointed to inspect the camp every day and report their findings to their brigade commanders. Furthermore, soldiers were ordered to keep themselves clean and neat in appearance, trimming their hair to a decent length, eating well-cooked food, and sleeping off of the cold ground.[62]

As important, the forces encamped in Peekskill would have time to drill and train as companies and regiments. Putnam ordered all soldiers not on fatigue detail to train regularly. Companies were to drill the manual exercise and their maneuvers three times a day. Brigades were ordered to maneuver their regiments twice a week.[63] One brigade commander explicitly stated in his general orders that the King's Manual Exercise of 1764 would be used for training and that officers needed to practice the manual exercise, as well. All officers of the regiments were required to drill with their soldiers and train their sergeants.[64] By July 1777, regiments under Putnam's command were ordering their sergeants major to arrest sergeants failing to obey orders or discipline their soldiers. If soldiers were slow to muster on the parade ground for drill, sergeants would be punished, and soldiers failing to follow the orders of their sergeants would likewise face consequences. These orders appeared to have had some success, as regiments began regularly training together in brigades, firing field pieces and in platoon volleys to practice skirmishing and regular maneuvers.[65]

At the same time, Washington continued to experience difficulties with his field officers while on campaign in Pennsylvania. In August one major was tried in a general court-martial for neglecting his duties while acting as a brigade major. He repeatedly refused to present himself to the commander's headquarters for the daily issuance of general orders and was sentenced to a public reprimand in the general orders. In the reprimand, Washington stated it pained him to so frequently be forced to censure his officers for failing to follow orders. Officers must, through their actions, illustrate diligence and discipline to the rank and file. If another brigade major failed to perform his duties, Washington would suspend his commission and ask Congress to give that commission to another officer.[66]

During this campaign to protect Philadelphia from General William Howe, Washington was forced to keep his army on the march, constantly alert for the landing of British forces from New York. He was aware of the invasion by Burgoyne to the north but uncertain of Howe's plans for the Middle Department. Following Howe's landing in Maryland, Washington marched his army south, fighting the British at Brandywine, Paoli's Tavern, and Germantown over the course of a month. While on the move, the commander of the "Grand Army" focused on administrative training and marching rather than tactical training. He was faced with regulating baggage allotments on wagons, disciplining wagon masters who impersonated officers, provisioning the army, and reducing the number of camp followers (particularly women). His was an army on the march, struggling to feed itself and maintain order and discipline. By September Washington realized part of the problem: only a very few companies actually maintained orderly books and so no records were kept of his general orders. Following this discovery, Washington warned his officers that if one of their soldiers could prove that they had disobeyed orders due to ignorance, the officer would be punished instead.[67] Washington was no longer simply admonishing his officers on this point, he was negotiating with them.

Early in October, following defeats at Brandywine and Paoli, Washington decided to attack the British in one last bid to force Howe's withdrawal from Philadelphia. On October 3, 1777, Washington issued his orders for an attack on British forces encamped at Germantown. His plan split his forces into four columns with Continental divisions in the center two columns and the militia on the flanks. White paper was ordered displayed on soldiers' hats to prevent fratricide, with light cavalry used for communications.[68] While this final battle of the season ended in failure, as well, the Grand Army did well at the beginning of the battle, but several factors worked against success. The morning began with a very thick fog, obscuring the view of the battlefield and making a concerted effort by all four columns very difficult. At one point, the two Continental brigades converged and began firing at one another. Furthermore, Washington made a mistake following the initial attack, committing his reserve to attack an enemy force barricaded in a stone mansion, which produced severe losses to his reserve. Yet the key problem for the Continental Army was the complexity of the plan itself.

At no point prior to this battle did Washington's orders focus on tactical training. While Nathanael Greene congratulated his division for their courage during the fight, he did address a particular lesson his forces needed to learn from that day. Sometimes it was necessary for officers to order a retreat during a battle, but those orders were meant to reposition the regiments for another attack. These commands did not mean the army was in general retreat. It was important for soldiers to listen to all the commands given, to obey quietly and quickly in order to allow the army to take advantage of their new positions.[69] Greene's comments point to a few important facts. Washington's plan, while audacious and important to improving the morale of the Grand Army, was far too complicated for an army with some experience but with inadequate training together as a united force. And Greene, at least, had found it necessary to negotiate with his soldiers in regard to their willingness to follow orders. He recognized their need to understand *why* some orders were being given if they were going to commit to following them.

Almost immediately, Washington recognized the need to focus on tactical training and his orders reflected this change in priorities. On October 10, 1777, he admonished his army for not following orders immediately. A soldier's job was to obey orders promptly, not to question why an order was given or require an explanation before an order was followed. An army, he said, was like a clock. If the pieces of a clock worked as directed, the clock operated in a rational and efficient manner. When the parts did not work well, the clock failed.[70] Two days later, Washington told his officers this was the time to instill discipline. Every day, weather permitting, the troops would be turned out to exercise priming and loading, advancing, forming, retreating, breaking, and rallying.[71] A week later, the brigades were ordered to exercise their formations every day, focusing on actions in wooded terrain: advancing in a line, forming into columns to march through defiles and openings in fences, and backing into lines. The brigade commanders were to do the same while in a retreat.[72] And on October 26, he asked for a council of generals to decide if it would be proper for the inspector general of the army to devise a new training manual since the adjutant general appeared too busy to do so.[73] They all agreed it was proper and necessary.[74]

This renewed focus on training both the manual exercise and maneuvers at the company, regimental, and brigade levels continued into the winter encampment of the Grand Army at Valley Forge. Washington consolidated forces from the New York Highlands with his immediate forces within the Middle Department. With the arrival of a former member of the Prussian Army, Friedrich Wilhelm von Steuben, Washington established a new standard for training in the army, set forth in the *Regulations for the Order and Discipline of the Troops of the United States*, known as the "Blue Book." On March 17, 1778, a hundred soldiers from each of the state lines present (Massachusetts, Connecticut, New Hampshire, Rhode Island, New York, New Jersey, Pennsylvania, Delaware, and Maryland) were ordered to the general's guard for training. The Virginia Line was exempted because they provided a hundred soldiers for the guard already.[75] For the remainder of the war, this would become the standard for training throughout the Continental Army.

The new manual contained a systematic approach for training new soldiers in the specifics of drill as they arrived in the army. Soldiers would first learn the facing movements and marching without arms.[76] The manual exercise consisted of twenty-seven separate commands (much fewer than in any of the other manuals in use, thus both streamlining the training regimen and giving the soldiers less commands to learn) and, while priming and loading the musket were broken down into separate commands, there was a separate section for priming and loading under fire that was trained separately in fifteen steps (thus allowing the soldiers to train the full motions of these tasks during regular drill instruction but allowing for a more efficient and faster method for loading to be trained after the initial manual exercise was mastered). The state lines were standardized to form in two lines when fighting (instead of three which was common in some manuals) and taught to use the bayonet in combat.[77] Not only were officers directed to take part during training, they were trained to empower their noncommissioned officers to enforce discipline and take charge in training. Maneuvers were explained at the company, regiment, brigade, and army levels.

And while these tactical tasks formed the basis for the drill manual, other important standards were enumerated. Standards for baggage trains and camp cleanliness were established.[78] Roll calls were explained, along with standards of uniforms and accoutrements.[79] The proper care of weapons and ammunition were explained, along with the standards for treating the sick.[80] And for the first time, every position in the army, from regimental commander to private soldier was fully described, setting the standard by which each man would be judged in his performance.[81] In short, and for the first time, the manual acted as a contract between the commanders and their soldiers for the standard and uniform conduct of the Continental Army in every situation (administrative, organizational, and tactical). The key to every article was the full participation by every element in the army, from the privates to the generals.

For the next few months, Washington continued to enforce regular and frequent exercises by the brigades, reiterating other parts of the manual and discouraging deviations. Commanders were told to stop training until the new manual could be disseminated to their regiments.[82] All majors, captains, and one subaltern officer per company were ordered to report to Major Samuel Cabell to observe the model companies drilling in the new manual.[83] On March 24, 1778, all the brigades were ordered to begin training in the new manual exercises that next morning at nine o'clock and again that afternoon, at four o'clock. The brigade commanders were notified the new inspector general, the Baron von Steuben, would be present to observe.[84] Field officers were appointed as brigade inspectors to ensure compliance with the new standard and every officer was told his leadership was required to ensure the success of the new standard.[85]

Washington did not reserve his commands solely for the officer corps. Recognizing the need for their commitment, the commanding general demanded adherence to the new regulations from the noncommissioned officers, as well. In April 1778, Washington focused for a time on the cleanliness of both the encampment at Valley Forge and individual soldiers. As stated in the Blue Book, soldiers were required to keep their uniforms and their bodies clean at all times, washing their faces and hands daily and grooming their hair and beards. The key to the soldiers' health was the enforcement of standards by their noncommissioned officers. It was the responsibility of the noncommissioned officers to ensure the cleanliness of their men. These corporals and sergeants held their rank by virtue of being better soldiers than the privates. Their example was key to compliance with the new standards by the rest of the army. If a noncommissioned officer was unable to enforce those standards among his soldiers, he would be reduced in the ranks and another soldier capable of leading his fellows would be promoted.[86]

For the next two months, in April and May 1778, the Grand Army directly under Washington's command practiced the "Prussian drill," as many diarists of that period called it, and exercised maneuvers. As Joseph Plumb Martin found when he returned after spending the winter on foraging duty, "After I had joined my regiment I was kept constantly, when off other duty, engaged in learning the Baron von Steuben's new Prussian exercise. It was a continual drill."[87] On Sunday, May 3, 1778, Washington ordered his brigades to conduct an exercise together, for two hours in the morning and an hour in the evening on that Monday. Their instructions were to conduct those exercises exactly according to the new regulation, for any deviation would create havoc on the field of battle. The brigades and their regiments would compete, in front of the inspectors, each striving to become the first to master the new system.[88] The first true test of the increasing skill among the regiments began the very next day, May 5, 1778. The cause was not conflict but a celebration. The French had decided to openly support the rebellion. In recognition of this important news, the Grand Army was instructed to conduct a feu de joie, marching together, in battalions, loading and firing their muskets in a running fire from the left to the right, first line and then second line, all coordinated by the firing of artillery.[89]

Shortly thereafter, Washington's forces removed from their winter encampment and followed the retreating British Army from Philadelphia back to New York. At the Battle of Monmouth Courthouse, the Continental Army succeeded in fighting the British in a conventional battle that included artillery barrages, tactical withdrawals, and linear charges, which proved they could succeed on the battlefield using their newly acquired skills. While the battle ended in an operational success for General Charles Cornwallis (his objective as the rear guard was to protect the British main forces, and he did), this was a tactical draw and the American forces rallied, maneuvered, and fought with discipline. While Private Martin complained of his return to the life of a regular soldier, when it came time to fight that summer, he remembered that the soldiers of his regiment were excited to meet the British. Placed in a light infantry regiment comprised of soldiers from a multitude of regiments, Martin wrote that the soldiers of the invalid unit refused to give up their weapons, wanting desperately to join the battle.[90]

This engagement directly after the intensive training of Valley Forge was crucial to the acceptance and commitment of the army to the new regulations. While a council of war, meeting on June 24, 1778, decided against a general engagement with the retreating British Army, Major General Greene wrote a separate letter to Washington as a caveat to his position. He understood the risk but felt a failure of the Continental Army to engage the enemy after all the work completed during the spring would both demoralize the army and damage its reputation with the American people.[91] Brigadier General Anthony Wayne concurred with this assessment in a separate letter.[92] Washington took their advice, deciding to attack the portion of the British Army most at risk. Despite Major General Charles Lee's initial rout, Washington rallied the troops who fought well until Cornwallis followed Henry Clinton in his continued retreat to New York. And after the battle, "General Lee's conduct was so dissatisfactory to the officers and Men that were out with him in the Morning that General Scott and General Wayne . . . entered a formal complaint against him" resulting in a court-martial.[93]

In his general orders the following day, the general congratulated his army for their success, highlighting the coolness under fire of the infantry regiments and the effectiveness of Henry Knox's artillery.[94] This first successful use of the new training under fire acted as a final agreement for the army that the new regulations would remain. Throughout the final five years of the war, the Blue Book was the standard. While military operations in the Northern and Middle Departments settled into a state of observation, training continued in the American encampments under the watchful eyes of generals and their inspectors. Nathanael Greene, acting as the commander in chief while Washington was away in Hartford, congratulated the army on their proficiency in the evolutions and maneuvers in September 1780. In the same order, he acknowledged the treason of Benedict Arnold but claimed this only reinforced the reality of the army's strengths. The British, unable to succeed on the battlefield, were now forced to gain through sabotage what they had failed to achieve in battle.[95]

Certainly, this last comment on treason was partly an attempt to raise morale following the devastating news concerning the betrayal by one of America's most popular generals, but it does point to a significant change in the army's level of training and discipline. Training continued while portions of the army remained encamped throughout New England and New York, and while on campaigns in the South. The commander of the Second Rhode Island Regiment, Colonel Israel Angell, described the parade of his regiment in front of the Baron von Steuben on August 10, 1780. He commanded his regiment in maneuvers the next day. Ten days later he repeated this training, exercising his regiment on the parade field.[96] While serving as part of the Army of Observation in Rhode Island following the Battle of Monmouth, Sergeant Jeremiah Greenman repeatedly noted drills and maneuvers, including ". . . a Genl. Revew and a Sham fight / fir'd a Nom of Cannon."[97] First Lieutenant Francis Brooke reported drilling and exercising his troops in the Virginia Line throughout 1781.[98]

Following the surrender of Cornwallis in October 1781, Washington remained focused on training as a method for retaining soldier morale and confidence while keeping the remaining British forces contained in New York City. In May 1782, Washington planned a grand tour of his forces encamped throughout the New York Highlands. He directed von Steuben to visit the regiments and determine which sequence of maneuvers they would all follow for the inspections. Over the course of a month, the commander visited each of his encampments, with favorable results. On June 18, 1782, he expressed his appreciation for the quality of training apparent throughout the army. He stated the soldiers all looked disciplined, in good spirits, and maintaining a high degree of esprit de corps. While some regiments performed their maneuvers better than others, those regiments located in especially rugged terrain encountered difficulties exercising on such close terrain. The brigade commanders were ordered to continue their training regimen throughout the year. While they were permitted to change the maneuvers they exercised from those specified during the inspection, they were reminded to stay within the "established principles" and always focus on priming and loading, leveling, and taking aim. These were the most important fundamentals.[99]

THE CONTINENTAL ARMY, as an institution, only lasted eight years, all in a state of war. Prior to June 1775, there were military traditions that existed in reality and in memory for many colonists preparing to revolt, but these traditions were different one from another. As part of those traditions, the standards for training were not the same and the leadership within the forming regiments of the Continental Army understood those training standards to varying degrees. Over the course of the first three years, the leaders and the followers of this new American institution struggled to come to an understanding of how the army should operate, how leaders and the led should interact, and how to learn to fight on the battlefield and trust one another under fire. Finally, after several years of trial, a standard was reached, tested under fire, and accepted by all.

The importance of this may not be fully understood, either by those involved or those historians looking back. Over the course of the remaining five years, officers, noncommissioned officers, and soldiers struggled with lack of food, clothing, and pay, either constantly on the move or stultified with boredom in encampments. One of the biggest binding agents between these men was their shared experiences, their shared exercises and drilling, and their formation into a cohesive team. The Blue Book standards established a written contract for how each member of the army was supposed to act, how they were supposed to form in battle, and how they were supposed to interact with one another. With so little experience prior to the war, these codes of conduct and methods for preparing for combat created trust, gave soldiers expectations of their leadership, and taught junior leaders techniques for gaining the respect of their men.

Washington knew in 1782 that the war was winding down. The surrender of Cornwallis at Yorktown was the final blow he had been trying to strike since Germantown. While he certainly needed his army to remain trained, ready to meet the British should they attempt to break out of New York City, his summer tour of the regiments and brigades in 1782 was more than a simple inspection of training. Washington had learned the power of training in creating cohesion within a unit. He understood there were going to be many boring days ahead, possibly with little pay or food. As will be discussed shortly, he had already experienced the Line Mutinies of 1781 and the complaints of groups of officers and soldiers against Congress and the state governments. He needed the army to remain an institution with esprit de corps and loyalty to each other and the leadership. Training and exhibiting excellence was a tried and true method to keep soldiers focused on their duty and off their hardships. As will be explored next, these attempts to keep the army together worked but with some interesting consequences in both discipline and morale.

Four

Morale in
the Continental Army

THE LIMITS TO EXERCISING AUTHORITY

D ESPITE BETTER TRAINING AND INCREASED EFFECTIVENESS ON the battlefield, by 1780 the Continental Army was showing serious fissures in discipline. On May 25, 1780, half of the Connecticut Line mutinied at Morristown, New Jersey. Following the morning muster, men from the Eighth Connecticut Regiment refused to leave the parade ground with their officers, as was customary, to start the day's other duties. The regimental adjutant remained as well to give the orders of the day to the orderly sergeants. An altercation ensued between the adjutant and one of the sergeants, leading the officer to loudly declare the noncommissioned officer a "mutinous rascal" and storm off. When the sergeant hit the butt of his musket on the ground and yelled "Who will parade with me?" the entire rank and file of the regiment fell into formation.[1]

The Eighth Connecticut Regiment was soon joined by the Fourth Connecticut and they marched together to convince their brothers in the Third and Sixth Connecticut to join them in protest against perceived maltreatment at the hands of their officers, their countrymen, and their government. Warned of the impending disaster, Colonel

Samuel Wyllys and Colonel Return J. Meigs attempted to place guards between their soldiers and their weapons and a fight broke out. Colonel Meigs was wounded, stabbed in the side with a bayonet. While the unplanned violence tempered the men from the other two regiments, the Fourth and Eighth Connecticut refused to put down their weapons and officers from the Pennsylvania Line attempted to gather their regiments to surround the mutineers. This plan did not have the desired result. Elements of the Pennsylvania regiments appeared more willing to join the mutiny than quell it and the officers were forced to march their men back to their huts. In the end, the Connecticut soldiers were only calmed when an officer they respected (Colonel Walter Stewart from the Pennsylvania Line) came to hear their grievances. His concern for their demands and assurance that their issues were both shared by their officers and would be addressed immediately eventually led the soldiers to disperse.[2]

This would not be the final mutiny of a regiment or regiments in the Continental Army during the Revolution. A much larger crisis involving both the Pennsylvania and New Jersey Lines was in the making, along with other protests from Massachusetts and Connecticut soldiers. Certainly, by 1780, Continental soldiers and officers had much to complain about, against both their government and their fellow countrymen. Throughout the army soldiers were rarely paid and, when they were, the currency that constituted their pay depreciated faster than they could spend it. Food, clothing, and supplies were always scarce, due to a rather ineffective administrative apparatus in both the army and in Congress, the refusal of state governments to allow military impressment of civilian property, and the unwillingness of local civilians to sell their goods for Continental dollars. The result was poverty and misery for both officers and soldiers throughout the war.

Yet the Continental Army remained in the field throughout the eight years it took to expel the British from the Eastern Seaboard of North America. No American army during the colonial wars had been required to remain in the field for such a long period nor did colonial governments have the administrative and logistical infrastructure necessary to do (and it will be seen that the Continental

Congress can be included in this group). Why did Continental soldiers remain in the face of defeat, privation, and poverty? It is possible they gave some deference to those in leadership who demanded
they remain to fight. Certainly state and martial laws sought to compel soldiers to stay. These men had agreed to (or been pressured into)
long-term enlistment contracts that made it illegal for them to leave,
no matter the cost. Additionally, by 1780, these were hardened,
trained veterans used to the rigors of war. Many soldiers may not
have had many prospects outside the army and so remained despite
the conditions. And most states passed laws protecting debtors as
long as they served in the army. Taken together, these were strong in-
centives for a soldier to remain in the service but they do not fully
explain why the army continued to fight. Tales of men leaving trails
of blood in the snow as they staggered into Valley Forge and descriptions of soldiers marching to battle in rags barely illustrates the difficulties faced or the methods needed to keep these men from
evaporating in front of General Washington's eyes.

A stronger explanation for the reason soldiers remained in the
army despite the lack of general support was that army leaders often
managed to maintain morale at a level high enough to convince the
majority of soldiers to stay and fight. Generally, morale is defined as
"the mental and emotional condition (as of enthusiasm, confidence,
or loyalty) of an individual or group with regard to the function or
tasks at hand."[3] For soldiers in the Continental Army, their levels of
enthusiasm, confidence, and loyalty were most often determined by
their belief that their leadership, their governments, and their fellow
citizens were meeting their expectations. Military leadership as a cultural negotiation of authority created many of those expectations,
especially regarding right conduct and treatment from their officers.
The ability of a leader in the army to maintain morale was determined by his ability and willingness to meet those expectations set
through cultural negotiation and deemed legitimate by his followers.
In particular, this meant officers honoring contracts, maintaining discipline, conducting themselves in accordance with standards, achieving success on the battlefield, and representing their men's grievances
to state governments and Congress. When combined with the unit

cohesion formed between the soldiers of all ranks within their companies and regiments, the ability of officers to meet soldiers' expectations could be powerful indeed. Despite the extreme difficulties faced by officers to meet these expectations, many were able to do so (and those that were not often paid a heavy price).

Studies of the Continental Army usually investigate the challenges faced by these soldiers and their responses; they often do not focus specifically on morale to determine why some regiments experienced lower esprit than others. Allen Bowman did conduct an instructive investigation of the morale within the Continental Army in 1943 as an attempt to aid the Committee for National Morale in understanding how resolve is gained and maintained. He examined the physical and psychological impediments to a soldier's mettle and then explored the effects of absenteeism and desertion to better understand how morale was maintained. He identified the quality of soldiers, lack of supplies, prevalence of disease, and depreciation of wages as the physical causes for lower morale.[4] Within his examination of psychological factors, Bowman highlighted the provincialism of the regiments and the individualism of the soldiers.[5] In the end, when he summed up all of the challenges, all of the deprivation experienced by officers and soldiers alike, Bowman came to one conclusion: the Continental Army remained intact due to the soldiers' devotion to the Revolutionary cause, a "crusade divinely blessed against a cruel oppressor."[6]

Other historians have come to similar conclusions to explain the activities of the soldiers and found that the army was bound together in common cause despite the disagreements between officers and soldiers over the ramifications of republican ideology. Investigating the motivation for service among the men of Massachusetts, one historian found that while a broad spectrum of society joined in the fight for liberty, they often did so for political and ideological reasons that become clear when viewed through the lens of town meetings.[7] Another scholar argued that as the requirements of the war changed how the Continental Army was organized, officers and soldiers agreed that while these changes were necessary, they were also a violation of their republican ideology.[8] The implication here is that there was a general agreement by all members of the Continental Army that they were working together to achieve a common goal. This sense of commonality was sufficient to overcome differences between the ranks and maintained morale despite a general lack of support.

There were other reasons for soldiers to remain in the army despite low morale and lacking supplies. Some scholars found no linkage between officers and soldiers, no common cause that would bind them. Instead, while officers and soldiers suffered alike, social differences and the deference common to late colonial America precluded anything more than a desire by Washington and his officers to exercise as much coercive authority as possible to deter desertions and mutinies. This perception of an insurmountable social gulf between officers and the rank and file implies that unit cohesion, the devotion of the men to each other, is an explanation for why soldiers continued to fight and also why they increasingly protested their plight through mutinies.[9]

Other scholars have agreed, deciding that the experience of military service during the Revolution pitted lower-class soldiers against the leading elites in a fight over the meaning of revolutionary ideology. In Pennsylvania, patriotism lost out to egalitarianism among the privates of the state though they were ultimately disappointed in a final demonstration during the Fort Wilson Riot of 1779.[10] And if patriotism and ideology were elitist conceptions then common men fought for localized reasons that colored their perception of the war.[11] From this perspective of class separation, motivation and morale in the Continental Army necessarily rested on a foundation of cohesion among like groups of soldiers serving together.

While these various explanations for why soldiers continued to fight during the Revolution help us understand the power of both ideology and unit cohesion, they fail to adequately discuss the relationship between the leaders of the army and those who followed them. In either overview, the maintenance of morale was left to unconscious or extraneous forces at work to explain why the army failed to fall apart in the face of extraordinary challenges. The first argument assumes ideology was strong enough to overcome years of privation and neglect experienced by officers and soldiers at the hands of their government and countrymen. The other position implies soldiers' commitment to the war effort during periods of low morale occurred in spite of the officers who led them. Neither thesis acknowledges that a strong relationship developed between the leaders and the led in the army over eight years of war. Belief in a common cause was certainly necessary for all to agree that their actions had meaning and worth. And unit cohesion and esprit de corps did exist among soldiers serving through hard times together. Yet these forces could have been mobilized to steer the army (or separate state lines) in very different directions. There were several examples when morale dropped, discipline suffered, and entire units of soldiers decided to go home or revolt. Still, those instances were relatively few and they were almost always redirected back to the issue at hand: defeating the British Army.

The idea that the officer corps actively led their soldiers has not been adequately explored to explain why the army continued in generally the same direction. The decisions made by officers to care for their soldiers and motivate them to continue in the face of hardships and defeat added more to the success of Washington's Fabian strategy than any other contributing factor. Washington personally set many examples to maintain the loyalty of his soldiers. Self-sacrificing and stalwart, the commander in chief only left the army when he deemed it necessary to visit Congress in person. He was otherwise constantly in the field and at camp with his men. And he demanded much the same from his subordinate officers. In most cases, they followed his example.

When viewed over the entire eight years of the war, it is certain the Continental Army disbanded greatly demoralized compared to the heady days of its establishment. And it would be easy to assume that the morale of the army could be determined by its performance on the battlefield. Certainly the First Establishment experienced a true low point following its defeat at New York in the fall of 1776. It was in this milieu that Washington was forced to recruit for the Second Establishment. Additionally, the Second Establishment experienced a series of highs and lows as separate departments experienced varying degrees of success. The Northern Department became the example of victory Washington was forced to rely upon during his less-than-successful campaign in Pennsylvania in 1777.[12] The relative success at Monmouth in 1778 increased morale in the entire army following the difficulties of Valley Forge while the flight of Horatio Gates from Camden in 1780 was certainly a new low, reached at a point when the army would have to reenlist many of its core veterans who had enlisted in 1777 for three years.

And a new period of tribulation existed after Lord Cornwallis was defeated in 1781. For the next two years the army encamped in New York was forced to remain in the Highlands north of New York City while Henry Clinton and what remained of the British Army held fast until the signing of the Paris Peace Treaty. Throughout the Revolution, soldiers' protests increased as the war progressed and the large majority of their group protests (executed in the form of mutinies) resulted from the lack of food, clothing, and pay and not from battlefield defeats.[13] Morale ebbed and flowed throughout the war, presenting the army's leadership with continuous challenges. Only by convincing the soldiers that they cared, that despite the apparent apathy of the government and society, officers appreciated the sacrifices made by their soldiers, did the Continental Army manage to persevere.

IF MORALE CAN BE DEFINED as the feelings generated among a group when expectations are met or not, Washington certainly benefitted from his reputation and the strong support for the Revolutionary cause when he first took command. His lack of understanding concerning the expectations of men from New England could have led to disaster early on. To be sure, he pushed very hard to change how the army was managed and reshape soldiers' expectations from the outset. The result was consternation on the part of many in the army. According to a Loyalist from Boston, Benjamin Thompson:

> Notwithstanding the indefatigable indeavours of Mr. Washington and the other generals, and particularly of Adjutant General

Gates, to arrange and discipline the army, yet any tolerable degree of order and subordination is what they are totally unacquainted with in the rebel camp. And the doctrines of independence and levellism have been so effectually sown throughout the country, and so universally imbibed by all ranks of men, that I apprehend it will be with the greatest difficulty that the inferior officers and soldiers will be ever brought to any tolerable degree of subjection to the commands of their superiors.[14]

Only the advice of Washington's senior officers from New England, and his willingness to follow that advice, averted the probable alienation of the commander Congress had appointed to take control.

Officers and soldiers alike refused to accept many of Washington's initial reforms. His generals, when asked to determine how to promote the best among the officers (outside the number of soldiers recruited), refused to give him an answer.[15] The committee sent from Congress to confer with Washington, his generals, and the representatives from the various state governments supplying soldiers refused to accept an adoption of the British Articles of War.[16] The men refused to enlist under officers they did not know.[17] And officers continued to fight with one another over recruits in the belief this would determine their rank.[18] By May 1776, Washington realized to maintain morale he would have to meet current expectations and, over time, change those expectations to meet his standards.[19]

During the year that the First Establishment existed, Washington and other leaders faced issues with morale that stemmed from more than a lack of success on the fields of battle. While the British withdrawal from Boston was a cause for celebration, defeats in Canada and at New York sobered those who believed there would be a quick end to the war and impacted the willingness of men to enlist in the regular army. Yet soldiers already serving in the army reacted more strongly to events that occurred outside of combat. In the Northern Department, Major General Philip Schuyler faced a mass desertion by his bateaux men after regimental officers blamed them for not transporting the regiments north in a timely manner. Schuyler was forced to arrest a regimental commander, Colonel William Irvine, for abusing his waggoners who also threatened to leave.[20] A general fear of smallpox led many soldiers in the North to disobey orders and convince local physicians to inoculate them, resulting in further defeats in Canada when these soldiers were no longer able to fight as they recovered from the vaccinations.[21] Furthermore, soldiers from regiments of the different states were fighting amongst themselves.[22] Philip Schuyler himself threatened to resign following his withdrawal from Crown Point, claiming many officers were attempting to damage his reputation and he demanded Congress hold a court of inquiry to clear his name.[23]

The forces under Washington's direct control in New York suffered similar problems with morale. Before the British landed on Long Island, soldiers in regiments from different states fought with one another.[24] Officers convinced Doctor Azor Betts to inoculate them for smallpox against Washington's direct orders (he could not afford to lose men while they recovered).[25] Soldiers complained consistently of overtaxing fatigue details in preparation for New York's defense.[26] Once British forces did land in New York, and particularly after the initial defeat at Long Island, soldiers lost confidence in many of their officers to care for their needs and senior officers lost confidence in their soldiers to stand and fight.[27]

It was in this environment of severely damaged morale that Washington was forced to contemplate the reorganization of the army for the Second Establishment as 1776 came to a close. He had received many of the reforms he had asked for from Congress. Enlistments were lengthened, pay was standardized at $6 and 2/3 and the Articles of War were made stronger and more comprehensive. Initial estimates from recruiting officers were that soldier enlistments would drop precipitously. Understanding that the future of the Continental Army (and the Revolution) were at stake, Washington decided to surprise British forces in New Jersey on Christmas and New Years 1776 to 1777. Despite his success at forcing the withdrawal of British forces from New Jersey, the impact of that victory on recruiting and morale was mixed. Washington was forced to ask those in service but refusing to reenlist to remain six weeks past their contracted service. Some, like David How from Methuen, Massachusetts, refused to stay despite experiencing success at Trenton.[28] At least one regiment refused to march into battle on December 31, 1776, until their officers agreed that the soldiers had done enough and would be released the following day when their enlistments expired.[29] Still, many did agree to stay the extended time, including the Nineteenth Continental Regiment (Connecticut), though they did so after they were offered an addition $10 bounty.[30] And, at least in Massachusetts, the continued threat of British invasion provided the impetus to enlist more men in 1777 than had been enlisted during the previous two years.[31]

While morale in the Continental Army never again reached the high point of 1775, it certainly did recover from the dark times of the following year. In particular, the victory at Saratoga late in 1777 and the success at Monmouth in the spring of 1778 led to increased confidence by both the officers and the soldiers that the overall success of the Revolution was attainable. The new training regimen established at Valley Forge convinced soldiers to such a degree that men left invalid by that harsh winter had to be forcibly restrained from joining the fight in New Jersey.[32] Yet these sporadic victories were not enough to overcome the debilitating realities of insufficient support from the government and local inhabitants. The most frequently cited reasons for low morale were the absence of pay, clothing, and food. Defeats on the battlefield, while certainly demoralizing, rarely warranted mention in soldiers' diaries or memoirs when recounting their reasons for protesting their conditions. While it can be justifiably surmised that victory at some point was an expectation for soldiers in the army, their strongest expectations centered on the promises made to them when they enlisted. The inability or unwillingness of their fellow countrymen to make good on those promises was always the greatest cause for discontent among those serving in uniform. Though new victories in 1781 again raised morale, the final two years of the war would bring about further demoralization as soldiers waited for the word that the war was at an end and their time in the army was likewise concluded.

———————

FROM THE VERY BEGINNING OF THE REVOLUTION, soldiers' pay was a serious issue with regard to morale. While the army consisted almost exclusively of regiments from New England, soldiers were paid on a fairly consistent basis or received back pay at the conclusion of their service. Troubles over pay began when regiments from the middle states joined forces with the rest of the Continental Army. Though men from different states often did not like one another, they certainly shared information across the regiments. Both in New York City and in Albany, soldiers from New York and Pennsylvania began to complain that their salary of $5 per month was lower than that of New England soldiers paid $6 and 2/3 per month. Washington was forced to promise soldiers from Pennsylvania they would be paid the higher amount before they would march north to Albany and months before Congress officially decided to do so.[33] From that point until the end of the war (and for decades after) pay and money would be the chief source of discontent among soldiers and officers.

Once army pay was standardized, the real problems surfaced. Initially, the challenge was paying soldiers in a regular fashion. Pay in the Continental Army was given in Continental dollars until 1781, a currency printed or authorized by the Congress and supported by little more than the promise of a Revolutionary victory. In some cases, as with Captain Bloomfield's command on the frontier in 1776, pay was often months late though this could be explained by the remote location of the command.[34] A lump sum payment of four months' pay still created a challenge for the commander, as soldiers experienced long bouts of dearth and then suddenly became flush with cash. Sutlers provided alcohol and other foodstuffs to supplement a bland army diet of beef and flour, forwarding credit to soldiers until they were paid. For Bloomfield, the result was an outburst of ill-disciplined behavior.[35]

As early as July 1777, soldiers were contemplating protests over the failure to consistently receive their pay.[36] By 1778, protests did occur in several regiments as an attempt to secure months (and soon years) of back pay. Yet the situation became worse by 1780 when the depreciation of the Continental dollar created an inflationary crisis that threatened to beggar all soldiers and ruin even the wealthiest of officers. When a young lieutenant, Francis Brooke of Virginia, joined his regiment late in 1780, he claimed he was paid $33,000 and 2/3 in paper in lieu of the $33 and 2/3 he was due because prices made the latter amount worthless. His uniform coat cost him $2,000 and the buttons $1,500.[37] Lieutenant Benjamin Gilbert expressed empathy for his soldiers in January 1781, claiming many of them had not been paid since December 1779.[38] In New York, Lieutenant John Barr answered accusations that he was working as a teacher while at home recovering from an injury by stating he would be a fool to stay outside of camp for longer than necessary. The cost of living at home far outstripped his wages in Continental dollars.[39]

To make matters worse, the commissary department of the army was completely inefficient, often incapable of supplying the necessary food and goods to units spread across the three departments. To supplement the needs of the soldiers, officers allowed sutlers to accompany their forces, but these men were certainly not above taking advantage of a captured market. Not only did these merchants artificially raise prices, they were a constant source of aggravation when they supplied soldiers with large amounts of alcohol. Additionally, food remained scarce despite the relative abundance of food production throughout the regions the army occupied. Many civilians were simply unwilling to sell their produce to the army for currency they had little faith in.[40] Finally, Congress failed to honor their enlistment promises for clothing and blankets. Soldiers were promised an annual resupply of two linen hunting shirts, two overalls, a waistcoat, hat, breeches, two pair of hose, and two pair of shoes. If the soldier supplied these clothes, he would be given $20 instead.[41] Congress lacked the ability to produce these articles or the infrastructure to supply them. By December 1779, Congress shifted responsibility to the states, requiring the state governments to supply their regiments with clothing and food.[42]

Given the deplorable state of supplying the army, it was not surprising soldiers responded at times with desertion, plundering, and mutiny. Desertion rates have been difficult to determine, due to the inaccurate and inconsistent manner with which muster rolls were collected. A study of Charles Lesser's research does allow for some analysis. During the terrible winter of 1779 to 1780, when the Continental Army was encamped at Morristown, New Jersey, the Massachusetts Line reported 79 soldiers deserted and 132 soldiers were sick and absent out of a total 4,738 soldiers. This constituted about 4 percent of its total force on the rolls at that time. The rolls of Connecticut (17 deserted, 180 sick and absent out of a 2,526 total), Pennsylvania (50 deserted, 71 sick and absent out of a 2,593 total), New York (13 deserted, 62 sick and absent out of a 1,407 total), Virginia (7 deserted, 35 sick and absent out of a 2,237 total), Maryland (72 deserted, 85 sick and absent out of a 2,112 total), and New Jersey (16 deserted, 66 sick and absent out of a 1,187 total) range between 5–7 percent reported absent from the winter encampment that might never return.[43] While these numbers increase dramatically when the numbers of soldiers on furlough are included, the official numbers of soldiers reported as absent without leave were actually quite low.

It is certain these numbers were inaccurate. Washington continuously berated his officers for failing to report their numbers in a timely fashion. Still, by the winter of 1779 to 1780, regimental officers were becoming more reliable and it was much easier to maintain accountability in winter camp than while on campaign. If the muster rolls are to be taken as even somewhat accurate, desertion rates within the Continental Army were not the problem some historians have come to believe. And this fact might explain the leniency often exhibited when deserters were captured and returned to the army, as officers found less of a reason to punish offenders harshly as a deterrent to others. It would be better for the soldiers to reform those who had been returned to the regiments and better for the army to keep a trained soldier (albeit one in need of reform).

Much more prevalent, at least within the general orders of the day, was the habit soldiers had of plundering local inhabitants for food and supplies. Washington's orders addressed this problem consistently from 1776 through the end of the war. Soldiers, frustrated by the sight of civilians spending their winters in relative comfort while the army faced harsh conditions with little clothing and food, decided to take matters into their own hands and relieve their condition through theft. Soon after establishing winter quarters at Valley Forge, Washington was forced to address civilian complaints against soldiers stealing food.[44] Farmers continued to complain that officers and soldiers took more food despite being shown certificates that food had already been given.[45] Late in the spring, Washington was still receiving reports of unauthorized foraging; farmers claimed soldiers were using Washington's name to demand gifts of food and clothing.[46]

The problem was even worse when regiments from Pennsylvania and New York came back into friendly territory following a season on campaign in the West. Major General John Sullivan led an expedition into Iroquois territory in the summer of 1779. His objective was to attempt the capture of Fort Niagara, but lacking the logistical means necessary to take his four thousand soldiers that far west, he instead defeated a force of Loyalists and Iroquois at Newtown and conducted a scorched-earth strategy for the season, burning crops and villages, utterly destroying the ability of the Six Nations to remain. When he returned to Easton, Pennsylvania, his soldiers appeared to have difficulty shedding habits developed over the previous summer. Sullivan initially gave orders that soldiers were to refrain from burning property and railings as they moved south.[47] Within two days of arriving back in Pennsylvania, locals began complaining of looting and violence. Sullivan threatened to place a guard around the camp even if that meant half the camp would remain on duty at any given time.[48] These orders were clearly not heeded as, a few weeks later, a soldier was wounded while attempting to rob a civilian, soldiers were reported firing at civilians while conducting their looting, and officers were failing to uphold order in the camp at Pompton, New Jersey. At this point, Sullivan ordered no one was to leave camp at night.[49] When these orders failed to have the desired effect, guards were placed in a circle around the encampment, field officers were placed in charge of the guards, and brigades were assigned patrols throughout the night.[50] One of the regiments involved, the Fourth New York Regiment, soon thereafter experienced the mass resignation of sixty-four officers as a petition against ill treatment from their "State and Assembly."[51]

While desertion was an issue for concern (given the low number of enlistments) and plundering was alarming (with its potential to turn the citizenry against their army), Washington's most dangerous problem connected to low morale came in the form of mutinies, whether from a single regiment or entire state lines. Mutiny for the Continental Army almost always meant a form of group protest against perceived failures by those in leadership to meet soldiers' expectations concerning pay, food, and clothing. At the risk of anachronism, these were a form of labor strike. During none of the various mutinies studied did soldiers seriously attempt to replace their officers with new leadership from among the noncommissioned officers or privates. Instead, for a period of time, the officers and some of the noncommissioned officers lost the ability to command the majority of their regiments while those in charge of the mutiny illustrated the temporary authority to direct a protest and demand fairer treatment.

The first mutiny occurred in September 1775 when a company of Virginia riflemen attempted to break out one of their fellows from the main guard at Cambridge.[52] More alarming, in December 1775, Connecticut soldiers marched home against orders from Washington and in violation of their enlistment contracts. Washington viewed this protest as a mass desertion from Israel Putnam's division. The soldiers from these regiments claimed their enlistments were at an end and they ran for home taking their weapons and ammunition with them.[53] Jonathan Trumbull, the governor of Connecticut, responded that these men were accustomed to liberty, making them disagreeable to discipline and subordination. Still, they had violated their contract and would be dealt with accordingly.[54] While the soldiers claimed they had the right to leave, all these men knew when their enlistments expired (January 1, 1776). It is clear they left for other reasons, though whether it was in protest to Washington's reforms or due to homesickness is not known.

In 1776, regiments refused to follow orders on several occasions. As stated previously, some regiments refused to march north until they were promised pay equal to that of New England troops. Others refused to continue fighting on the last day of their enlistments until promised release on the next day. In the winter of 1777 to 1778, at

Valley Forge, soldiers and camp followers from the Second and Tenth Virginia Regiments attempted a mutiny in protest of their deplorable conditions. Mary Johnson was found guilty in a division court-martial of mutiny and attempting to desert to the enemy. She was sentenced to a hundred lashes and was drummed out of the army. Eight of her coconspirators (all male) were also found guilty, though only Jeremiah Bride was given a hundred lashes as punishment. The other seven soldiers were sentenced to a hundred lashes but their punishments were reprieved. Three other people (two soldiers and one female camp follower) were acquitted of all charges.[55]

Still, protests of this kind did not seriously threaten the integrity of the army until the Connecticut Line Mutiny of 1780. As stated earlier, the protest embroiled two regiments, almost included another two, and had the potential to include regiments from Pennsylvania, as well. The end result of the exhibition was that soldiers received immediate support in the form of clothing and food.[56] Less than seven months later, the most serious of mutinies occurred. In early January 1781, first the Pennsylvania Line and then the New Jersey Line mutinied in mass over issues of pay, food, and enlistment terms. For soldiers from the Pennsylvania Line, many of whom were German and Irish immigrants, there was a dispute over whether their terms of enlistment were for three years or the duration of the war. The state government insisted these soldiers had enlisted for the longer of the two terms. Since most of these soldiers initially enlisted in 1777, those who believed they had enlisted for only three years insisted their time was over.[57] Furthermore, Pennsylvania was still working through the legislation required to pay these soldiers in Pennsylvania currency, the new requirement once Congress admitted the Continental dollar was no longer a viable form of payment.[58] The end result was a complete breakdown in discipline, the death of at least two officers, the wounding of many others, and an accommodation by the Pennsylvania government to release those no longer willing to serve and a new enlistment bounty to those who would.[59]

The New Jersey Line Mutiny that followed a few days later would end much differently (as would two other smaller mutinies at Yorktown and in New York over the next year). When a portion of the soldiers of New Jersey's First and Second Regiments encamped at Pompton saw what they believed to be the success of the Pennsylvanian protest, they too decided to march toward Philadelphia. First they agreed to head to Chatham to enlist more soldiers in the Third New Jersey Regiment for the protest. Their leader, Sergeant Major George Grant, was only days before a member of the Third Regiment but had been moved in a reorganization of the line.[60] The leadership within the New Jersey Line was somewhat confused in these first weeks of 1781. The line was consolidating three regiments into two. The commander of the Third Regiment, Colonel Elias Dayton, was considered a very capable officer and was taking command of the Second Regiment.[61] He was located with many of his soldiers originally from the Third Regiment at Chatham.[62] The former commander of the Second Regiment, Colonel Israel Shreve, was retiring but still in the field at Pompton.[63] He followed behind his soldiers as they marched to Chatham. When Sergeant Major Grant and his fellow mutineers arrived at Chatham, they met with Colonel Dayton and some commissioners from the New Jersey Assembly who listened to their complaints. Colonel Dayton told the mutineers of pay advances that were soon to be given, refused to allow the men to leave the service upon a sworn oath that their enlistments had expired, and convinced them to return to their duty and await a redress for their grievances. The mutineers agreed and marched back to Pompton under the command of Colonel Shreve.[64]

While Colonel Dayton was working to avert disaster, Washington put in motion a plan to make an example of the New Jersey Line. The quick succession of events was too much for him and he ordered regiments from the Massachusetts Line to march south under the command of Major General Robert Howe. They surrounded the protesters, executed two members of the mutiny (sparing the life of Sergeant Major Grant), and quashed further resistance.[65] In that same year, in the Southern Department, troops from Virginia also mutinied when told to join General Nathanael Greene's forces. They too had not been paid in close to a year. Again the mutiny was forcefully put down. Sergeant Hagarltoy was impaled with Captain Shelton's sword and the Second Virginia Regiment commander, Colonel Christian Febiger, ordered that the barracks be burned to the ground.[66]

The effectiveness of soldier protests varied over the eight years of war. Desertion was usually an individual form of protest or, at times, a method for a few soldiers to decide conditions were no longer acceptable.[67] Plundering was often viewed as necessary by the soldiery due to the failed supply systems of Congress and the army, though it rarely relieved more than the direst of needs. Group protests, mutinies and the threat of them, appeared to be much more effective, at least until 1781. Before the incident with the troops of New Jersey, these events almost always ended with an accommodation to the demands of the soldiers in revolt. The change in strategy for handling this challenge to authority by higher-ranking officers would mark a new and final point in the negotiations over the meaning of military leadership in the Continental Army and suggests not only a limit to the willingness of officers to negotiate with soldiers but also an agreement by those soldiers used to quell mutinies that this method of protest no longer served as a proper form of negotiation.

WASHINGTON ALWAYS WISHED for more control over the administration of the army. He wanted the ability to commission company officers. He asked for more authority to punish soldiers as he thought necessary. He wanted states to initiate more drafts to lower his reliance on militia support. In the end, he never received the authority he thought he needed. Yet he also never wanted certain powers he always believed should remain within the purview of his political leadership. The republican and Whig ideological beliefs that separated military authority from civil authority, and placed the former under the latter, were central to Washington's own political values. That these separations remained throughout the war also meant that officers in the Continental Army were both limited in their abilities to meet the expectations of their soldiers and protected in some regard from the ire of their troops when those expectations were not met.

Furthermore, officers suffered from many of the same failed expectations as their soldiers. When soldiers were not paid, officers were also not paid. When the Continental dollar lost all value, officers too were left begging family and local civilians for support.

Lieutenant Benjamin Gilbert expressed his sympathy for the soldiers who were not receiving pay, claiming in a letter to his father that this was also true for the officers. For this reason, he asked his parents to send him white yarn and thread to fix his socks and clothing.[68] In Philadelphia a soldier and officer were charged with begging from locals for necessary supplies for the sick.[69] In February 1778, one officer, Lieutenant Alexander Guy in Colonel John Lamb's Second Continental Artillery Regiment, was found guilty of conducting robbery with one of his privates. He was sentenced to having his sword broken over his head and dismissed from the army with infamy.[70] Still, officers received certain privileges soldiers did not and it was when they abused those privileges to avoid the travails of their soldiers that they lost the respect of their soldiers and morale in their units plummeted.

Joseph Plumb Martin's memoirs contain several examples of this fact. Shortly after arriving at their winter quarters near Redding, Connecticut, in 1779, Israel Putnam led soldiers on a failed patrol to find the enemy. Unable to return to their encampment before dark, the officers took up quarters in some nearby lodgings and left the soldiers to camp in the woods. When it began to rain hard after midnight, soldiers began firing their weapons in an attempt to force the officers from their cozy lodgings. When this failed to work, Martin concluded it was because the officers did not care for their men.[71] A short time later, while still encamped within Connecticut, this same regiment began a mutiny over pay, clothing, and food. The soldiers (perhaps not surprisingly) believed their officers were not doing enough to address this problem with the state. They mustered several times over the course of a month, threatening to march to Hartford and deal with the government on their own terms. The regimental commander berated his soldiers, but when this failed to quiet them, he did promise to go to Hartford and represent the soldiers. Still, one night the troops loaded a gun barrel with powder, placed it in one of the barracks, and set it off with a slow match. The resultant explosion sent the officers scrambling from their huts. When none of the men would admit to the prank, the officers returned to their quarters and the soldiers repeated the joke. This continued several times until the officers simply ignored them.[72] These were the same men who mutinied again in May 1780.

While examples of this kind could suggest the very separation highlighted by other historians between officers and soldiers in the Continental Army, other examples exist that counter this argument. Included in this same account of the Revolutionary War, Martin described his platoon commander giving a short inspirational speech prior to the Battle of Monmouth. The soldiers viewed this leader as a brave officer, afraid of nothing, a man these soldiers would gladly follow into any battle.[73] Furthermore, during the mutiny in 1780, two of the Connecticut regiments were dissuaded from joining the protest after they wounded Colonel Meigs. Martin described Meigs as a well-respected officer and believed the wounding to be accidental. Finally, the uprising was finished when Colonel Walter Stewart from Pennsylvania agreed to discuss the grievances with the soldiers. Colonel Stewart was apparently very well liked by soldiers in both the Pennsylvania and Connecticut lines and his assurances that both the officers and men were suffering alike and that he would bring the matter up to the Connecticut officers was enough to calm the soldiers down and return them to their duty.[74]

It is curious an officer from another state line would maintain enough trust with these Connecticut men to diffuse such a dangerous situation. This fact points to a situation in the Eighth Connecticut, the regiment that began the protest, which has not been covered in other histories of mutinies during the war. The first commander, Colonel John Chandler, fell ill after less than a year in command and was forced to resign. His second-in-command also fell ill at the same time and was absent for the entire winter of 1777 to 1778, resigning a month after Chandler. The vacancies in leadership positions forced the promotion of the regimental major, Joseph Hait, to lieutenant colonel and Giles Russell (the lieutenant colonel of the Fourth Connecticut) was promoted as the new regimental commander. But stability in leadership continued to elude the Eighth Connecticut. Colonel Russell died on October 28, 1779, reportedly due to complications arising from wounds sustained during the French and Indian War. Joseph Hait was transferred to the Second Connecticut and

Lieutenant Colonel Isaac Sherman was moved in from the Second Connecticut to command the regiment just months before the mutiny in May 1780.[75] The turbulence in senior leadership within the Connecticut Line meant that officers they did not know and who did not know them led these soldiers and this situation was a contributing factor to their low morale.[76]

What becomes apparent from many of the accounts throughout the war was that officers who illustrated for soldiers they were willing to both share in the difficulties of war with their men and represent them to the higher authorities when expectations were not met became the leaders capable of maintaining morale even in the worst of conditions. Colonel Stewart appeared several times to help his soldiers and calm their protests. At Valley Forge, Washington ordered his company commanders to visit their sick at the hospitals, with a captain appointed each day to visit the sick, inspect the hospitals, and ensure their men were receiving the necessary care.[77] After several weeks of visiting the hospital, Colonel Stewart realized these orders were being ignored. He decided to ensure his men were taken care of personally. From that point forward, the captains appointed for hospital duty would report directly to Colonel Stewart daily and report their findings and actions to care for the soldiers to him.[78] In addition to his role during the Connecticut Line Mutiny, it was Stewart who was called forward to Anthony Wayne's temporary headquarters during the Pennsylvania Line Mutiny because it was known the soldiers trusted him and would listen to him.[79]

Washington understood the need to share his soldiers' travails and clearly show his support for them. He never took a furlough in the entire eight years of war. He issued orders to his officers to not abuse furloughs as a method for avoiding the difficulties of winter encampments.[80] Furthermore, to protect his soldiers from unscrupulous sutlers, Washington and his generals established public markets where the officers fixed prices to allow soldiers to buy tobacco, liquor, sugar, and other necessaries at reasonable prices.[81] And, as stated earlier, officers were ordered to visit their sick in the hospitals, attend to their needs when possible, and certainly keep an account of hospital shortages.[82]

Actions like those above and others, to include setting the example of marching with the soldiers on campaign, legitimized officer authority and granted them the ability to command the respect necessary to maintain morale. To be sure, officers from some state lines succeeded in this endeavor better than others. Looking at the instances of mutinies conducted and other examples of group protests, most state lines experienced troubles. Besides the cases of Connecticut, Pennsylvania, Virginia, and New Jersey previously discussed, Massachusetts, Maryland, Rhode Island, New York, and South Carolina also experienced varying degrees of protests that resulted in mass officer resignations, refusals to march, or mass desertions. For Massachusetts, approximately a hundred men marched home from West Point, New York, on January 1, 1780. Yet it was the Massachusetts Line Washington chose a year later to suppress the New Jersey Line during their mutiny. The reasons the mutiny was little more than a company strong and why Washington felt he could trust these men a year later can be explained by examining the response of Massachusetts's officers to their soldiers' grievances and their government's response to their appeals.

On January 19, 1779, the four brigades from Massachusetts sent a petition to the General Court. That petition laid before the assembly the complaints of officers and soldiers regarding the depreciation of their pay and the impact on their ability to feed and clothe themselves and their families.[83] In response, the General Court ordered towns to support their soldiers with credit, to be repaid once the soldiers were paid.[84] A few months later, Colonel Rufus Putnam sent a petition requesting those soldiers serving in the regiments but not citizens of the state also be included in all resolves to provide support. The court agreed.[85] Still, in September 1779, Major General William Heath sent a letter to the court that spurred them to appoint a three-man committee to meet with the officers and soldiers at West Point to hear their grievances. Political leaders were facing a serious problem at this juncture; the majority of their soldiers had enlisted for three years in 1777 and those enlistments would soon be completed. The committee was authorized to offer a reenlistment bonus of $300 to those willing to reenlist for the duration of the war and to promise all soldiers and officers that as much of their back pay as the state could provide would be paid to them by January 1, 1780. The remainder would be given when available.[86]

The committee traveled to New York, met with all the officers and the men at West Point, and returned to submit their report on November 12, 1779. The report was not encouraging. Both the officers and the enlisted soldiers were unhappy with their treatment by their government and unwilling to remain in the service. Officers were broke, spending their own money to feed their soldiers. The families of both officers and soldiers were now destitute, reliant on the generosity of their towns for support. Deserters were not pursued; to the contrary, they were hired by the towns as laborers and protected from being forcibly returned to the army. While the committee did its best to promise restitution was coming and that there was a sizeable bonus for those who reenlisted, they did not feel enlistments would be substantial unless the state rectified the immediate need for food and clothing. Finally, the committee reported that the officers were very concerned that the men who served and counted in the state's quota but were citizens from other states be included in any and all benefits agreed upon.[87]

While these discussions, in reality, never amounted to much (officers and soldiers remained unpaid for long periods of time and, as will be shown later, both officers and men left the army in 1783 greatly disillusioned by the treatment from both the government and their countrymen), the combined knowledge that their officers suffered with them and that those same officers supported them went far to ameliorate the damage done to morale. Contrasted to the case of the Pennsylvania Line Mutiny of 1781, it is apparent that the appearance of the committee in November 1779 quite possibly averted a similar event occurring a year earlier in what were arguably the most radical units in the army with a reputation from the French and Indian War of marching home when contractual expectations were not met.

In the case of the Pennsylvania Line, its government was also working to solve the riddle of paying for its soldiers once the Continental dollar collapsed. Where Massachusetts decided to fund its soldiers through a lottery,[88] Pennsylvania chose to use the promised sale of seized Loyalist real estate as collateral for the issuance of state notes. Yet while the Pennsylvania Assembly worked to pass a law that would fund a state currency, backed by the promise of land sales, and authorized a team of auditors to determine the back pay due to its soldiers, to include accounting for depreciation, the soldiers of the regiments decided to take matters into their own hands.[89] There is no record of petitions sent to the Pennsylvania Assembly by officers in support of their soldiers prior to the mutiny. There are no records to show the soldiers knew of the new resolutions passed to attempt their relief. Instead, Joseph Reed rode up to Princeton from Philadelphia to meet with Major General Anthony Wayne and the leaders of the revolt with this information after the protest began. He arrived with the power to promise those who believed they had enlisted for three years the ability to leave the service or reenlist for an additional bounty. Once this information was given to the soldiers, to include the promise of new clothing and more food, the mutiny ended and the soldiers either marched back to Morristown or were marched home to await a rendezvous in Carlisle the following spring.[90] The mutiny that winter was as much a failure of leadership on the part of both senior officers and politicians as it was a necessary protest to resolve legitimate grievances.

Still, if leadership is a cultural negotiation of authority and the officers were products of the same colonial cultures and military traditions as their men, why would the soldiers from these different state lines appear to act in similar ways to similarly failed expectations? The reason for this was that by 1780 much of the Continental Army had come together to form its own military tradition, a new set of standards and expectations, built over the shared experiences of the previous five years, that required officers to answer the needs of their soldiers in a similar fashion, despite their own understanding of their place in society.[91] Key to this joining, as discussed earlier, was training. Training set the standard of conduct for officers, noncommissioned officers, and soldiers alike. Another force bringing these men together was simply the experience of serving together in the same region and on the same battlefields. Soldiers were often placed on special duties that forced them to work with other officers and other soldiers from the various regiments and states. A melding of culture and expectations was not, therefore, surprising. Still, while this evolution of traditions was important, perhaps the strongest force that drew soldiers from across the army into a common military culture was the revolutionary rhetoric of Washington and his officers.

Starting with the reading of the Declaration of Independence a few days after its signing, soldiers were inundated with revolutionary ideology as a way to motivate them before a battle, to entreat them toward better behavior in camp, and to lift their morale following a defeat. Washington's general orders are replete with calls to defend liberty, to uphold the right to private property, and to guard against tyranny. Prior to the Battle of Long Island, Washington told his army that they fought not for their specific states but for the single cause of liberty. "Let all distinctions of Nations, Countries, and Provinces, therefore be lost in the generous contest, who shall behave with the most Courage against the enemy, and the most kindness and good humor to each other."[92] Now was the time for every soldier to do his duty, to fight for liberty, property, life, and honor, for his wife, his children, and his country (America).[93] Prior to the beginning of the campaign in 1778, Washington assured his soldiers of their imminent victory, for they were free citizens in arms fighting against the mercenaries and forces of a king intent on ravaging their lands and their rights.[94]

Washington was certainly not the sole provider of revolutionary fervor. Leaders down to the company level were inspired by this revolutionary rhetoric and acted in concert with those ideals. Following the death of one of his soldiers, Captain Bloomfield held a military funeral with all officers in attendance. Five soldiers fired three shots in salute. The soldiers from Bloomfield's regiment were impressed at the respect shown a private soldier.[95] Over the summer of 1776, Bloomfield and his soldiers built Fort Dayton, north of German Flatts, and following the successful conclusion of its construction, the entire unit raised a sixty-foot pole, flew a flag atop it with "Liberty" on one side and "Property" on the other. They then gathered around a barrel of grog, the officers toasted the success of the fort, the soldiers gave nine cheers, they all fired shots through the portholes, marched around the fort, gathered back around the grog, gave more patriotic toasts, and then dispersed.[96] It is impossible to know how many of the soldiers there that day were present almost five years later when Washington ordered members of the New Jersey Line to shoot to death two of their own for leading the Mutiny of 1781, but the ideology of life, liberty, and property surely survived those first heady days in the summer of 1776.

The experience of serving in the Continental Army was radicalizing, especially for soldiers serving from states where those ideals were not even close to being practiced in reality. It should be no wonder, then, that the failures of the Congress, the state governments, the local populace, and, at times, the leaders of the army caused soldiers to come together to protest violations of the ideals for which they fought. The wonder is that it happened so infrequently and usually was diffused before their protests exploded into mob violence or mass desertions and defections. The best explanation for why that was the case is the leadership of many of the officers to care for their men, address their needs when possible, and represent those men to higher authorities when needed.

Yet by 1781 Washington and other generals found that accommodation had its limits, especially in the face of the enemy. While the Pennsylvania Line refused British attempts to turn the protest to their advantage, the quick succession of first the Pennsylvania mutiny and then the New Jersey mutiny convinced Washington he had to respond more forcefully with the second protest. Despite the success of Colonel Dayton to diffuse the situation, Washington marched five hundred soldiers of the Massachusetts Line down from West Point to Pompton, surrounded the offenders, and forced the execution of two ringleaders by twelve fellow mutineers.[97]

For the rest of the war, these forms of protest no longer brought accommodation; they brought executions. The two times when mutiny again threatened the army, it occurred in the same regiments where it had occurred before. Regiments of the Pennsylvania Line attempted mutiny at Yorktown, claiming correctly that the promises made to them earlier had not been kept. Anthony Wayne violently suppressed this revolt in front of the enemy by executing several members of the mutiny while in commission of instigating the re-volt.[98] In May 1782, the Connecticut Line again planned a mutiny but a soldier revealed the plot to seize artillery and march to Hart-ford, resulting in the execution of one plot leader.[99] While caring for soldiers, leading them by the example of perseverance, and represent-ing them remained the cornerstone to maintaining morale, accom-modation to mutiny was no longer tolerated in the Continental Army.

AS THE WAR DREW TO A CLOSE, Washington and the other officers of the army faced their final challenge to morale: a waning sense of pur-pose. Following the victory at Yorktown, the army was forced to re-main encamped in the New York Highlands to maintain a careful watch over British forces still occupying New York City. For the of-ficers and soldiers remaining in the army, this was a tense time, one of small skirmishes, foraging parties, no pay, little food, and an un-certain future. In order to maintain morale, Washington was forced to get creative.

His first order of business was to keep the soldiers spread across the Highlands busy. He organized a tour of his forces and he ordered them to perform a specific set of exercises, given to them by von Steuben. Washington would inspect every unit and critique them on their tactical abilities. Following the inspection, Washington issued general orders congratulating the officers and soldiers on their per-formance. All units looked professional (except a few regiments that had yet to receive hats) and all performed their exercises well (except a few that had difficulty conducting their training on such rugged terrain). Washington thanked von Steuben for all his hard work and encouraged regimental commanders to continue training and to change the routine of maneuvers but also to stay true to the estab-lished principles of the Blue Book.[100]

Washington then created two new forms of recognition for his soldiers. The first was a thin white stripe of cloth, cut in an angular fashion, and worn on the left sleeve of the uniform coat. It would symbolize three years of brave and faithful service. Those soldiers who served for six years wore two stripes sewed parallel to one another. The second award was for any soldier or noncommissioned officer who served gallantly in a singular meritorious action. These men would be awarded a purple heart, cut from cloth, and sewed on the facings of his left breast. To be awarded such an honor, the soldier's commander was required to certify the action with General Washington personally. The wearer of the Purple Heart would receive the privilege of passing the guards as officers did.[101] These two distinctions are still in use in the modern US Army, though the Purple Heart now signifies that a soldier has been wounded in combat. His or her service stripes still represent three years of dedicated service each.

Washington had one final project to keep the men busy as they waited for the signing of the final peace treaty to end the war. On Christmas Day in 1782, Washington approved the suggestion of Reverend Dr. Israel Evans, the chaplain for the New Hampshire Brigade, who proposed the construction of a great public building for the common use of worship.[102] For the next few months, officers and soldiers from across the army came together to collect the materials and expertise necessary. Colonel Tupper of the Massachusetts Line was placed in charge and the building was complete in early March 1783.[103] It is perhaps ironic that the first meeting ever held there would later be called the Newburgh Conspiracy.

In the first week of March 1783 a letter circulated among the officers remaining in the army announcing a meeting to be held at the new public building to discuss the future of the officers and their soldiers. A few months earlier, in December, Major General Alexander McDougall, Colonel Matthias Ogden, and Colonel John Brooks traveled to Philadelphia as a committee representing the grievances of the army to Congress. Their desire to secure the pay owed everyone in the army and commute a promised pension to a lump sum payment for the officers was debated but not decided over the winter. Back at Newburgh, tensions were running high as all men in uniform contemplated the upcoming peace, the definite dissolution of the army, and the threat that they would all be forced to return home without a settlement of their accounts. Some officers decided more pressure was necessary to force Congress to honor its promises.

The letter sent to the officers, known as the Newburgh Address, was an emotional appeal, listing the wrongs done to the officers by Congress and declaring that only two options remained if Congress refused to resolve these issues regarding pay. If peace was declared, the officers could lead the army to Philadelphia and refuse to lay down their arms and disperse until their accounts were settled and commutation given. If the war did not end, the officers could lead the army west, leaving Congress vulnerable to British attacks.[104] Washington immediately took control of the situation, issued a general order stopping the proposed meeting, and announced a meeting the next Saturday to discuss a report from McDougall's committee. He assumed no officers would have attended the earlier meeting due to its "irregular" announcement but he requested that all officers attend his meeting with the senior officer in attendance to act as president. The president was to report the results of the meeting to Washington upon its conclusion.[105]

The general order implied Washington would not attend the meeting personally. Major General Gates chaired the meeting as president, but before the discussions could begin, Washington walked into the building and began to attack the anonymous letter as emotional and dangerous. The two options presented in the letter were preposterous. If the army marched on Philadelphia, every objective of the Revolution would be compromised. If the officers marched the army west, they would not only leave Congress vulnerable, they would also place their families at risk. The only rational decision was to remain patient, trust that Congress would honor its responsibilities, and continue to lead the army to a victorious conclusion of the war.[106] Following this appeal to his officers' sense of commitment to the Revolution and their new country, Washington read the report from McDougall stating congressional support to address the army's grievances. The officers unanimously agreed to support the Congress and a potential crisis was averted.[107]

Several scholars have debated the importance of this sole example of a mutiny by the officers of the Continental Army. Richard H. Kohn asserts this event was the result of a conspiracy between young nationalists in Congress and young "Turks" in the army (led by Horatio Gates) who attempted to use the army to further their aims at centralizing national power in Congress. While these politicians and officers never wished for a military coup d'etat, they were willing to risk revolt in order to force the issue of pay and commutation paid for by a national tax to fund a national debt.[108] Historian Paul D. Nelson, a biographer of Horatio Gates, argues Gates and his protégés never intended a coup. Instead, while perhaps politically naïve, their intentions were solely to place pressure on Congress and were never of a treasonous nature.[109] Historian C. Edward Skeen took Nelson's argument one step further, depicting the Newburgh Address as misunderstood by Washington. The entire affair was fomented by politicians in Philadelphia who were attempting to excite the army to their own nationalist agenda while the officers involved only ever wished for a stronger remonstrance to congressional failures. Washington, receiving letters from Alexander Hamilton and a Virginia congressman, Joseph Jones, became convinced the address was originally written in Philadelphia and delivered to Newburgh by Colonel Walter Stewart. He then overreacted during his meeting on March 15, 1783, crushing any attempts to pressure Congress for legitimate redress and ending what was actually a non-event.[110]

Regardless, the events of early March 1783 highlighted the extreme distress of all in the army during those final days over the issues of failed expectations. While Washington's reaction illustrated the limits to which he would go, the Newburgh Conspiracy showed that the officers in the army suffered the same plight as their men and were willing to continue their support to care for their soldiers. Whatever the intentions of the address, everyone knew of the continued attempts to speak with Congress and receive due compensation while the petitions included demands for both soldiers and officers. And despite the failure of Congress to come to a resolution, the army at Newburgh did not revolt.

All of these actions at Newburgh over the final months of the war point to another important fact. Washington had changed his view of his army, as they had conveyed their trust and loyalty to him. By March 1783, the vast majority of his army came from New England. Of the nineteen regiments remaining, fourteen were from the four

New England states, and eight came from Massachusetts alone. His decisions to create the army's first official recognitions for soldiers' service and actions were not cynical attempts to ameliorate failures from governments to meet their obligations. These were recognitions that his soldiers were men worthy of his respect and appreciation. Furthermore, his most trusted officers were Nathanael Greene, Henry Knox, William Heath, Rufus Putnam, and John Brooks (commander of the Seventh Massachusetts), all officers from New England. And these were the men he relied upon to support him when he decided to end the Newburgh Conspiracy in no uncertain terms.[111]

The last days of the Continental Army were not ones of high morale. Washington thanked all who served with him over the duration of the war in one of his last general orders. He asked all to remember their time in the army with pride, knowing they helped erect a "fabric of freedom and empire on the broad basis of independency."[112] Yet despite his best efforts to the contrary, most officers and soldiers left the army with little more than their weapons, their uniforms, and promissory notes. Many of them were forced to sell those notes immediately, at a depreciated value, to be able to afford their transport home. Lieutenant Gilbert, forced to remain in camp until he received some payment, described the plight of many soldiers and officers as they were furloughed in the summer of 1783. Disillusioned by the ingratitude he witnessed from American citizens toward the soldiers, he described for his brother-in-law the scenes of soldiers who served for four to eight years leaving the army without a penny in their pocket. These men were forced to beg for money from the very people they had fought for and died to protect. For Gilbert the scene was impossible to bear.[113]

Conditions for the solders of the Continental Army were terrible. Without the logistical or administrative infrastructure to support the army, pay, food, clothing, and other necessaries were never adequately provided. The military traditions of colonial America never demanded the ability to support an army year-round and certainly not to do so for almost a decade constantly in the field. Yet stirred by the revolutionary rhetoric that convinced them they were fighting for liberty against slavery and tyranny, the final decision made by those last soldiers in the Continental Army not to take the Revolution to the doorsteps of their state assemblies and the Continental Congress for redress is hard to explain without acknowledging the leadership of their officers in service with them. And while that leadership failed to adequately protect soldiers from the apathy of government and country, the result of eight years of war was a new American military tradition that would define the relationship between leaders and led in the army for centuries to come.

CONCLUSION

The War of Independence ended in September 1783 and the Continental Army was largely dissolved. Only a single regiment, known as the First American Regiment, remained to guard the frontier against Indian attacks as the American population continued its move westward into Ohio, Kentucky, and territories farther west. This small force was not equal to the task.[1] The political weaknesses of the Congress under the Articles of Confederation and the republican politics that were strengthened by the success of the Revolution required the new nation to rely more heavily on state militias for defense. Though Washington suggested a method for regulating the militia that would centralize control at the national level, it was rejected.[2] The idea of a peacetime establishment was debated during the Constitutional Convention and, while it was eventually declared constitutional, still the country relied heavily on state militias for defense. In effect, according to historian Don Higginbotham, the new Constitution created a dual military system of state militias (the old colonial tradition) and a standing army (maintaining the lessons learned from the Continental Army).[3]

While this system appears to illustrate a break in traditions and practices between the Continental Army and the American armies that followed, this is not the case. The United States Militia Act of

1792 maintained states' control of their militia forces but also mandated the use of *The Regulations for the Order and Discipline of the Troops of the United States* from 1779 for organization and training. Some officers from the Revolution remained in the small standing force while others entered politics during the early republic. Many of them blamed their experiences of insufficient support during the Revolution on a weak central government and became ardent Federalists.[4] In 1792, the army recruited approximately four thousand soldiers to fight under the command of Major General Anthony Wayne to protect settlers in the Northwest Territory. At the Battle of Fallen Timbers in 1794, Wayne decisively defeated his Native American opponents and ended the war for the Northwest Territory.[5]

During President Washington's administration, he and Alexander Hamilton advocated for a military academy to educate and train officers, especially in the military art and in engineering. While Congress declined to debate this and several similar proposals over the course of the 1790s, President Thomas Jefferson did approve the establishment of the United States Military Academy at West Point in 1802, though historians debate his reasons. Some historians argue Jefferson sought to establish a three-tiered educational system that included desperately needed professional schools to teach mathematics, science, and engineering. The United States Military Academy was part of his educational vision.[6] But as historian Theodore Crackel has skillfully shown, Jefferson's strongest reason lay in his desire to "Republicanize" the army. Following the Military Peace Establishment Act of 1802, Jefferson and his secretary of war, Henry Dearborn (who served for New Hampshire as a captain, major, and lieutenant colonel in the Continental Army), worked through a reorganization of the army to rid the senior ranks of Federalists, promote the lieutenant colonels to colonels (thus winning over many who were moderates), and reinstitute the rank of ensign in the infantry regiments to create many new offices for the Republican Party to fill. As a part of this reorganization, the United States Military Academy at West Point provided the means to educate future officers in proper, republican leadership, while the free education and political appointments ensured young men of merit were appointed who also maintained the proper political leanings.[7] It was at West Point that continuity was maintained between the Continental Army and what became the United States Army.

The debates and decisions concerning the American army that came to light in the early republic show a continued negotiation over the issues of military service and authority that began with the adoption of the Continental Army in the summer of 1775. Over the course of the War of Independence, the officers and soldiers of the Continental Army wrestled with what it meant to lead and follow during the most active parts of the Revolution. As the commander in chief of this army, Washington had great influence over these debates but so too did his soldiers and junior officers. He took command of a New England army at the heart of the revolt and he left command again in charge of a largely New England army. The final garrison for the Continental Army became the future sight of the United States Military Academy and its final agreement on military leadership lived on in the publication and early adherence to the Blue Book.

The United States Army continued, from the Revolution until the creation of the all-volunteer force in 1972, to work in this dual system of a small standing army and a larger state militia system whereby a small core of professionals stood by ready to incorporate citizen-soldiers in times of need. This system maintained a requirement to negotiate the use of military authority as large numbers of citizens entered the regular service to support their nation in times of war. Even during the American Civil War, regiments remained delineated by the states from which they were formed. Still, many of the officers continued to be educated and trained at one school, West Point. And the agreements reached in the Continental Army persevered. In particular, the idea prevailed that American soldiers were autonomous individuals, unwilling to follow leaders simply because they had been granted the authority to lead by their government. This belief remains the foundation on which is built our understanding of leadership today.

In 1879, following a hazing scandal at the academy, a former superintendent and then commander of the US Army, Major General John M. Schofield, gave an address to the Corps of Cadets. A portion of his speech, known as "Schofield's Definition of Discipline," is still required to be memorized by every cadet as he or she begins their four years of training and education.

> The discipline which makes the soldiers of a free country reliable in battle is not to be gained by harsh or tyrannical treatment. On the contrary, such treatment is far more likely to destroy than to make an army. It is possible to impart instruction and to give commands in such a manner and such a tone of voice to inspire in the soldier no feelings but an intense desire to obey, while the opposite manner and tone of voice cannot fail to excite strong resentment and a desire to disobey. The one mode or the other of dealing with subordinates springs from a corresponding spirit in the breast of the commander. He who feels the respect which is due to others cannot fail to inspire in them regard for himself, while he who feels, and hence manifests, disrespect toward others, especially his inferiors, cannot fail to inspire hatred against himself.[8]

This commitment to the agreement reached between the officers and soldiers in the Continental Army is the Revolution's greatest legacy to the United States Army today.

NOTES

INTRODUCTION

1. George Washington, "General Orders, Cambridge, July 3, 1775," in *The Papers of George Washington Digital Edition*, edited by Thomas J, Crackel (Charlottesville: University Press of Virginia , Rotunda, 2008), http://0-rotunda.upress.virginia.edu.usmalibrary.usma.edu/founders/GEWN-03-01-02-0025.

2. Washington, "General Orders, Cambridge, July 4, 1775," *PGWD*, http://0-rotunda.upress.virginia.edu.usmalibrary.usma.edu/founders/GEWN-03-01-02-0027.

3. Washington, "General Orders, Cambridge, July 7, 1775," *PGWD*, http://0-rotunda.upress.virginia.edu.usmalibrary.usma.edu/founders/GEWN-03-01-02-0040.

4. Charles H. Lesser, *The Sinews of Independence: Monthly Strength Reports of the Continental Army* (Chicago: University of Chicago Press, 1976), 4-5.

5. Washington, "Letter to Lund Washington, Cambridge, August 20, 1775," *PGWD*, http://0-rotunda.upress.virginia.edu.usmalibrary.usma.edu/founders/GEWN-03-01-02-0234.

6. Washington, "Letter to George William Fairfax, Philadelphia, May 31, 1775," *PGWD*, http://0-rotunda.upress.virginia.edu.usmalibrary.usma.edu/founders/GEWN-02-10-02-0281.

7. Paul Lockhart, *The Whites of Their Eyes: Bunker Hill, the First American Army, and the Emergence of George Washington* (New York: HarperCollins, 2011), 84-88.

8. David How, *Diary of David How, a Private in Colonel Paul Dudley Sargent's Regiment of the Massachusetts Line, in the Army of the American Revolution* (Morrisania, NY: H.D Houghton, 1865), ix.

9. Ibid., 1, 4-5.

10. Ibid., 4, 6, 10.

11. Ibid., 7.

12. Ibid., 5.

13. Lesser, 4-5.

14. *The Spirit of 'Seventy-Six: The Story of the American Revolution as Told by Participants*, edited by Henry Steele Commager and Richard B. Morris (New York: Harper and Row, 1967), 152.

15. Ibid., 154.

16. Washington, "Letter to Robert Dinwiddie, Winchester, April 16, 1756," *PGWD*, http://0-rotunda.upress.virginia.edu.usmalibrary.usma.edu/founders/GEWN-02-03-02-0001-0001.

17. Washington, "Letter to Robert Dinwiddie, Winchester, April 18, 1756," *PGWD*, http://0-rotunda.upress.virginia.edu.usmalibrary.usma.edu/founders/GEWN-02-03-02-0010.

18. Bertram Wyatt Brown, *Southern Honor: Ethics and Behavior in the Old South* (New York: Oxford University Press, 1982), 14-15.

19. *Leadership in the American Revolution* (Washington, DC: Library of Congress, 1974), 7.

20. Ibid., 8.

21. Ibid., 45-46.

22. Ibid., 64.

23. Ibid., 67.

24. Ibid., 91.

25. Ibid., 94-95.

26. Ibid., 96.

27. Ibid., 99.

28. Ibid., 102-107.

29. Max Weber, "Economically Determined Power and the Social Order," in *From Max Weber: Essays in Sociology*, trans. and ed. H.H. Gerth and C. Wright Mills (New York: Oxford University Press, 1946), 180.

30. Edmund S. Morgan, *Inventing the People: The Rise of Popular Sovereignty in England and America* (New York: W.W. Norton, 1988), 13-15.

31. John Lynn, *Battle: A History of Combat and Culture* (Boulder, CO: Westview Press, 2003), 365-368.

32. James M. Hadden, *Hadden's Journal and Orderly Books: A Journal Kept in Canada and Upon Burgoyne's Campaign in 1776 and 1777*, ed. Horatio Rogers (Boston: Gregg Press, 1972), lxx-lxxiii; Frederick William von Steuben, *Regulations for the Order and Discipline of the Troops of the United States to Which is Added, an Appendix, Containing the United States Militia Act, Passed by Congress, May, 1792* (Boston: Henry Ranlet, 1794), 67-78.

33. John Brewer, *The Sinews of Power: War, Money, and the English State, 1688-1783* (New York: Alfred A, Knopf, 1989), 29-37, 88-91.

34. I.F. Burton and A.N. Newman, "Sir John Cope: Promotion in the Eighteenth-Century Army," *English Historical Review* Vol. 78, No. 309 (Oct. 1963): 668.

35. J.A. Houlding, *Fit for Service: The Training of the British Army, 1715-1795* (Oxford: Clarendon Press, 1981), 100.

36. Ibid., 104-105.

37. Sylvia R. Frey, *The British Soldier in America: A Social History of Military Life in the Revolutionary Period* (Austin: University of Texas Press, 1981), 6.

38. Ibid., 4-5; Houlding, 117-118.

39. Frey, 133-134.

40. Scott N. Hendrix, "The Spirit of the Corps: The British Army and the Pan-European Military World and the Origins of American Martial Culture, 1754-1783" (Pittsburgh: University of Pittsburgh, 2005), 73-74.

41. Frey, 120, 134-135.

42. Matthew C. Ward, *Breaking the Backcountry: The Seven Years' War in Virginia and Pennsylvania, 1754-1765* (Pittsburgh: University of Pittsburgh Press, 2003), 92.

43. James Titus, *The Old Dominion at War: Society, Politics, and Warfare in Late Colonial Virginia* (Columbia: University of South Carolina Press, 1991), 25-30.

44. Washington, "Letter to Robert Dinwiddie, Winchester, April 16, 1756," *PGWD*, http://0-rotunda.upress.virginia.edu.usmalibrary.usma.edu/founders/GEWN-02-03-02-0001-0001.

45. Titus, 109-125.

46. Washington, "Orders, Winchester, May 1, 1756," *PGWD*, http://0-rotunda.upress.virginia.edu.usmalibrary.usma.edu/founders/GEWN-02-03-02-0062.

47. Titus, 46-72.

48. Ibid., 126-141.

49. Ibid., 134-135.

50. Steven Charles Eames, "Rustic Warriors: Warfare and the Provincial Soldier on the Northern Frontier, 1689-1748" (University of New Hampshire, 1989), 27-29.

51. For a narrative of Massachusetts' successful assault on the fortress at Louisbourg, see Fairfax Downey, *Louisbourg: A Key to a Continent* (Englewood Cliffs, NJ: Prentice Hall, 1965), 73-102.

52. Kyle F. Zelner, *A Rabble in Arms: Massachusetts Towns and Militamen During King Philip's War* (New York: New York University Press, 2009), 213-217.

53. Wyllis E. Wright, *Colonel Ephraim Williams: A Documentary Life* (Pittsfield: Berkshire County Historical Society, 1970), 26-27.

54. Fred Anderson, *A People's Army: Massachusetts Soldiers and Society in the Seven Years' War* (Chapel Hill: University of North Carolina Press, 1984), 167-180.

55. Ibid., 26-50.

56. Ibid., 111-141.

57. Eames, 323-327.

58. Seth Pomeroy, *The Journal and Papers of Seth Pomeroy, Sometime General in the Colonial Service*, ed. Louis Effingham de Forest (New York: Society of Colonial War in the State of New York, 1926), 117, 121-123.

59. Rufus Putnam, *Memoirs of Rufus Putnam* (Boston: Houghton Mifflin, 1903), 11.

60. Ward, 29-31, 92.

61. Samuel J. Newland, *The Pennsylvania Militia: The Early Years, 1669-1792* (Annville, PA: Commonwealth of Pennsylvania Department of Military and Veterans Affairs, 1997), 41-47.

62. R.S. Stephenson, "Pennsylvania Provincial Soldiers in the Seven Years' War," *Pennsylvania History* 62 (1995): 196-200.

63. Ward, 97.

64. Ibid., 200-204.

65. Ward, 113-120.

66. Ibid., 204-209.

67. Harold E. Selesky, *War and Society in Colonial Connecticut* (New Haven: Yale University Press), 47-65.

68. Ibid., 144-145.

69. Ibid., 155-156.

70. Ibid., 172.

71. Ibid., 194-196, 201.

72. Ibid., 197.

73. Ibid., 207, 215.

74. Lesser, 4-5.

75. Washington, "Letter to John Hancock, Cambridge, July 10-11, 1775," *PGWD*, http://0-rotunda.upress.virginia.edu.usmalibrary.usma.edu/founders/ GEWN-03-01-02-0047-0003.

76. Richard M. Ketchum, *Decisive Day: The Battle for Bunker Hill* (Garden City, NY: Doubleday, 1973), 190.

77. Lockhart, *The Whites of Their Eyes*, 299.

78. Ibid., 302.

79. Ketchum, 181.

80. Guy Chet, *Conquering the American Wilderness: The Triumph of European Warfare in the Colonial Northeast* (Amherst: University of Massachusetts Press, 2003), 100-140.

81. Don Higginbotham, "Military Leadership in the American Revolution," in *Leadership in the American Revolution* (Washington, DC: Library of Congress, 1974), 91-109.

82. James K. Martin and Mark E. Lender, *A Respectable Army: The Military Origins of the Republic, 1763-1789*, 3rd Edition (Malden, MA: Wiley-Blackwell, 2015), 19.

83. Ibid., 95-96.

84. John A. Ruddiman, *Becoming Men of Some Consequence: Youth and Military Service in the Revolutionary War* (Charlottesville: University Pressof Virginia, 2014), 12.

CHAPTER ONE: OFFICERSHIP IN THE CONTINENTAL ARMY

1. Scott N. Hendrix, "The Spirit of the Corps: The British Army and the Pre-National Pan-European Military World and the Origins of American Martial Culture, 1754-1783" (PhD Diss., University of Michigan, 2005), xiii.

2. Ibid., 22-23.

3. Ibid., 299-328.

4. Caroline Cox, *A Proper Sense of Honor: Service and Sacrifice in George Washington's Army* (Chapel Hill: University of North Carolina Press, 2004), 38.

5. Ibid., 100-101.

6. See Don Higginbotham, *George Washington and the American Military Tradition* (Athens: University of Georgia Press, 1985).

7. See E.Wayne Carp, *To Starve the Army at Pleasure: Continental Army Administration and American Political Culture, 1775-1783* (Chapel Hill: University of North Carolina Press, 1984).

8. John Barker, *The British in Boston: The Diary of Lt. John Barker* (New York: Arno Press, 1969), 26-27.

9. Thomas Anburey, *With Burgoyne from Quebec: An Account of the Life at Quebec and of the Famous Battle at Saratoga* (Toronto: Macmillan of Canada, 1963), 83-84.

10. Ibid., 85-86.

11. Washington, "Letter to John Robinson, Winchester, April 18, 1756," *PGWD*, http://0-rotunda.upress.virginia.edu.usmalibrary.usma.edu/founders/GEWN-02-03-02-0011.

12. Landon Carter, "Letter to George Washington, Sabine Hall, April 21, 1756," *PGWD*, http://0-rotunda.upress.virginia.edu.usmalibrary.usma.edu/founders/GEWN-02-03-02-0031.

13. Washington, "General Orders, Cambridge, October 31, 1775," *PGWD*, http://0-rotunda.upress.virginia.edu.usmalibrary.usma.edu/founders/GEWN-03-02-02-0247.

14. Washington, "Letter to Colonel William Woodford, Cambridge, November 10, 1775," *PGWD*, http://0-rotunda.upress.virginia.edu.usmalibrary.usma.edu/founders/GEWN-03-02-02-0320.

15. "Proceedings of the Committee of Conference, Cambridge, October 18-24, 1775," *PGWD*, http://0-rotunda.upress.virginia.edu.usmalibrary.usma.edu/founders/GEWN-03-02-02-0175-0003.

16. Thomas Lynch, "Letter to George Washington, Philadelphia, November 13, 1775," *PGWD*, http://0-rotunda.upress.virginia.edu.usmalibrary.usma.edu/founders/GEWN-03-02-02-0337.

17. Washington, "Letter to John Hancock, Cambridge, November 8, 1775," *PGWD*, http://0-rotunda.upress.virginia.edu.usmalibrary.usma.edu/founders/GEWN-03-02-02-0304.

18. Washington, "Letter to Lieutenant Colonel Joseph Reed, Cambridge, November 28, 1775," *PGWD*, http://0-rotunda.upress.virginia.edu.usmalibrary.usma.edu/founders/GEWN-03-02-02-0406.

19. Washington, "General Orders, Cambridge, November 22, 1775," *PGWD*, http://0-rotunda.upress.virginia.edu.usmalibrary.usma.edu/founders/GEWN-03-02-02-0381.

20. "From the Soldiers of Captain Thomas Mighill's Company, October 9, 1775," *PGWD*, http://0-rotunda.upress.virginia.edu.usmalibrary.usma.edu/founders/GEWN-03-02-02-0122.

21. Pomeroy, 124.

22. Putnam, *The Memoirs of Rufus Putnam*, 11.

23. Ibid., 16-21.

24. Ibid., 22.

25. Ibid., 25-32.

26. Ibid., 32-33.

27. Stephen Cross, Sarah E. Mulliken, ed., "Journal of Stephen Cross, of Newburyport, Entitled Up to Ontario, the Activities of Newburyport Shipbuilders in Canada in 1756," *Essex Institute Historical Collections* LXXV (1939): 337.

28. Josiah Perry, "The Orderly Book of Sergeant Josiah Perry," *New England Historical and Genealogical Register* LIV (1900): 74.

29. Putnam, *The Memoirs of Rufus Putnam*, 11.

30. Washington, "General Orders, Cambridge, November 5, 1775," *PGWD*, http://0-rotunda.upress.virginia.edu.usmalibrary.usma.edu/founders/GEWN-03-02-02-0279.

31. Washington, "General Orders, Head Quarters, Cambridge, February 7, 1776," *PGWD*, http://0-rotunda.upress.virginia.edu.usmalibrary.usma.edu/founders/GEWN-03-03-02-0190.

32. Lesser, 4, 27.

33. Joseph Seymour, *The Pennsylvania Associators, 1747-1777* (Yardley, PA: Westholme Publishing, 2012), 45.

34. Ibid., 126-144.

35. Ibid., 150.

36. Washington, "General Orders, Cambridge, March 3, 1776," *PGWD*, http://0-rotunda.upress.virginia.edu.usmalibrary.usma.edu/founders/GEWN-03-03-02-0293.

37. "Address from the Massachusetts General Court, Watertown, March 28, 1776," *PGWD*, http://0-rotunda.upress.virginia.edu.usmalibrary.usma.edu/founders/GEWN-03-03-02-0416.

38. Washington, "General Orders, Head Quarters, New York, July 9, 1776," *PGWD*, http://0-rotunda.upress.virginia.edu.usmalibrary.usma.edu/founders/GEWN-03-05-02-0176.

39. Washington, "Letter to Lieutenant Colonel Joseph Reed, Cambridge, November 28, 1775," *PGWD*, http://0-rotunda.upress.virginia.edu.usmalibrary.usma.edu/founders/GEWN-03-02-02-0406.

40. Washington, "Letter to John Hancock, Cambridge, November 28, 1775," *PGWD*, http://0-rotunda.upress.virginia.edu.usmalibrary.usma.edu/founders/GEWN-03-02-02-0404.

41. Washington, "Letter to Richard Henry Lee, Cambridge, August 29, 1775," *PGWD*, http://0-rotunda.upress.virginia.edu.usmalibrary.usma.edu/founders/GEWN-03-01-02-0270.

42. Washington, "Circular Letter to the General Officers, Cambridge, October 5, 1775," *PGWD*, http://0-rotunda.upress.virginia.edu.usmalibrary.usma.edu/founders/GEWN-03-02-02-0096.

43. "Council of War, Cambridge, October 8, 1775," *PGWD*, http://0-rotunda.upress.virginia.edu.usmalibrary.usma.edu/founders/GEWN-03-02-02-0115.

44. Washington, "General Orders, Cambridge, November 16, 1775," *PGWD*, http://0-rotunda.upress.virginia.edu.usmalibrary.usma.edu/founders/GEWN-03-02-02-0349.

45. James Thacher, *A Military Journal During the American Revolutionary War, from 1775 to 1783* (Boston: Richardson and Lord, 1823), 82-83.

46. Joseph Bloomfield, *Citizen-Soldier: The Revolutionary War Journal of Joseph Bloomfield*, ed. Mark E. Lender and James Kirby Martin (Newark: New Jersey Historical Society, 1982), 1-28.

47. Ibid., 38.

48. Ibid., 41-42.

49. Ibid., 68-70.

50. Washington, "Letter to Brigadier General Joseph Spencer, Cambridge, September 26, 1775," *PGWD*, http://0-rotunda.upress.virginia.edu.usmalibrary. usma.edu/founders/GEWN-03-02-02-0048.

51. Washington, "Letter to John Hancock, New York, May 5, 1776," *PGWD*, http://0-rotunda.upress.virginia.edu.usmalibrary.usma.edu/founders/GEWN-03-04-02-0176.

52. Washington, "Letter to John Hancock, New York, May 11, 1776," *PGWD*, http://0-rotunda.upress.virginia.edu.usmalibrary.usma.edu/founders/GEWN-03-04-02-0217.

53. Ibid.

54. Ibid.

55. Washington, "General Orders, Head Quarters, New York, August 13, 1776," *PGWD*, http://0-rotunda.upress.virginia.edu.usmalibrary.usma.edu/founders/GEWN-03-06-02-0001.

56. Joseph Plumb Martin, *Ordinary Courage: The Revolutionary War Adventures of Joseph Plumb Martin*, 4th Edition, ed. James Kirby Martin (Malden, MA: Wiley-Blackwell, 2013), 29.

57. Almon W. Lauber, ed., *Orderly Books of the Fourth New York Regiment, 1778-1780 [&] the Second New York Regiment, 1780-1783 by Samuel Tallmadge and Others with Diaries of Samuel Tallmadge, 1780-1782 and John Barr, 1779-1782* (Albany: University of the State of New York, 1932), 137.

58. Martin, 82.

59. George Weedon, *Valley Forge Orderly Book of General George Weedon* (New York: Arno Press, 1971), 300.

60. Lauber, 97.

61. Martin, 17.

62. Ibid., 26.

63. Washington, "Orders to Major General Israel Putnam, New York, August 25, 1776," *PGWD*, http://0-rotunda.upress.virginia.edu.usmalibrary.usma.edu/founders/GEWN-03-06-02-0113.

64. Washington, "General Orders, Head Quarters, New York, August 31, 1776," *PGWD*, http://0-rotunda.upress.virginia.edu.usmalibrary.usma.edu/founders/GEWN-03-06-02-0143.

65. Washington, "To Colonel Fisher Gay, New York, September 4, 1776," *PGWD*, http://0-rotunda.upress.virginia.edu.usmalibrary.usma.edu/founders/GEWN-03-06-02-0174.

66. Weedon, 83-84.

67. Ibid., 135-136.

68. Ibid., 162-163, 223-224, 225-229, 231-232, 235-236, 236-237.

69. Ibid., 209-211.

70. Lauber, 193.

71. Weedon, 256-257.

72. Israel Putnam, *General Orders Issued by Major-General Israel Putnam, When in Command of the Highlands, In the Summer and Fall of 1777*, ed. Worthington Chauncy Ford (Boston: Gregg Press, 1972), 8-10.
73. Weedon, 200-201.
74. Ibid., 45-46, 70-71.
75. Ibid., 46-47.
76. Ibid., 243.
77. Isaac Bangs, *Journal of Lieutenant Isaac Bangs, April 1 to July 29, 1776* (New York: Arno Press, 1968), 20-21.
78. Ibid., 38-39.
79. Weedon, 231-232, 238-239.
80. Lauber, 837-840, 845.
81. Philip Schuyler, "Letter to George Washington, Albany, August 18, 1776," *PGWD*, http://0-rotunda.upress.virginia.edu.usmalibrary.usma.edu/founders/GEWN-03-06-02-0063.
82. Caleb Stark, *Memoir and Official Correspondence of Gen. John Stark* (Concord: G. Parker Lyon, 1860), 42.
83. Washington, "Letter to John Hancock, New York, August 14, 1776," *PGWD*, http://0-rotunda.upress.virginia.edu.usmalibrary.usma.edu/founders/GEWN-03-06-02-0018.
84. Weedon, 280-281.
85. Bloomfield, 70-71, 78.
86. Martin, 154-155.
87. Washington, "Letter to John Hancock, July 29, 1776," *PGWD*, http://0-rotunda.upress.virginia.edu.usmalibrary.usma.edu/founders/GEWN-03-05-02-0371.
88. Martin, 44-45.
89. Barnard Elliott, "Barnard Elliott's Recruiting Journal, 1775," *South Carolina Historical and Genealogical Magazine* 17, no. 3 (July 1916): 98.
90. John Joseph Henry, *Account of Arnold's Campaign Against Quebec* (New York: Arno Press, 1968), 23.
91. Lemuel Roberts, *The Memoirs of Captain Lemuel Roberts* (New York: Arno Press, 1969), 39-40.
92. Washington, "General Orders, Head Quarters, Cambridge, February 6, 1776," *PGWD*, http://0-rotunda.upress.virginia.edu.usmalibrary.usma.edu/founders/GEWN-03-03-02-0188.
93. Roberts, 40.
94. Benjamin Gilbert, *Winding Down: The Revolutionary War Letters of Lt. Benjamin Gilbert of Massachusetts, 1780-1783*, ed. John Shy (Ann Arbor: University of Michigan Press, 1989), 10, 19.
95. Von Steuben, *Regulations*, 67-69.
96. Ibid., 67-69, 72-73, 74, 75-78.
97. Ibid., 77-78.

CHAPTER TWO: RECRUITING FOR THE CONTINENTAL ARMY

1. Elliott, "Recruiting Journal," 95-98.

2. Rhys Isaac, *The Transformation of Virginia, 1740-1790* (Chapel Hill: University of North Carolina Press, 1982), 111-114.

3. Ibid., 97-98.

4. Michael A. McDonnell, *The Politics of War: Race, Class, and Conflict in Revolutionary Virginia* (Chapel Hill: University of North Carolina Press, 2007), 34.

5. Ibid., 46.

6. Charles Neimeyer, "'Town Born, Turn Out:' Town Militias, Tories, and the Struggle for Control of the Massachusetts Backcountry," in *War and Society in the American Revolution: Mobilization and Home Fronts*, edited by John Resch and Walter Sargent (De Kalb: Northern Illinois University Press, 2007), 37.

7. Washington, "Circular Letter to the General Officers, Cambridge, October 5, 1775," *PGWD*, http://0-rotunda.upress.virginia.edu.usmalibrary.usma.edu/founders/GEWN-03-02-02-0096.

8. "Council of War, Cambridge, October 8, 1776," *PGWD*, http://0-rotunda.upress.virginia.edu.usmalibrary.usma.edu/founders/GEWN-03-02-02-0115.

9. Ibid.

10. Henshaw, "Letter to Washington, Cambridge, October 8, 1775," *PGWD*, http://0-rotunda.upress.virginia.edu.usmalibrary.usma.edu/founders/GEWN-03-02-02-0116.

11. "Minutes of the Conference, Cambridge, 18-24 October 1775," *PGWD*, http://0-rotunda.upress.virginia.edu.usmalibrary.usma.edu/founders/GEWN-03-02-02-0175-0003.

12. Lesser, 15-16.

13. Washington, "Letter to Major General Artemus Ward, New York, May 13, 1776," *PGWD*, http://0-rotunda.upress.virginia.edu.usmalibrary.usma.edu/founders/GEWN-03-04-02-0233.

14. Artemus Ward, "Letter to General Washington, Boston, May 19, 1776," *PGWD*, http://0-rotunda.upress.virginia.edu.usmalibrary.usma.edu/founders/GEWN-03-04-02-0279.

15. *A Historical Collection, from Official Records, Files. Etc., of the Part Sustained by Connecticut, During the War of the Revolution*, compiled by Royal R. Hinman, Secretary of State (Hartford: E. Gleason, 1842), 164-165; Richard Buel, Jr., *Dear Liberty: Connecticut's Mobilization for the Revolutionary War* (Middletown, CT: Wesleyan University Press, 1980), 37-39.

16. Buel, 50-52.

17. Washington, "Letter to Jonathan Trumbull, Sr., Cambridge, December 2, 1775," *PGWD*, http://0-rotunda.upress.virginia.edu.usmalibrary.usma.edu/founders/GEWN-03-02-02-0428; Washington, "Letter to John Hancock, Cambridge, December 4, 1775," *PGWD*, http://0-rotunda.upress.virginia.edu.usmalibrary.usma.edu/founders/GEWN-03-02-02-0437.

18. Buel, 56.

19. *Spirit of Seventy-Six*, 158-159.

20. Jonathan Trumbull, Sr., "Letter from Jonathan Trumbull Sr., Lebanon, Conn., December 7, 1775," *PGWD*, http://0-rotunda.upress.virginia.edu.usmalibrary. usma.edu/founders/GEWN-03-02-02-0462.

21. Washington, "Circular to the New England Governments, Cambridge, December 7, 1775," *PGWD*, http://0-rotunda.upress.virginia.edu.usmalibrary.usma.edu/founders/GEWN-03-02-02-0443.

22. Hinman, 193-194, 197.

23. Buel, 59.

24. Martin, 12.

25. James T. Mitchell and Henry Flanders, ed., *Statutes at Large of Pennsylvania from 1682 to 1801*, VIII (1766-1776) (Philadelphia: William Stanley Ray, 1903), 485-486, 492-493.

26. Ibid., 499-516.

27. John B.B. Trussell, Jr., *The Pennsylvania Line: Regimental Organization and Operations, 1776-1783* (Harrisburg: Pennsylvania Historical and Museum Commission, 1977), 21.

28. Gregory T. Knouff, *The Soldiers' Revolution: Pennsylvanians in Arms and the Forging of Early American Identity* (University Park: Pennsylvania State University Press, 2004), 39.

29. Ibid., 41-43.

30. John B. Franz and William Pencak, "Introduction: Pennsylvania and Its Three Revolutions," in *Beyond Philadelphia: The American Revolution in the Pennsylvania Hinterland*, edited by John B. Franz and William Pencak (University Park: Pennsylvania State University Press, 1998), xix-xxi.

31. William Waller Hening, *Hening's Statutes at Large: Being a Collection of all the Laws of Virginia from the first session of the Legislature, in the Year 1619*, IX (1775-1778) (Richmond: W.W. Gray, 1819), 10-17.

32. Ibid., 75-81, 91.

33. Lesser, 32-33.

34. McDonnell, *The Politics of War*, 110-111.

35. Ibid., 164.

36. Washington, "Letter to John Hancock, Cambridge, February 9, 1776," *PGWD*, http://0-rotunda.upress.virginia.edu.usmalibrary.usma.edu/founders/GEWN-03-03-02-0201.

37. Lord Stirling, "Letter to Washington, New York, March 27, 1776," *PGWD*, http://0-rotunda.upress.virginia.edu.usmalibrary.usma.edu/founders/GEWN-03-03-02-0413.

38. Washington, "Letter to John Hancock, Camp Above Trenton Falls, December 20, 1776," *PGWD*, http://0-rotunda.upress.virginia.edu.usmalibrary.usma.edu/founders/GEWN-03-07-02-0305; Joseph Reed, "Letter from Colonel Joseph Reed, Bristol, PA, December 22, 1776," *PGWD*, http://0-rotunda.upress.virginia.edu.usmalibrary.usma.edu/founders/GEWN-03-07-02-0324.

39. Washington, "General Orders, Headquarters, Newton, PA, December 27, 1776," *PGWD*, http://0-rotunda.upress.virginia.edu.usmalibrary.usma.edu/founders/GEWN-03-07-02-0351.

40. Washington, "Letter to John Hancock, White Plains, NY, November 6, 1776," *PGWD*, http://0-rotunda.upress.virginia.edu.usmalibrary.usma.edu/founders/GEWN-03-07-02-0067.

41. "From the Field Officers of the Connecticut Light Horse, New York, July 16, 1776," *PGWD*, http://0-rotunda.upress.virginia.edu.usmalibrary.usma.edu/founders/GEWN-03-05-02-0244.

42. Washington, "To the Field Officers of the Connecticut Light Horse, New York, July 16, 1776," *PGWD*, http://0-rotunda.upress.virginia.edu.usmalibrary.usma.edu/founders/GEWN-03-05-02-0245.

43. John F. Grimke, "Journal of the Campaign to the Southward, May 9th to July 14th, 1778," *South Carolina Historical and Genealogical Magazine* 12, no. 4 (October 1911): 194-206.

44. *The Acts and Resolves, Public and Private, of the Province of the Massachusetts Bay: To Which are Prefixed the Charters of the Province*, V (1769-1780) (Boston: Wright & Potter Printing Company, 1886), 680.

45. Ibid., 681-682.

46. Ibid., 179-184.

47. Washington, "Letter to John Hancock, Peekskill, NY, November 11, 1776," *PGWD*, http://0-rotunda.upress.virginia.edu.usmalibrary.usma.edu/founders/GEWN-03-07-02-0102.

48. *The Acts and Resolves of Massachusetts Bay*, 683-684.

49. Ibid., 684; Charles J. Hoadly, ed., *The Public Records of the State of Connecticut, from October 1776 to February 1778, inclusive, with the Journal of the Council of Safety from October 11, 1776 to May 6, 1778, inclusive, and an Appendix* (Hartford: Lockwood & Brainard Company, 1894), 65-66, 70.

50. Washington, "Letter to John Hancock, New York, April 25-26, 1776," *PGWD*, http://0-rotunda.upress.virginia.edu.usmalibrary.usma.edu/founders/GEWN-03-04-02-0106.

51. Walter Sargent, "The Massachusetts Rank and File of 1777," in *War and Society in the American Revolution: Mobilizations and Home Fronts*, edited by John Resch and Walter Sargent (De Kalb: Northern Illinois University Press, 2007), 53-55.

52. *The Acts and Resolves of Massachusetts Bay*, 812.

53. Ibid., 983.

54. *The Public Records of Connecticut*, 106.

55. Ibid., 126-128.

56. Ibid., 193-194.

57. Ibid., 207-209.

58. Ibid., 240-242.

59. Ibid., 405-406.

60. Ibid., 419.

61. Buel, 108-109.

62. *The Public Records of Connecticut*, 474-475.

63. Lesser, 46.

64. Hening, 275-280.

65. Michael A. McDonnell, "'Fit for Common Service?': Class, Race, and Recruitment in Revolutionary Virginia," in *War and Society in the American Revolution: Mobilizations and Home Fronts*, edited by John Resch and Walter Sargent (De Kalb: Northern Illinois University Press, 2007), 110-112.

66. Henning., 337-349.

67. Lesser, 54-55.

68. Ibid., 454-456.

69. Ibid., 588-592.

70. Trussell, vi, 237.

71. Gregory T. Knouff, *The Soldiers' Revolution: Pennsylvanians in Arms and the Forging of Early American Identity* (University Park: Pennsylvania State University Press, 2004), 39-41.

72. Trussell, 250.

73. Ibid., 1282-1283; William Heath, *Memoirs of Major-General William Heath by Himself* (New York: Arno Press, 1968), 204.

74. *The Acts and Resolves of Massachusetts Bay*, 1284-1286.

75. Buel, 230-232.

76. Ibid., 248-253.

77. William Waller Hening, *Hening's Statutes at Large: Being a Collection of all the Laws of Virginia from the first session of the Legislature, in the Year 1619*, X (1779-1781) (Richmond: W.W. Gray, 1819), 326-337.

78. Ibid., 433-434.

79. Sargent, "The Massachusetts Rank and File of 1777," 44.

80. Ibid., 54.

81. Ibid., 57-58.

82. Ibid., 61.

83. Ibid., 60.

84. Selesky, 144, 155.

85. Martin, 40-41.

86. Allan Kulikoff, *The Agrarian Origins of American Capitalism* (Charlottesville: University of Virginia Press, 1992), 159-169.

87. Ibid., 70-71.

88. Gilbert, 25-26.

89. Ibid., 41-43.

CHAPTER THREE: THE USE OF DISCIPLINE IN THE CONTINENTAL ARMY

1. *Constitutional Gazette*, New York, June 29, 1776 (Issue 96): 3-4.

2. Washington, "To Colonels Alexander Spotswood, Alexander McClanachan, and Abraham Bowman and Lieutenant Colonel Christian Febiger, Head Quarters, Morris Town, April 30, 1777," *PGWD*, http://rotunda.upress.virginia.edu. usmalibrary.idm.oclc.org/founders/GEWN-03-09-02-0301.

3. "Arrest Warrant from a Secret Committee of the New York Provincial Congress, New York, June 21, 1776," *PGWD*, http://0-rotunda.upress.virginia.edu. usmalibrary.usma.edu/founders/GEWN-03-05-02-0042.

4. "Court Martial for the trial of Thomas Hickey and others," *American Archives: Documents of the American Revolution, 1774-1776*, http://lincoln. lib.niu.edu/cgi-bin/amarch/getdoc.pl?/var/lib/philologic/databases/amarch/ 17512#.

5. It is possible the recorder of the court-martial documents annotated the second offense incorrectly, meaning instead to record a violation of the thirty-first article,

prohibiting anyone in the Army from compelling their commanders to surrender or abandon fortifications to the enemy. This was a capital crime at the time and would remain so.

6. Washington, "General Orders, Head Quarters, New York, June 27, 1776," *PGWD*, http://0-rotunda.upress.virginia.edu.usmalibrary.usma.edu/founders/GEWN-03-05-02-0073.

7. Washington, "General Orders, Head Quarters, New York, June 28, 1776," *PGWD*, http://0-rotunda.upress.virginia.edu.usmalibrary.usma.edu/founders/GEWN-03-05-02-0086.

8. *Constitutional Gazette*, New York, June 29, 1776 (Issue 96): 4.

9. Thomas Simes, *The Military Guide for Young Officers, in Two Volumes* (London, printed in Philadelphia: Humphreys, Bell, and Aiken, 1776), 1-3.

10. Washington, "General Orders, Head Quarters, Cambridge, January 1, 1776," *PGWD*, http://0-rotunda.upress.virginia.edu.usmalibrary.usma.edu/founders/GEWN-03-03-02-0001.

11. Titus, *The Old Dominion at War*, 91-92.

12. Cox, 96-98.

13. Anderson, *A People's Army*, 123-125.

14. Stephen Cross, Sarah E. Mulliken, ed., "Journal of Stephen Cross, of Newburyport, Entitled Up to Ontario, the Activities of Newburyport Shipbuilders in Canada in 1756," *Essex Institute Historical Collections* LXXVI (1940): 14-17.

15. Anderson, 125.

16. Seymour, *The Pennsylvania Associators*, 139; *Statutes at Large of Pennsylvania* VIII (1766-1776): 509.

17. *Statutes at Large of Pennsylvania* VIII (1766-1776): 510.

18. Samuel J. Newland, *The Pennsylvania Militia: The Early Years, 1669-1792*, (Annville, PA: Department of Military and Veterans Affairs, 1997), 130.

19. Stephenson, "Pennsylvania Provincial Soldiers," 200-209.

20. "Journals of the Continental Congress—Articles of War, June 30, 1775," *The Avalon Project*, Yale Law School, http://avalon.law.yale.edu/18th_century/contcong_06-30-75.asp.

21. Richard Henry Lee, "Letter to Washington, Philadelphia, June 29, 1775," *PGWD*, http://0-rotunda.upress.virginia.edu.usmalibrary.usma.edu/founders/GEWN-03-01-02-0022; Washington, "Letter to John Hancock, Cambridge, July 10-11, 1775," *PGWD*, http://0-rotunda.upress.virginia.edu.usmalibrary.usma.edu/founders/GEWN-03-01-02-0047-0003.

22. "Proceedings of the Committee of Conference, Cambridge, October 18-24, 1775," *PGWD*, http://0-rotunda.upress.virginia.edu.usmalibrary.usma.edu/founders/GEWN-03-02-02-0175-0003.

23. Washington, "General Orders, Head Quarters, Cambridge, January 1, 1776," *PGWD*, http://0-rotunda.upress.virginia.edu.usmalibrary.usma.edu/founders/GEWN-03-03-02-0001; Washington, "General Orders, Head Quarters, Cambridge, January 3, 1776," *PGWD*, http://0-rotunda.upress.virginia.edu.usmalibrary.usma.edu/founders/GEWN-03-03-02-0008; Washington, "General Orders, Head Quarters, Cambridge, January 9, 1776," *PGWD*, http://0-ro-

tunda.upress.virginia.edu.usmalibrary.usma.edu/founders/GEWN-03-03-02-0036; Washington, "General Orders, Head Quarters, Cambridge, February 27, 1776," *PGWD*, http://0-rotunda.upress.virginia.edu.usmalibrary.usma.edu/founders/GEWN-03-03-02-0275; Washington, "General Orders, Head Quarters, Cambridge, March 13, 1776," *PGWD*, http://0-rotunda.upress.virginia.edu.usmalibrary.usma.edu/founders/GEWN-03-03-02-0336.

24. Washington, "General Orders, Head Quarters, Cambridge, January 1, 1776," *PGWD*, http://0-rotunda.upress.virginia.edu.usmalibrary.usma.edu/founders/GEWN-03-03-02-0001; Washington, "General Orders, Head Quarters, Cambridge, January 3, 1776," *PGWD*, http://0-rotunda.upress.virginia.edu.usmalibrary.usma.edu/founders/GEWN-03-03-02-0008.

25. Washington, "General Orders, Head Quarters, Cambridge, January 8, 1776," *PGWD*, http://0-rotunda.upress.virginia.edu.usmalibrary.usma.edu/founders/GEWN-03-03-02-0032; Washington, "General Orders, Head Quarters, Cambridge, January 12, 1776," *PGWD*, http://0-rotunda.upress.virginia.edu.usmalibrary.usma.edu/founders/GEWN-03-03-02-0048.

26. Washington, "General Orders, Head Quarters, Cambridge, February 27, 1776," *PGWD*, http://0-rotunda.upress.virginia.edu.usmalibrary.usma.edu/founders/GEWN-03-03-02-0275.

27. Washington, "Letter to Lieutenant Colonel Joseph Reed, Cambridge, February 1, 1776," *PGWD*, http://0-rotunda.upress.virginia.edu.usmalibrary.usma.edu/founders/GEWN-03-03-02-0171.

28. Washington, "Letter to John Hancock, Cambridge, February 9, 1776," *PGWD*, http://0-rotunda.upress.virginia.edu.usmalibrary.usma.edu/founders/GEWN-03-03-02-0201.

29. Washington, "General Orders, Head Quarters, New York, April 27, 1776," *PGWD*, http://0-rotunda.upress.virginia.edu.usmalibrary.usma.edu/founders/GEWN-03-04-02-0114.

30. Washington, General Orders, Head Quarters, New York, July 10, 1776," *PGWD*, http://0-rotunda.upress.virginia.edu.usmalibrary.usma.edu/founders/GEWN-03-05-02-0185.

31. Bangs, *Journal of Lieutenant Isaac Bangs*, 57.

32. Bloomfield, *Citizen-Soldier*, 40-44.

33. Ibid., 70-71.

34. Ibid., 76.

35. Ibid., 73, 75.

36. Ibid., 89-90, 93.

37. Ibid., 103-104.

38. Ibid., 115-116.

39. George B. Davis, *A Treatise on the Military Law of the United States* (New York: Wiley & Sons, 1913), 341; William Winthrop, *Military Law and Precedents* (Washington, DC: Government Printing Office, 1920), 22.

40. "Journals of the Continental Congress—Articles of War, June 30, 1775," *The Avalon Project*, Yale Law School, http://avalon.law.yale.edu/18th_century/contcong_06-30-75.asp; "Journals of the Continental Congress—Articles of War,

September 20, 1776," *The Avalon Project*, Yale Law School, http://avalon.law. yale.edu/18th_century/contcong_09-20-76.asp.

41. Ibid.

42. Ibid.

43. John Hancock, "Letter from John Hancock, Philadelphia, September 24, 1776," *PGWD*, http://0-rotunda.upress.virginia.edu.usmalibrary.usma.edu/ founders/GEWN-03-06-02-0301.

44. Washington, "General Orders, Head Quarters, Harlem Heights, September 28, 1776," *PGWD*, http://0-rotunda.upress.virginia.edu.usmalibrary. usma.edu/ founders/GEWN-03-06-02-0323.

45. Washington, "General Orders, Head Quarters, Harlem Heights, October 2, 1776," *PGWD*, http://0-rotunda.upress.virginia.edu.usmalibrary.usma.edu/ founders/GEWN-03-06-02-0348.

46. Edmund S. Morgan, *American Slavery, American Freedom* (New York: W.W. Norton, 1975), 330-333.

47. Barry Levy, *Town Born: The Political Economy of New England from Its Founding to the Revolution* (Philadelphia: University of Pennsylvania Press, 2009), 52-54.

48. Jeremiah Greenman, *Diary of a Common Soldier in the American Revolution, 1775-1783: An Annotated Edition of the Military Journal of Jeremiah Greenman*, ed. Robert C. Bray and Paul E. Bushnell (De Kalb: Northern Illinois University Press, 1978), 72-73.

49. James C. Neagles, *Summer Soldiers: A Survey and Index of Revolutionary War Courts-Martial* (Salt Lake City, UT: Ancestry Incorporated, 1986), 68-120.

50. Stephen Adye, *A Treatise on Courts Martial* (New York: H. Gaines, 1769), 112-123.

51. Weedon, 245-247.

52. Washington, "General Orders, Head-Quarters, Valley Forge, March 1, 1778," *PGWD*, http://0-rotunda.upress.virginia.edu.usmalibrary.usma.edu/ founders/GEWN-03-14-02-0001; Washington, "General Orders, Head-Quarters, Valley Forge, March 2, 1778," *PGWD*, http://0-rotunda.upress.virginia. edu.usmalibrary.usma.edu/founders/GEWN-03-14-02-0014.

53. Weedon, 309-310.

54. Putnam, *General Orders Issued by Major-General Israel Putnam*, 37-38, 48-50.

55. Ibid, 33-35.

56. Ibid, 43-44.

57. Ibid, 69-71.

58. Ibid.

59. Ibid, 33-35, 43-44, 53, 62, 72; Greenman, 78; John Smith, "Diary of Sergeant John Smith," American Antiquarian Society of Worcester, MA, transcribed by Bob McDonald, http://www.revwar75.com/library/bob/smith.htm.

60. Stark, *Memoir of General John Stark*, 296-297.

61. Sargent, "The Massachusetts Rank and File," 53, 62.

62. Gilbert, 25-26.

63. Weedon, 212-215, 252-253.

64. John F. Grimké, "Journal of the Campaign to the Southward, May 9th to July 14th, 1778," *South Carolina Historical and Genealogical Magazine* 12, no. 2 (April 1911): 64-67.

65. Israel Angell, *Diary of Colonel Israel Angell* (New York: Arno Press, 1971), 108-109; Greenman, 180.

66. Martin, 29.

67. Ibid., 99-100.

68. Ibid., 109-112.

69. Gilbert, 23-24.

70. Ibid., 31-32.

71. Martin, 132-134.

72. Ibid.

73. John Barr, "John Barr's Diary," in *Orderly Books of the Fourth New York Regiment, 1778-1780 [&] the Second New York Regiment, 1780-1783 by Samuel Tallmadge and Others with Diaries of Samuel Tallmadge, 1780-1782 and John Barr, 1779-1782*, ed. Almon W. Lauber (Albany: University of the State of New York, 1932), 830-831.

74. Gilbert, 35; Heath, *Memoirs*, 251-252.

75. E. Wayne Carp, *To Starve the Army at Pleasure: Continental Army Administration and American Political Culture, 1775-1783* (Chapel Hill: University of North Carolina Press, 1984), 14.

CHAPTER FOUR: TRAINING IN THE CONTINENTAL ARMY

1. Jesse Lukens, "Letter to Mr. John Shaw, Prospect Hill, September 13, 1775," in *The Spirit of Seventy-Six: The Story of the American Revolution as Told by Participants*, ed. Henry Steele Commager and Robert B. Morris (New York: Da Capo Press, 1995), 156-157.

2. Ibid.

3. Benjamin Thompson, "The American Soldiers are Dirty, Nasty, Insubordinate, and Quarrelsome," in *The Spirit of 'Seventy-Six: The Story of the American Revolution as Told by Participants*, ed. Henry Steele Commager and Robert B. Morris (New York: Da Capo Press, 1995), 155.

4. Ibid., 156.

5. Martin, 81.

6. Ibid., 83.

7. Ibid., 85.

8. Ibid., 85-86.

9. Anburey, *With Burgoyne from Quebec*, 88-90, 95.

10. Thomas Hughes, *A Journal by Thomas Hughes: For his Amusement, and Designed only for his Perusal by the Time he Attains the Age of 50 if he Lives so Long* (Cambridge: Cambridge University Press, 1947), 6.

11. For a discussion on the British Army's evolution from firearms engagement to a reliance on the bayonet charge in America, see Matthew H. Springer, *With Zeal and with Bayonets Only: The British Army on Campaign in North America, 1775-1783* (Norman: University of Oklahoma Press, 2008), 138-168.

12. Martin and Lender, *A Respectable Army*, 17-20.

13. David Hackett Fischer, *Paul Revere's Ride* (New York: Oxford University Press, 1994), 151-154.

14. Newland, *The Pennsylvania Militia*, 130-132.

15. Seymour, *The Pennsylvania Associators*, 124-125.

16. Ibid., 133.

17. Ibid., 138-139.

18. J.A. Houlding, *Fit for Service: The Training of the British Army, 1715-1795* (Oxford: Clarendon Press, 1981), 207.

19. William Windham, *A Plan of Discipline Composed for the Use of the Militia of the County of Norfolk* (London: The Sun, 1760), xx-xxvi.

20. Houlding, 214-215.

21. Ibid., 208-209.

22. Ibid., 214-215.

23. Thomas Pickering, *An Easy Plan of Discipline for a Militia* (Salem: Samuel and Ebenezer Hall, 1775), 6-7.

24. Windham, 3.

25. Ibid., 8.

26. Pickering, 32-33.

27. This was regular practice in the British Army, where two companies were added to infantry regiments (a company of light infantry and a company of grenadiers) who were then detached from their regiments to form ad hoc battalions of light infantry and grenadiers for the duration of a battle. It is no coincidence that the first units of Continental light infantry created in this manner appeared in 1778 after the adoption of von Steuben's reforms.

28. Matthew H. Spring, *With Zeal and with Bayonets Only: The British Army on Campaign in North America, 1775-1783* (Norman: University of Oklahoma Press, 2008), 174-175.

29. Hadden, *Hadden's Journal and Orderly Books*, 70-77.

30. Windham, 37-54, 177-186.

31. Weedon, 273-274.

32. Ketchum, *Decisive Day*, 137-84, 190; Bernard Bailyn, "The Battle of Bunker Hill," http://www.masshist.org/bh/essay.html.

33. Washington, "General Orders, Cambridge, January 2, 1776," *PGWD*, http://0-rotunda.upress.virginia.edu.usmalibrary.usma.edu/founders/GEWN-03-03-02-0005.

34. Washington, "General Orders, Cambridge, October 5, 1776," *PGWD*, http://0-rotunda.upress.virginia.edu.usmalibrary.usma.edu/founders/GEWN-03-06-02-0362.

35. Washington, "General Orders, Cambridge, October 3, 1776," *PGWD*, http://0-rotunda.upress.virginia.edu.usmalibrary.usma.edu/founders/GEWN-03-06-02-0352.

36. How, 30, 36.

37. Elisha Bostwick, "A Connecticut Soldier under Washington: Elisha Bostwick's Memoirs of the First Years of the Revolution," *William and Mary Quarterly*, 3rd Series, 6 (1949): 106.

38. Washington, "General Orders, Head Quarters, Cambridge, January 21, 1776," *PGWD*, http://0-rotunda.upress.virginia.edu.usmalibrary.usma.edu/founders/GEWN-03-03-02-0110.

39. Washington, "General Orders, Head Quarters, Cambridge, February 20, 1776," *PGWD*, http://0-rotunda.upress.virginia.edu.usmalibrary.usma.edu/founders/GEWN-03-03-02-0247.

40. Washington, "General Orders, Head Quarters, Cambridge, February 24, 1776," *PGWD*, http://0-rotunda.upress.virginia.edu.usmalibrary.usma.edu/founders/GEWN-03-03-02-0262.

41. Washington, "General Orders, Head Quarters, Cambridge, February 27, 1776," *PGWD*, http://0-rotunda.upress.virginia.edu.usmalibrary.usma.edu/founders/GEWN-03-03-02-0275.

42. John Hancock, "Letter to Washington, Philadelphia, March 6, 1776," *PGWD*, http://0-rotunda.upress.virginia.edu.usmalibrary.usma.edu/founders/GEWN-03-03-02-0305.

43. Cox, *A Proper Sense of Honor*, 42-43; Sylvia R. Frey, *The British Soldier in America: A Social History of Military Life in the Revolutionary Period* (Austin: The University of Texas Press, 1981), 95-97.

44. Washington, "General Orders, Head Quarters, New York, April 14, 1776," *PGWD*, http://0-rotunda.upress.virginia.edu.usmalibrary.usma.edu/founders/GEWN-03-04-02-0047; Washington, "General Orders, Head Quarters, New York, April 20, 1776," *PGWD*, http://0-rotunda.upress.virginia.edu.usmalibrary.usma.edu/founders/GEWN-03-04-02-0076.

45. Washington, "General Orders, Head Quarters, New York, April 28, 1776," *PGWD*, http://0-rotunda.upress.virginia.edu.usmalibrary.usma.edu/founders/GEWN-03-04-02-0125; Washington, "General Orders, Head Quarters, New York, August 7, 1776," *PGWD*, http://0-rotunda.upress.virginia.edu.usmalibrary.usma.edu/founders/GEWN-03-05-02-0446; Washington, "General Orders, Head Quarters, New York, August 16, 1776," *PGWD*, http://0-rotunda.upress.virginia.edu.usmalibrary.usma.edu/founders/GEWN-03-06-02-0029.

46. Lesser, *The Sinews of Independence*, 24-25.

47. Washington, "Orders and Instructions to Major General Horatio Gates, Head Quarters, New York, June 24, 1776," *PGWD*, http://0-rotunda.upress.virginia.edu.usmalibrary.usma.edu/founders/GEWN-03-05-02-0054.

48. Washington, "General Orders, Head Quarters, New York, June 30, 1776," *PGWD*, http://0-rotunda.upress.virginia.edu.usmalibrary.usma.edu/founders/GEWN-03-05-02-0104.

49. Washington, "General Orders, Head Quarters, New York, July 1, 1776," *PGWD*, http://0-rotunda.upress.virginia.edu.usmalibrary.usma.edu/founders/GEWN-03-05-02-0110.

50. Bangs, *Journal of Lieutenant Isaac Bangs*, 29-30, 37.

51. Ibid., 37.

52. Ibid., 46-54.

53. Ibid., 55.

54. Ibid., 58-60.

55. Nathanael Greene, "Letter to Washington, Long Island, August 9, 1776," *PGWD*, http://0-rotunda.upress.virginia.edu.usmalibrary.usma.edu/founders/ GEWN-03-05-02-0486.

56. Nathanael Greene, "Letter to Washington, Long Island, August 15, 1776," *PGWD*, http://0-rotunda.upress.virginia.edu.usmalibrary.usma.edu/founders/ GEWN-03-06-02-0024.

57. Washington, "General Orders, Head Quarters, New York, August 11, 1776," *PGWD*, http://0-rotunda.upress.virginia.edu.usmalibrary.usma.edu/ founders/GEWN-03-05-02-0502.

58. Washington, "General Orders, Head Quarters, New York, August 30, 1776," *PGWD*, http://0-rotunda.upress.virginia.edu.usmalibrary.usma.edu/ founders/GEWN-03-06-02-0136.

59. Washington, "Orders to Major General Israel Putnam, New York, August 25, 1776," *PGWD*, http://0-rotunda.upress.virginia.edu.usmalibrary.usma.edu/ founders/GEWN-03-06-02-0113.

60. Washington, "General Orders, Head Quarters, New York, September 6, 1776," *PGWD*, http://0-rotunda.upress.virginia.edu.usmalibrary.usma.edu/ founders/GEWN-03-06-02-0185.

61. Putnam, *General Orders Issued by Major-General Israel Putnam*, 15-17.

62. Ibid., 20-21, 27.

63. Ibid., 28.

64. Ibid., 29-31.

65. Ibid., 66-67.

66. Weedon, 12-14.

67. Ibid., 58-59.

68. Ibid., 72-74.

69. Ibid., 70-71.

70. Ibid., 77-79.

71. Ibid., 83-84.

72. Ibid., 95-96.

73. George Washington, "Circular to the General Officers, Head Quarters, Whitpain Township, PA, October 26, 1777," *PGWD*, http://rotunda.upress.virginia .edu.usmalibrary.idm.oclc.org/founders/GEWN-03-12-02-0002.

74. "Council of War, Whitpain Township, PA, October 29, 1777," *PGWD*, http://rotunda.upress.virginia.edu.usmalibrary.idm.oclc.org/founders/GEWN 03-12-02-0040.

75. Weedon, 263.

76. Von Steuben, *Regulations*, 5-8.

77. Ibid., 16, 31.

78. Ibid., 40-47.

79. Ibid., 47-48.

80. Ibid., 62-65.

81. Ibid., 67-80.

82. Weedon, 266.

83. Ibid., 268.

84. Ibid.

85. Ibid., 273-275.

86. Ibid., 283-284.

87. Martin, 77.

88. Weedon, 305.

89. Ibid., 307-309.

90. Martin, 83.

91. Nathanael Greene, "From Major General Nathanael Greene, Hopewell, NJ, June 24, 1778," *PGWD*, http://0-rotunda.upress.virginia.edu.usmalibrary.usma.edu/founders/GEWN-03-15-02-0550.

92. Anthony Wayne, "From Brigadier General Anthony Wayne, Hopewell, NJ, June 24, 1778," *PGWD*, http://0-rotunda.upress.virginia.edu.usmalibrary.usma.edu/founders/GEWN-03-15-02-0563.

93. Nathanael Greene, "To Jacob Greene, Camp at Brunswick, NJ, July 2, 1778," *The Papers of General Nathanael Greene*, Vol. II (1 January 1777-16 October 1778), edited by Richard K. Showman (Chapel Hill: University of North Carolina Press, 1980), 449-452.

94. George Washington, "General Orders, Head Quarters, Freehold (Monmouth County), June 29, 1778," *PGWD*, http://0-rotunda.upress.virginia.edu.usmalibrary.usma.edu/founders/GEWN-03-15-02-0632.

95. Lauber, 142-3.

96. Angell, *Diary of Colonel Israel Angell*, 103-104, 106-107.

97. Greenman, *Diary of a Common Soldier*, 122.

98. Francis H. Brooke, *A Family Narrative: Being the Reminiscences of a Revolutionary Officer* (New York: Arno Press, 1971), 20.

99. *General Orders of George Washington Commander-in-Chief of the Army of the Revolution Issued at Newburgh on the Hudson, 1782-1783*, edited by Edward Boynton, 1909 (Reprint Harrison, NY: Harbor Hill Books, 1973), 21, 30-31.

CHAPTER FIVE: MORALE IN THE CONTINENTAL ARMY

1. Martin, 118-119.

2. Ibid., 119-122.

3. "Morale," *Merriam-Webster Online Dictionary*, http://www.merriam-webster.com/dictionary/morale (accessed on February 22, 2015).

4. Allen Bowman, *The Morale of the American Revolutionary Army* (Washington, DC: American Council on Public Affairs, 1943), 13-26.

5. Ibid., 26-29, 30.

6. Ibid., 61, 102.

7. Sargent, "The Massachusetts Rank and File," 44.

8. Royster, *A Revolutionary People at War*, 25-54.

9. Martin and Lender, *A Respectable Army*, 127-134.

10. Steven Rosswurm, *Arms, Country and Class: The Philadelphia Militia and the "Lower Sort" during the American Revolution, 1775-1783* (New Brunswick, NJ: Rutgers University Press, 1987), 109-112.

11. Knouff, *The Soldiers' Revolution*, 36-37.

12. Weedon, *Valley Forge Orderly Book*, 89-90.

13. John A. Nagy, *Rebellion in the Ranks: Mutinies of the American Revolution* (Yardley, PA: Westholme Publishing, 2008), 294.

14. Thompson, "The American Soldiers," in *The Spirit of 'Seventy-Six*, 155.

15. "Proceedings from the Council of War, Cambridge, October 8, 1775," *PGWD*, http://0-rotunda.upress.virginia.edu.usmalibrary.usma.edu/founders/GEWN-03-02-02-0115.

16. "Proceedings of the Committee of Conference, Cambridge, October 18-24, 1775," *PGWD*, http://0-rotunda.upress.virginia.edu.usmalibrary.usma.edu/founders/GEWN-03-02-02-0175-0003.

17. Washington, "Letter to Lieutenant Colonel Joseph Reed, Cambridge, November 28, 1775," *PGWD*, http://0-rotunda.upress.virginia.edu.usmalibrary.usma.edu/founders/GEWN-03-02-02-0406.

18. Washington, "General Orders, Cambridge, November 22, 1775," *PGWD*, http://0-rotunda.upress.virginia.edu.usmalibrary.usma.edu/founders/GEWN-03-02-02-0381.

19. Washington, "Letter to John Hancock, New York, May 11, 1776," *PGWD*, http://0-rotunda.upress.virginia.edu.usmalibrary.usma.edu/founders/GEWN-03-04-02-0217.

20. Philip Schuyler, "Letter to General Washington, Albany, June 15, 1776," *PGWD*, http://0-rotunda.upress.virginia.edu.usmalibrary.usma.edu/founders/GEWN-03-04-02-0417.

21. Roberts, *Memoirs of Captain Lemuel Roberts*, 28-29.

22. Washington, "Letter to Major General Philip Schuyler, New York, July 17-18, 1776," *PGWD*, http://0-rotunda.upress.virginia.edu.usmalibrary.usma.edu/founders/GEWN-03-05-02-0267.

23. Philip Schuyler, "Letter to General Washington, Albany, August 18, 1776," *PGWD*, http://0-rotunda.upress.virginia.edu.usmalibrary.usma.edu/founders/GEWN-03-06-02-0063.

24. Washington, "General Orders, Head Quarters, New York, August 1, 1776," *PGWD*, http://0-rotunda.upress.virginia.edu.usmalibrary.usma.edu/founders/GEWN-03-05-02-0396.

25. Washington, "General Orders, Head Quarters, New York, May 26, 1776," *PGWD*, http://0-rotunda.upress.virginia.edu.usmalibrary.usma.edu/founders/GEWN-03-04-02-0312.

26. Bangs, *Journal of Lieutenant Isaac Bangs*, 37.

27. Martin, 17, 25-26, 29; William Heath, "Letter to General Washington," Kingsbridge, September 3, 1776.

28. How, *Diary of David How*, 41-42.

29. Roberts, 40.

30. Bostwick, "A Connecticut Soldier," 103.

31. Sargent, 54.

32. Martin, 83.

33. Washington, "Letter to Colonel William Irvine, New York, April 26, 1776," *PGWD*, http://0-rotunda.upress.virginia.edu.usmalibrary.usma.edu/founders/GEWN-03-04-02-0112.

34. Bloomfield, 102.

35. Ibid., 103.

36. Greenman, 76.

37. Brooke, 21.

38. Gilbert, 31-32.

39. Barr, "John Barr's Diary," in *Orderly Books of the Fourth New York Regiment, 1778-1780 [&] the Second New York Regiment, 1780-1783*, 829-830.

40. Carp, *To Starve the Army at Pleasure*, 172.

41. *The Acts and Resolves of the Massachusetts Bay*, 680-681.

42. Carp, 179.

43. These statistics were collated from the rolls found in Lesser, *The Sinews of Independence*.

44. Weedon, 167-169.

45. Ibid., 205-207.

46. Ibid., 297-298.

47. Lauber, 94.

48. Ibid., 98.

49. Ibid., 114-115.

50. Ibid., 115-116.

51. Ibid., 818.

52. Lukens, "Virginia Regiment," 156-157.

53. Washington, "Letter to Jonathan Trumbull, Sr., Cambridge, December 2, 1775," *PGWD*, http://0-rotunda.upress.virginia.edu.usmalibrary.usma.edu/founders/GEWN-03-02-02-0428.

54. Jonathan Trumbull, Sr., "Letter to General George Washington, Lebanon, December 7, 1775," *PGWD*, http://0-rotunda.upress.virginia.edu.usmalibrary.usma.edu/founders/GEWN-03-02-02-0462.

55. Weedon, 215-216.

56. Martin, 122.

57. Nagy, 77.

58. James T. Mitchell and Henry Flanders, *Statutes at Large of Pennsylvania from 1682 to 1801*, IX (1776-1781) (Philadelphia: William Stanley Ray, 1903), 233-238.

59. Nagy, 79, 158.

60. Ibid., 172.

61. Francis B. Heitman, *Historical Register of the Officers of the Continental Army During the War of the American Revolution, April 1775 to December 1781* (Washington, DC: Rare Book Shop Printing Company, 1914), 42-43. Colonel Elias Dayton was Captain Joseph Bloomfield's regimental commander in 1776. He served in the Jersey Blues as both an enlisted soldier and junior officer. He remained in the service of the Continental Army from 1776 to the end of the war when, in recognition for his service, Washington convinced Congress to promote him to Brigadier General.

62. Nagy, 172.

63. Heitman, 495.

64. Nagy, 172-3.

65. Ibid., 179-80; Gilbert, 33-34.

66. Brooke, 21.

67. And the records suggest that many deserters were not actually protesting their failed expectations; they were looking to take advantage of a rudimentary administrative process in the army to earn several bounties at once and then, perhaps, runaway with the cash.

68. Gilbert, 33-34.

69. Greenman, 243.

70. Weedon, 225-226.

71. Martin, 97.

72. Ibid., 99-100.

73. Ibid., 83.

74. Ibid., 119-122.

75. Heitman, 16-19.

76. This was similarly the case during the New Jersey Line Mutiny, where the relationships built between the officers and the men were altered as the regiments reorganized.

77. Weedon, 216-217.

78. Ibid., 243.

79. Nagy, 82.

80. Lauber, 193.

81. Putnam, *General Orders Issued by Major-General Israel Putnam*, 51, 54-55, 61, 66-67; Weedon, 200-201, 209-211, 225-229.

82. Weedon, 243.

83. *The Acts and Resolves of the Massachusetts Bay*, 1277-1278.

84. Ibid., 1278-1279.

85. Ibid., 1280.

86. Ibid., 1282-1283.

87. Ibid., 1284-1286.

88. Ibid., 983.

89. Mitchell and Flanders, *Statutes at Large of Pennsylvania* IX (1776-1781): 233-238.

90. Nagy, 158-159.

91. And in most cases, particularly in the regiments of New England, the company officers were really not that different in economic or social status from the start. As the war dragged on (due to their military service) the lack of pay and time spent fighting the war rather than attending to a private career had a leveling effect between soldiers and officers rather than increasing their disparity of condition.

92. Washington, "General Orders, Head Quarters, New York, August 1, 1776," *PGWD*, http://0-rotunda.upress.virginia.edu.usmalibrary.usma.edu/founders/GEWN-03-05-02-0396.

93. Washington, "General Orders, Head Quarters, New York, August 13, 1776," *PGWD*, http://0-rotunda.upress.virginia.edu.usmalibrary.usma.edu/founders/GEWN-03-06-02-0001.

94. Weedon, 245-256.

95. Bloomfield, 46.
96. Bloomfield, 101.
97. Gilbert, 35.
98. Charles Knowles Bolton, *The Private Soldier Under Washington* (New York: Scribner & Sons, 1902), 141.
99. Gilbert, 57-58.
100. Boynton, *General Orders of George Washington*, 30-31.
101. Ibid., 34-35.
102. Ibid., 62.
103. Ibid., 63-64.
104. Anonymous, "Officer's Letter at Newburgh," in Nagy, *Rebellion in the Ranks*, 314-315.
105. Boynton, 69-70.
106. Washington, "George Washington's Speech at Newburgh," in Nagy, *Rebellion in the Ranks*, 317-319.
107. Nagy, 209.
108. Richard H. Kohn, "The Inside History of the Newburgh Conspiracy: America and the Coup d'Etat," *William and Mary Quarterly* Vol. 27, No. 2 (Apr. 1970): 199-200.
109. Paul David Nelson, "Horatio Gates at Newburgh, 1783: A Misunderstood Role," *The William and Mary Quarterly* Vol. 29, No. 1 (Jan. 1972): 149-150.
110. C. Edward Skeen, "The Newburgh Conspiracy Reconsidered," *William and Mary Quarterly* Vol. 31, No. 2 (Apr. 1974): 282-288.
111. Ibid., 287; Kohn, 211.
112. Boynton, 78-79.
113. Gilbert, 107-108.

CONCLUSION

1. Russell F. Weigley, *The American Way of War: A History of United States Military Strategy and Policy* (Bloomington: Indiana University Press, 1973), 41.
2. Don Higginbotham, *The War of American Independence: Military Attitudes, Policies, and Practice 1763-1789* (Boston: Northeastern University Press, 1983), 441-444.
3. Ibid., 457.
4. Ibid., 438.
5. Weigley, 41.
6. Jennings L. Wagoner and Christine Coalwell McDonald, "Mr. Jefferson's Academy: An Educational Interpretation," in *Thomas Jefferson's Academy: Founding West Point*, edited by Robert M.S. McDonald (Charlottesville: University Press of Virginia, 2004), 120.
7. Theodore J. Crackel, "Jefferson, Politics, and the Army: An Examination of the Military Peace Establishment Act of 1802," *Journal of the Early Republic* Vol. 2, No. 1 (Spring, 1982): 25-36.
8. John M. Schofield, "Address to the Corps of Cadets, August 11, 1879," *Bugle Notes*, http://www.west-point.org/academy/malo-wa/inspirations/buglenotes.html.

BIBLIOGRAPHY

PRIMARY SOURCES

Adye, Stephen. *A Treatise on Courts Martial*. New York: H. Gaines, 1769.

Anburey, Thomas. *With Burgoyne from Quebec: An Account of the Life at Quebec and of the Famous Battle at Saratoga*. Toronto: Macmillan of Canada, 1963.

Angell, Israel. *Diary of Colonel Israel Angell*. New York: Arno Press, 1971.

Bangs, Isaac. *Journal of Lieutenant Isaac Bangs, April 1 to July 29, 1776*. New York: Arno Press, 1968.

Barker, John. *The British in Boston: The Diary of Lt. John Barker*. New York: Arno Press, 1969.

Bloomfield, Joseph. *Citizen-Soldier: The Revolutionary War Journal of Joseph Bloomfield*. Edited by Mark E. Lender and James Kirby Martin. Yardley, PA: Westholme Publishing, 2018.

Bostwick, Elisha. "A Connecticut Soldier under Washington: Elisha Bostwick's Memoirs of the First Years of the Revolution." *William and Mary Quarterly*, 3rd Series, 6 (1949): 94-107.

Boynton, Edward, ed. *General Orders of George Washington Commander-in-Chief of the Army of the Revolution Issued at Newburgh on the Hudson, 1782-1783*. 1909. Reprint Harrison, NY: Harbor Hill Books, 1973.

Brooke, Francis H. *A Family Narrative: Being the Reminiscences of a Revolutionary Officer*. New York: Arno Press, 1971.

Commager, Henry Steele and Morris, Robert B., ed. *The Spirit of 'Seventy-Six: The Story of the American Revolution as Told by Participants*. New York: Da Capo Press, 1995.

Crackel, Thomas J., ed. *The Papers of George Washington*. Charlottesville: University Press of Virginia, Rotunda, 2008.

Cross, Stephen. Sarah E. Mulliken, ed. "Journal of Stephen Cross, of Newburyport, Entitled Up to Ontario, the Activities of Newburyport Shipbuilders in Canada in 1756." *Essex Institute Historical Collections* LXXV (1939): 334-357.

_____. "Journal of Stephen Cross, of Newburyport, Entitled Up to Ontario, the Activities of Newburyport Shipbuilders in Canada in 1756." *Essex Institute Historical Collections* LXXVI (1940): 14-42.

Elliott, Barnard. "Barnard Elliott's Recruiting Journal, 1775." *South Carolina Historical and Genealogical Magazine*, Vol. 17, No. 3 (July 1916): 95-100.

Gilbert, Benjamin. *Winding Down: The Revolutionary War Letters of Lt. Benjamin Gilbert of Massachusetts, 1780-1783*. Edited by John Shy. Ann Arbor: University of Michigan Press, 1989.

Greenman, Jeremiah. *Diary of a Common Soldier in the American Revolution, 1775-1783: An Annotated Edition of the Military Journal of Jeremiah Greenman*. Edited by Robert C. Bray and Paul E. Bushnell. De Kalb: Northern Illinois University Press, 1978.

Grimké, John F. "Journal of the Campaign to the Southward, May 9th to July 14th, 1778." *South Carolina Historical and Genealogical Magazine*, Vol. 12, No. 2 (April 1911): 60-69.

_____. "Journal of the Campaign to the Southward, May 9th to July 14th, 1778." *South Carolina Historical and Genealogical Magazine* Vol. 12, No. 3 (July 1911): 118-134.

_____. "Journal of the Campaign to the Southward, May 9th to July 14th, 1778." *South Carolina Historical and Genealogical Magazine* Vol. 12, No. 4 (October 1911): 190-206.

Hadden, James M. *Hadden's Journal and Orderly Books: A Journal Kept in Canada and Upon Burgoyne's Campaign in 1776 and 1777*. Edited by Horatio Rogers. Boston: Gregg Press, 1972.

Heath, William. *Memoirs of Major-General William Heath by Himself*. New York: Arno Press, 1968.

Hening, William Waller, ed. *Hening's Statutes at Large: Being a Collection of all the Laws of Virginia from the first session of the Legislature, in the Year 1619*, Vol. IX (1775-1778). Richmond: W.W. Gray, 1819.

_____. *Hening's Statutes at Large: Being a Collection of all the Laws of Virginia from the first session of the Legislature, in the Year 1619*, Vol. X (1779-1781). Richmond: W.W. Gray, 1819.

Henry, John Joseph. *Account of Arnold's Campaign Against Quebec.* New York: Arno Press, 1968.

Hoadly, Charles J., ed. *The Public Records of the State of Connecticut, from October 1776 to February 1778, inclusive, with the Journal of the Council of Safety from October 11, 1776 to May 6, 1778, inclusive, and an Appendix.* Hartford: Lockwood & Brainard Company, 1894.

How, David. *Diary of David How, a Private in Colonel Paul Dudley Sargent's Regiment of the Massachusetts Line, in the Army of the American Revolution.* Morrisania, NY: H.D. Houghton, 1865.

Hughes, Thomas. *A Journal by Thomas Hughes: For his Amusement, and Designed only for his Perusal by the Time he Attains the Age of 50 if he Lives so Long.* Cambridge: Cambridge University Press, 1947.

Lauber, Almon W., ed. *Orderly Books of the Fourth New York Regiment, 1778-1780 [&] the Second New York Regiment, 1780-1783 by Samuel Tallmadge and Others with Diaries of Samuel Tallmadge, 1780-1782 and John Barr, 1779-1782.* Albany: University of the State of New York, 1932.

Lesser, Charles H. *The Sinews of Independence: Monthly Strength Reports of the Continental Army.* Chicago: University of Chicago Press, 1976.

Martin, Joseph Plumb. *Ordinary Courage: The Revolutionary War Adventures of Joseph Plumb Martin.* 4th Edition. Edited by James Kirby Martin. Malden, MA: Wiley-Blackwell, 2013.

_____. *Private Yankee Doodle: Being a Narrative of Some of the Adventures, Dangers and Sufferings of a Revolutionary Soldier.* Edited by George F. Scheer. Boston: Little, Brown, 1962.

Mitchell, James T. and Henry Flanders, ed. *Statutes at Large of Pennsylvania from 1682 to 1801.* Volume VIII (1766-1776). Philadelphia: William Stanley Ray, 1903.

_____. *Statutes at Large of Pennsylvania from 1682 to 1801.* Volume IX (1776-1781). Philadelphia: William Stanley Ray, 1903.

Perry, Josiah. "The Orderly Book of Sergeant Josiah Perry." *New England Historical and Genealogical Register* LIV (1900): 70-76.

Pickering, Thomas. *An Easy Plan of Discipline for a Militia.* Salem: Samuel and Ebenezer Hall, 1775.

Pomeroy, Seth. *The Journal and Papers of Seth Pomeroy, Sometime General in the Colonial Service.* Edited by Louis Effingham de Forest. New York: Society of Colonial War in the State of New York, 1926.

Putnam, Israel. *General Orders Issued by Major-General Israel Putnam, When in Command of the Highlands, In the Summer and Fall of 1777.* Edited by Worthington Chauncy Ford. Boston: Gregg Press, 1972.

Putnam, Rufus. *Memoirs of Rufus Putnam.* Boston: Houghton Mifflin, 1903.

Roberts, Lemuel. *The Memoirs of Captain Lemuel Roberts.* New York: Arno Press, 1969.

Schofield, John M. "Address to the Corps of Cadets, August 11, 1879." *Bugle Notes*, http://www.west-point.org/academy/malo-wa/inspirations/buglenotes.html. Accessed March 2, 2015.

Showman, Richard K., ed. *The Papers of General Nathanael Greene.* Volume II (1 January 1777-16 October 1778). Chapel Hill: University of North Carolina Press, 1980.

Simes, Thomas. *The Military Guide for Young Officers, in Two Volumes.* Philadelphia: Humphreys, Bell, and Aiken, 1776.

Smith, John. "Diary of Sergeant John Smith." American Antiquarian Society of Worcester, MA. Transcribed by Bob McDonald. http://www.revwar75.com/library/bob/smith.htm. Accessed November 10, 2014.

Stark, Caleb. *Memoir and Official Correspondence of Gen. John Stark.* Concord: G. Parker Lyon, 1860.

Thacher, James. *A Military Journal During the American Revolutionary War, from 1775 to 1783.* Boston: Richardson and Lord, 1823.

Von Steuben, Frederick William. *Regulations for the Order and Discipline of the Troops of the United States to Which is Added, an Appendix, Containing the United States Militia Act, Passed by Congress, May, 1792.* Boston: Henry Ranlet, 1794.

Weedon, George. *Valley Forge Orderly Book of General George Weedon*. New York: Arno Press, 1971.

Windham, William. *A Plan of Discipline Composed for the Use of the Militia of the County of Norfolk*. London: The Sun, 1760.

A Historical Collection, from Official Records, Files, Etc., of the Part Sustained by Connecticut, During the War of the Revolution. Compiled by Royal R. Hinman, Secretary of State. Hartford: E. Gleason, 1842.

The Acts and Resolves, Public and Private, of the Province of the Massachusetts Bay: To Which are Prefixed the Charters of the Province, Volume V (1769-1780). Boston: Wright & Potter Printing Company, 1886.

The Constitutional Gazette. Issue 96. New York. June 29, 1776.

"Court Martial for the trial of Thomas Hickey and others." *American Archives: Documents of the American Revolution, 1774-1776*. http://lincoln.lib.niu.edu/cgi-bin/amarch/getdoc.pl?/var/lib/philologic/databases/amarch/.17512#. Accessed October 1, 2014.

"Journals of the Continental Congress—Articles of War, June 30, 1775," *The Avalon Project*. Yale Law School. http://avalon.law.yale.edu/18th_century/contcong_06-30-75.asp. Accessed September 29, 2014.

"Journals of the Continental Congress—Articles of War, September 20, 1776," *The Avalon Project*. Yale Law School. http://avalon.law.yale.edu/18th_century/contcong_09-20-76.asp. Accessed September 29, 2014.

SECONDARY SOURCES

Anderson, Fred. *A People's Army: Massachusetts Soldiers and Society in the Seven Years' War*. Chapel Hill: University of North Carolina Press, 1984.

Bailyn, Bernard. "The Battle of Bunker Hill." http://www.masshist.org/bh/essay.html. Accessed October 1, 2014.

Bolton, Charles Knowles. *The Private Soldier Under Washington*. New York: Scribner & Sons, 1902.

Bowman, Allen. *The Morale of the American Revolutionary Army*. Washington, DC: American Council on Public Affairs, 1943.

Brewer, John. *The Sinews of Power: War, Money, and the English State, 1688-1783*. New York: Alfred A. Knopf, 1989.

Brown, Bertram Wyatt. *Southern Honor: Ethics and Behavior in the Old South*. New York: Oxford University Press, 1982.

Buel, Richard Jr. *Dear Liberty: Connecticut's Mobilization for the Revolutionary War*. Middletown, CT: Wesleyan University Press, 1980.

Burton, I. F. and Newman, A. N. "Sir John Cope: Promotion in the Eighteenth-Century Army," *English Historical Review* Vol. 78, No. 309 (Oct. 1963): 655-668.

Carp, E.Wayne. *To Starve the Army at Pleasure: Continental Army Administration and American Political Culture, 1775-1783*. Chapel Hill: University of North Carolina Press, 1984.

Chet, Guy. *Conquering the American Wilderness: The Triumph of European Warfare in the Colonial Northeast*. Amherst: University of Massachusetts Press, 2003.

Cox, Caroline. *A Proper Sense of Honor: Service and Sacrifice in George Washington's Army*. Chapel Hill: University of North Carolina Press, 2004.

Crackel, Theodore J. "Jefferson, Politics, and the Army: An Examination of the Military Peace Establishment Act of 1802," *Journal of the Early Republic* Vol. 2, No. 1 (Spring, 1982): 25-36.

Davis, George B. *A Treatise on the Military Law of the United States*. New York: Wiley & Sons, 1913.

Downey, Fairfax. *Louisbourg: A Key to a Continent*. Englewood Cliffs, NJ: Prentice Hall, 1965.

Fischer, David Hackett. *Paul Revere's Ride*. New York: Oxford University Press, 1994.

Franz, John B. and Pencak, William, ed. *Beyond Philadelphia: The American Revolution in the Pennsylvania Hinterland*. University Park: Pennsylvania State University Press, 1998.

Frey, Sylvia R. *The British Soldier in America: A Social History of Military Life in the Revolutionary Period*. Austin: University of Texas Press, 1981.

Heitman, Francis B. *Historical Register of the Officers of the Continental Army During the War of the American Revolution, April*

1775 to December 1781. Washington, DC: Rare Book Shop Printing Company, 1914.

Hendrix, Scott N. "The Spirit of the Corps: The British Army and the Pre-National Pan-European Military World and the Origins of American Martial Culture, 1754-1783." Pittsburgh: UMI, 2005.

Higginbotham, Don. *George Washington and the American Military Tradition*. Athens: University of Georgia Press, 1985.

_____. "Military Leadership in the American Revolution" in *Leadership in the American Revolution*. Washington, DC: Library of Congress, 1974.

_____. *The War of American Independence: Military Attitudes, Policies, and Practice 1763-1789*. Boston: Northeastern University Press, 1983.

Houlding, J.A. *Fit for Service: The Training of the British Army, 1715-1795*. Oxford: Clarendon Press, 1981.

Isaac, Rhys. *The Transformation of Virginia, 1740-1790*. Chapel Hill: The University of North Carolina Press, 1982.

Ketchum, Richard M. *Decisive Day: The Battle for Bunker Hill*. Garden City, NY: Doubleday, 1973.

Knouff, Gregory T. *The Soldiers' Revolution: Pennsylvanians in Arms and the Forging of American Identity*. University Park: Pennsylvania State University Press, 2004.

Kohn, Richard H. "The Inside History of the Newburgh Conspiracy: America and the Coup d'Etat," *William and Mary Quarterly* Vol. 27, No. 2 (Apr. 1970): 199-200.

Kulikoff, Allan. *The Agrarian Origins of American Capitalism*. Charlottesville: University Press of Virginia, 1992.

Levy, Barry. *Town Born: The Political Economy of New England from Its Founding to the Revolution*. Philadelphia: University of Pennsylvania Press, 2009.

Library of Congress. *Leadership in the American Revolution*. Washington, DC: Library of Congress, 1974.

Lockhart, Paul. *The Whites of Their Eyes: Bunker Hill, the First American Army, and the Emergence of George Washington*. New York: HarperCollins, 2011.

Lynn, John. *Battle: A History of Combat and Culture.* Boulder, CO: Westview Press, 2003.

Martin, James K. and Mark E. Lender. *A Respectable Army: The Military Origins of the Republic, 1763-1789.* 3rd Edition. Malden, MA: Wiley-Blackwell, 2015.

McDonald, Robert M.S., ed. *Thomas Jefferson's Academy: Founding West Point.* Charlottesville: University Press of Virginia, 2004.

McDonnell, Michael A. *The Politics of War: Race, Class, and Conflict in Revolutionary Virginia.* Chapel Hill: University of North Carolina Press, 2007.

"Morale." *Merriam-Webster Online Dictionary.* http://www.merriam-webster.com/dictionary/morale. Accessed February 22, 2015.

Morgan, Edmund S. *American Slavery, American Freedom.* New York: W.W. Norton, 1975.

_____. *Inventing the People: The Rise of Popular Sovereignty in England and America.* New York: W.W. Norton, 1988.

Nagy, John A. *Rebellion in the Ranks: Mutinies of the American Revolution.* Yardley, PA: Westholme Publishing, 2008.

Neagles, James C. *Summer Soldiers: A Survey and Index of Revolutionary War Courts-Martial.* Salt Lake City, UT: Ancestry Incorporated, 1986.

Nelson, Paul David. "Horatio Gates at Newburgh, 1783: A Misunderstood Role." *William and Mary Quarterly* Vol. 29, No. 1 (Jan. 1972): 149-150.

Newland, Samuel J. *The Pennsylvania Militia: The Early Years, 1669-1792.* Annville, PA: Department of Military and Veterans Affairs, 1997.

Resch, John and Walter Sargent, ed. *War and Society in the American Revolution: Mobilization and Home Fronts.* De Kalb, IL: Northern Illinois University Press, 2006.

Rosswurm, Steven. *Arms, Country and Class: The Philadelphia Militia and the "Lower Sort" during the American Revolution, 1775-1783.* New Brunswick, NJ: Rutgers University Press, 1987.

Royster, Charles. *A Revolutionary People at War: The Continental Army and American Character, 1775-1783.* Chapel Hill: University of North Carolina Press, 1979.

Ruddiman, John A. *Becoming Men of Some Consequence: Youth and Military Service in the Revolutionary War*. Charlottesville: University Press of Virginia, 2014.

Selesky, Harold E. *War and Society in Colonial Connecticut*. New Haven: Yale University Press.

Seymour, Joseph. *The Pennsylvania Associators, 1747-1777*. Yardley, PA: Westholme Publishing, 2012.

Skeen, C. Edward. "The Newburgh Conspiracy Reconsidered," *William and Mary Quarterly* Vol. 31, No. 2 (Apr. 1974): 282-288.

Springer, Matthew H. *With Zeal and with Bayonets Only: The British Army on Campaign in North America, 1775-1783*. Norman: University of Oklahoma Press, 2008.

Stephenson, R.S. "Pennsylvania Provincial Soldiers in the Seven Years' War." *Pennsylvania History*, Vol. 62 (1995): 196-213.

Titus, James. *The Old Dominion at War: Society, Politics, and Warfare in Late Colonial Virginia*. Columbia: University of South Carolina Press, 1991.

Trussell, John B. B. *The Pennsylvania Line: Regimental Organization and Operations, 1776-1783*. Harrisburg: Pennsylvania Historical and Museum Commission, 1977.

Weber, Max. *From Max Weber: Essays in Sociology*. Translated and edited by H.H. Gerth and C. Wright Mills. New York: Oxford University Press, 1946.

Weigley, Russell F. *The American Way of War: A History of United States Military Strategy and Policy*. Bloomington: Indiana University Press, 1973.

Winthrop, William. *Military Law and Precedents*. Washington, DC: Government Printing Office, 1920.

Wright, Wyllis E. *Colonel Ephraim Williams: A Documentary Life*. Pittsfield: Berkshire County Historical Society, 1970.

Zelner, Kyle F. *A Rabble in Arms: Massachusetts Towns and Militamen During King Philip's War*. New York: New York University Press, 2009.

ACKNOWLEDGMENTS

It is with much gratitude that I acknowledge the support and guidance given by many people to complete this book. As *Contest for Liberty* was born from my PhD dissertation, several faculty members at the University of Massachusetts and the surrounding Five Colleges were instrumental in getting this project started and brought to a "rough draft" conclusion. Both Barry Levy at UMass and Kevin Sweeney at Amherst College guided me through a masters thesis and the dissertation. They were the ones who encouraged me to move from the Seven Years' War into the Revolution and to continue in my higher education. Thank you for your mentorship, your friendship, and the inspiration to make the study of history my next career. Two other professors agreed to join the project with very little knowledge of who I am as a student and so took a big gamble with their time and energy. Guy Chet (teaching at North Texas State and so not even in the same region of the US as I was) and Steve Pendery (who does teach at UMass but in another department) took a chance and provided the guidance and discussions necessary to help me learn what I did not know. I could not have done this without your support.

As an officer on active duty, I wrote this book on my "free time" and I could not have accomplished this feat without the amazing support of the commanders I worked for over these last seven years. During this time, I have been a battalion executive officer, a brigade operations officer, and a program director at the Department of History, United States Military Academy. To my commanders at Fort Jackson—Colonel Mark Beiger, Colonel H. Clint Kirk, and Lieutenant Colonel J. Keith Purvis—thank you for your understanding and support. You gave me the time and mentorship to accomplish both our missions and my goal. And most especially I want to express gratitude to my current commanders, Colonel Gail Yoshitani and Colonel Ty Seidule. The completion of this project would not have been possible without your encouragement and inspiration. You selected me for my dream job and have spent the last three years providing me with the greatest example of military leadership I have ever encountered.

While I had this manuscript far along by the time I arrived at the academy in 2015, several members of the faculty in the History Department spent an inordinate amount of time helping me polish it for publication. Sam Watson took an immediate interest in my work, reading the rough draft and providing detailed notes on how I could improve both my writing and my scholarship. And during the academic year of 2017 to 2018, I had the incredible good fortune to spend ten months under the tutelage of James Kirby Martin during his tenure as our Ewing Chair Visiting Professor. Jim read my work, gave me important guidance to improve it, and then introduced me to Westholme Publishing. Jim, your mentorship has changed the course of my career and I thank you.

To my parents, Mary and Pat, I owe my love of history. They encouraged me from the very start to respect the past and learn from it. And over the past seven years, they have read what I read, read what I wrote, and volunteered to come on this journey with me. The gratitude I have for your support and love, both for this project and for me, cannot be expressed in words.

Finally, to my best friend and partner in life, Jenny, to whom I owe everything. For the past twenty-two years we have experienced the challenges that come with a military life together, including many years of separation during deployments. Your efforts to complete this project were equal to or greater than mine (including the winter you spent incorporating all the statistics of Continental Army muster rolls into a single database!). I could not have done this without you. I love you.

INDEX